Knowing China

A Twenty-First-Century Guide

FRANK N. PIEKE
Leiden University

CAMBRIDGE
UNIVERSITY PRESS

CAMBRIDGE
UNIVERSITY PRESS

University Printing House, Cambridge CB2 8BS, United Kingdom

Cambridge University Press is part of the University of Cambridge.

It furthers the University's mission by disseminating knowledge in the pursuit of education, learning and research at the highest international levels of excellence.

www.cambridge.org
Information on this title: www.cambridge.org/9781107587618

© Frank N. Pieke 2016

First published 2016

Printed in the United Kingdom by Clays, St Ives plc

A catalogue record for this publication is available from the British Library

ISBN 978-1-107-13274-0 Hardback
ISBN 978-1-107-58761-8 Paperback

For Klaas and René, who each made me half the man I am

Contents

Preface

As a student of contemporary China, I have long noticed the reluctance among my fellow China specialists to wield a broad brush. I have also become increasingly convinced of the necessity to do so. General discussions about contemporary China are often woefully ignorant of the vast store of specialist knowledge. Specialists themselves focus on a particular slice of Chinese reality and, with few exceptions, are reluctant to enter debates even within China studies that take them beyond their core expertise. This book is an attempt to fill this gap. Writing a book for both lay and specialist audiences at once comes with an obvious risk: you may find that you reach none of them. I certainly hope that I have avoided this pitfall and that both general readers and China specialists will take away useful knowledge or insights from this book. If they don't, I apologize, but at least I tried.

This book would never have seen the light of day without the support of many among my colleagues, friends and family. I would in particular like to thank those who have read and commented on parts of the manuscript: Alka Shah, Bill Callahan, Eric Thun, André Gerrits, Barend ter Haar, David Parkin, three anonymous reviewers and my editor, Lucy Rhymer, at Cambridge University Press. It goes without saying that I alone bear final responsibility for any remaining errors in this book.

Main Events in China, 1976–2015

1976 Death of Zhou Enlai and Mao Zedong
      Tian'anmen Incident
      Fall of Deng Xiaoping
      Tangshan earthquake
      Fall of Maoist 'Gang of Four'
      Official end of the Cultural Revolution
1977 Rehabilitation of Deng Xiaoping
1978 Third Plenum of the Eleventh Central Committee of the
      Chinese Communist Party (CCP)
      Start of the reforms
1989 People's movement at Tian'anmen Square in Beijing and
      other cities in China
      Fall of Zhao Ziyang
      Jiang Zemin becomes CCP general secretary
1992 Deng Xiaoping's Southern Tour and start of the second
      phase of the reforms
2001 China's accession to the World Trade Organization
2002 Hu Jintao becomes general secretary at the CCP's Sixteenth
      Party Congress
2008 Beijing Olympics
      Wenchuan earthquake
2010 Shanghai Expo
      Liu Xiaobo awarded Nobel Peace Prize
2012 Xi Jinping becomes general secretary at the CCP's
      Eighteenth Party Congress
2013 Bo Xilai sentenced to life imprisonment on charges of
      corruption

1 | *Introduction: Knowing China*

1.1 Why China?

On the evening of 3 June 1989, I rode my bike down to Beijing's Tian'anmen Square, China's political and symbolic centre. I had done so virtually every day since students from Peking University almost two months earlier had posted a giant, black-and-white portrait in commemoration of Hu Yaobang at the Monument for Revolutionary Heroes there. Hu had been secretary general of the Chinese Communist Party (CCP) from 1982 to 1987, when paramount leader Deng Xiaoping sacked him for his support of widespread student demonstrations the year before. Hu continued to serve on the CCP's Politburo, but on 9 April 1989 he suddenly and unexpectedly collapsed from a heart attack during a meeting of that body, dying a few days later. The students' commemorative act of political defiance on 15 April triggered an unprecedented national protest movement that involved at its peak on 17 May more than one million people in the capital alone, rocking the very foundations of CCP rule.[1]

My visit to Tian'anmen Square on 3 June was different from my previous ones: I knew it would be my last. Heavily armed units of the People's Liberation Army had already entered Beijing from the Northwest, making their way to the city centre battling largely unarmed and unorganized groups of civilians. Later that evening, other, only lightly armed troops suddenly appeared in streets or intersections much closer to the square, confronting the public in an eerie, silent and ominous stand-off, without moving or trying to do anything. A few hours later, after midnight on 4 June, the army units that had entered the city from the Northwest reached, sealed off and cleared the square. How many students died then and there is still not known. Many more civilians

[1] Pieke, Frank N. 1996. *The Ordinary and the Extraordinary: An Anthropological Study of Chinese Reform and the 1989 People's Movement in Beijing*. London: Kegan Paul International.

1

had died during the army's march through the city. Communist Party rule had become a military occupation.[2]

The Tian'anmen Movement – or June Fourth, as it is often known – impressed two conclusions upon me and many other people in China on that day. Despite ten years of reform, communist rule continued to be fundamentally violent, repressive and, in the final instance, based on the Party's control of the army. Furthermore, the Communist Party had lost whatever popular mandate it had and was on its last legs. Its demise would only be a matter of time.

Twenty-five years on, these conclusions have proven to be entirely wrong. From the rubble of military occupation, the CCP reinvented itself as a modernizing, technocratic and largely benign authoritarian regime presiding over thirty-five years of unprecedented economic growth. Violence and repression are no longer directed at the population as a whole but, are limited to specific targets that challenge the legitimacy of the regime, the sovereignty of the state or the integrity of the nation: Tibetan and Uighur separatists, the Falun Gong, dissidents and activists. The army has been professionalized and modernized, the political role of its top brass curtailed.

Two complementary sets of questions have routinely been asked about the CCP's recent successes. Is all this not just a facade, a velvet glove hiding the iron fist of continued totalitarian rule? And if the CCP indeed continues to be just a communist dictatorship, will it then eventually fall, crumbling under the weight of its own contradictions, just like the Soviet Union twenty-five years ago? In other words, will the post-Tian'anmen period ultimately not simply prove to be a stay of execution? Conversely, if the CCP has indeed genuinely changed its spots and managed to put its rule on a new and more solid footing, will the cumulative effect of market liberalization and incremental political changes eventually and unintentionally lead to fundamental political change? Differently put, is reform tantamount to democratization one little step at a time, a fall from power by a thousand cuts?

These are certainly not questions that just spring from the mind of Western thinkers, politicians or journalists who believe that multi-party democracy is the only political system compatible with

[2] Brook, Timothy. 1999. *Quelling the People: The Military Suppression of the Beijing Democracy Movement*. Stanford, CA: Stanford University Press.

advanced capitalism, the 'end of history' proclaimed by Francis Fukuyama during the fall of communism in Russia and Eastern Europe.[3] The belief in the contradiction between a socialist political system and a capitalist economy is in fact inherent to Marxist political thinking and communist political practice from Lenin to Stalin and from Mao to Deng Xiaoping.

Fears of the market heavily framed the debate within the CCP in the early phases of the reforms in the 1980s. The issue was only resolved, at least formally, with the adoption of the formula of a 'socialist market economy' at the Fourteenth Party Congress in 1994. Yet suspicions of the political implications of the development of a market economy have never quite disappeared, expressed every time when political key words such as *bourgeois liberalization, socialism with Chinese characteristics* or, more recently, *social management, consultative democracy* or *social governance* surface. However, the fundamental achievement has been that the contradiction between capitalism and socialism is no longer perceived as absolute. The question has become not if but rather how much and which kinds of freedom should be granted, and to whom. A degree of political liberalization has become a necessary complement to economic liberalization and socialist governance; a blank cheque of liberalism, however, is still a threat.

The purpose of this book is not to determine whether China is or will become capitalist or will remain socialist. It will not allay any fears or feed any hopes about the outcome of the Chinese experiment. Such questions – and their answers – are ultimately teleological: the judgement of what China is thought to become is conditioned by the conviction of what it ought to be. In this, neo-liberal economists declaring the victory of capitalism are just as misguided as CCP leaders insisting on the triumph of socialism.

Instead, I focus on what is actually going on. Socialism and capitalism are not monolithic and antithetical ideologies and systems but loose assemblages of specific ideas and institutions that are historically contingent and that vary from place to place. Aspects of capitalism like private entrepreneurship and a market economy may go together with

[3] Fukuyama, Francis. 1992. *The End of History and the Last Man.* New York: Free Press.

unambiguous property rights, the rule of law, multi-party democracy or human rights in some contexts but not necessarily so in others.[4]

If China teaches anything, it is that the dissembling and reassembling of specific elements does not stop at the ideologically drawn borders between capitalism and socialism. In China, some of the components of 'capitalism' can and do combine with 'socialist' institutions like democratic centralism, a Party-dominated system of bureaucratic appointments, state or collective ownership and 'fuzzy' property rights. When held up against a particular standard of how things ought to be, the nature of these assemblages may, depending on the observer, appear very different. Some will conclude that they have retained China's socialist essence; others will see in them the immanent superiority of capitalism.

To me, this seems a fruitless exercise, not more than an evaluation of what is new in terms of what has come before, a twentieth-century perspective on twenty-first-century phenomena. This book therefore proposes not to treat the processes of dissembling and assembling as departures from a norm but to give them centre stage in a *recombinant* view of the evolution of what I have termed China's neo-socialist political and social formations that seek answers to empirical rather than ideological questions. How are contradictions between specific institutions resolved or kept in check? Which path dependencies, choices or political agendas enable or constrain the assemblage of elements? Which actors are involved in the selection, adaptation and combination of institutions? What are the intended and unintended consequences of these choices, and how might these create new path dependencies for the future?

Questions such as these will make it possible to pursue an open-ended perspective on China's present and future. This, I believe, makes it possible to assess what the impact of China's rise might be. The future of and with China will not be determined by a simple clash of ideologies or civilizations. Recombination and evolution will produce new realities and ideas that will be recognizable and unfamiliar at the same time, not only in China but across the world. Not only will they require

---

[4] The possibility of a disconnect between capitalism and democracy has been acknowledged by several students of authoritarian regimes. For China, this argument has been made in Nathan, Andrew J. 2003. Authoritarian Resilience. *Journal of Democracy* 14,1:6–17.

new analytical concepts; they will also bring new expectations, apprehensions, fears, desires and, ultimately, ideologies.

1.2 Why This Book?

China is a cauldron in which the tension between socialist government, market economy, globalization, modernization and traditional culture produces forms of entrepreneurship, social organization, ways of life and governance that are at once new and unique, recognizably Chinese and generically modern. As a result, to outside observers, contemporary China appears both deceptively familiar and inexplicably different.

China's rise has triggered a virtual feeding frenzy among policy wonks, journalists, public intellectuals and (former) politicians. Their books, articles, comments and blogs ask the same questions over and over again: What explains China's economic growth which, despite a recent slowdown, continues at a pace that other countries can only dream about? Is a capitalist market economy compatible with socialist dictatorship? Will China replace the US and dominate the world? These questions and many of the answers are lodged within an antagonistic world view: Us versus Them. China may require an 'Asian pivot', active engagement or even containment, but it can never be treated as another large, rapidly developing country like India, Brazil or Indonesia.

To a large extent, this presentation of China's 'challenge' builds on two old Orientalist images. The first one, which goes all the way back to the eighteenth century, presents Chinese civilization as unchanging, superior and quintessentially different from the West. The other image represents the rise of China in exactly the opposite way. Dating from the nineteenth century, it paints a picture of China as a failed society, the 'sick man of Asia' that requires Western tutelage to have any hope of salvation.

In the twenty-first-century inflection of these images, China is represented as at last having awakened, rapidly becoming modern, capitalist and prosperous. This *mainstreaming* representation places China's transformation in a master narrative which assumes that reform and modernization are not only making China more successful and powerful but also transforming it into a place which no longer defies the predictions of normal development or even historical necessity. The distinctive features of China's modernization are distilled into a 'model' which is just one of the global varieties of capitalism. The Chinese model may contain valuable lessons for other developing countries but does not fundamentally challenge the general applicability of capitalist principles.

The mainstreaming picture of China is predicated on the inevitability of change that ultimately can and must take one direction only, turning China into a modern country just like all others. Increasingly, however, this expectation runs up against the older image of China: a giant civilization quintessentially different from the West. The representation and predictions of this *exceptionalist* image become more relevant as China's wealth and power are felt ever more strongly across the world, not least within China itself. In China, this image is translated into the necessity or mission to restore its rightful place, making a confrontation, or at least sustained competition, with the West inevitable.

China's rise is viewed in equal measure through these two contrasting images, which explains the often very sudden shifts and changes in opinion and debate in China and elsewhere. Is Chinese investment a desirable contribution to development in Africa or a threat to Western global dominance? Can China be trusted as a strategic partner, or is it a global competitor that the West should prepare against? Will it play by the rules of the established international order, or will it create a new one that better serves its purposes?

Despite the obvious importance of questions such as these, public debate and generalist academic research are almost entirely disconnected from the work of China specialists who might actually possess the knowledge to answer them. For the better part of two centuries, Western scholars in the humanities and social sciences (some, but by no means all, operating under the label of 'sinology') have immersed themselves in the language, history and culture of China. In the last twenty years they have been increasingly joined by scholars from or based in China itself. What primarily drives their research is a fascination with China, not a concern about its impact on the West. The expertise of contemporary China specialists therefore often seems myopically irrelevant to the big questions that politics, media and the general public in the West are asking. Specialists, in turn, regard such questions as beside the point, naive and trivial and find the highly polemical nature of public debate often more than a little unsettling. Ill-prepared to participate, many China specialists choose to stay well clear of debates about China. The few that enter the fray find that, to be heard, they too have to don the garb of stereotype and prejudice. Before long, their voices are barely distinguishable from those of people without any claim to specialist knowledge.

Nevertheless, debate and decision making across the world (including in China itself) have much to gain from the perspective of China specialists. Avoiding both Orientalist stereotype and the Procrustean bed of the social sciences, this book endeavours to take China specialist research out of the seclusion of area studies and put it squarely inside the arena of public and academic debate.[5] This is not to say that China specialists know it all. We certainly have our own blinders when we obsess about arcane details of Chinese politics, religion or culture. More seriously, in many ways, we have happily continued our work as if China is still in some remote and isolated corner of the world. Some people even allege that our long involvement in China may make it awkward to do research on topics that the authorities don't like or to be openly critical of the government.[6]

Despite these real or imagined shortcomings, China specialists have a vital contribution to make. China-centric insights, concepts and theories that emerge from the Chinese experience reveal China in ways that are not conditioned by Western preoccupations, desires or fears. China-centric research is based at least in part on accounts of how China is experienced by people living there. Although a 'native's point of view' is the hallmark of the author's own discipline of social anthropology, all China specialists view China through Chinese eyes regardless of their disciplinary orientation or the nature of the sources or data they use. What anthropologists perhaps do more than, say, economists or political scientists is to lay bare the connections between the myriad social, political, economic and cultural aspects of contemporary Chinese society, and this book is no exception.

Although the research of China specialists used throughout this book is based on Chinese materials (documents, archives, interviews, observations, statistical data, surveys), the references have been limited

[5] See Vukovich, Daniel F. 2012. *China and Orientalism: Western Knowledge Production and the P.R.C.* London: Routledge.
[6] See Carsten Holz's polemical piece in the *Far Eastern Economic Review* some years ago. Holz, Carsten A. 2007. Have China Scholars All Been Bought? *Far Eastern Economic Review* 170,3:36–40.

to secondary literature in English, unless a specific fact or figure was only available from a primary source or in a Chinese-language work. I have chosen to limit direct references in notes to specific facts or viewpoints, saving information on the books and articles that I have drawn on for a separate bibliographic section at the end of the book. In this way, I hope to have improved the accessibility of the book somewhat, while still giving the reader systematic access to the extensive specialist literature on contemporary China.

A China-centric approach is not simply a Chinese approach but one that starts from Chinese realities rather than non-Chinese (usually Western) examples, norms, concepts or expectations. Chinese and Western readers will find things in it that they instantly recognize but also much that they may find novel or puzzling. A China-centric approach is also not the same as a China-friendly approach. This book paints a warts-and-all picture of Chinese society that is essential to understanding China. It shows that China is a society that works for the vast majority of people living in it, sometimes with difficulty, sometimes with surprising ease. Moreover, as a functioning and evolving set of institutions, it is very likely to continue to do so. Like all societies, it might not be ideal, but there is no practical reason why it should collapse or transform, regardless of the principled objections that observers in democratic countries may have.

1.3 Neo-socialism and New Technologies of Power

From the perspective of the CCP, market reform is only a means towards a more important end: a vigorous Party leading a strong state that governs a healthy nation and represents a powerful country. Socialist governance, a capitalist economy and nationalist pride are locked in a symbiotic relationship. Authoritarian socialism as a form of practical governance has made capitalism possible, while the future of socialist rule depends on the continued success of capitalist development. Both in turn are needed to make China a strong nation and a powerful country.

To the CCP, only its own continued rule thus guarantees that China will be strong and prosperous. Rather than breeding conservatism, this conviction has inspired a pragmatism and willingness on the part of the Party constantly to reinvent itself, while retaining core Leninist principles that guarantee its authoritarian leading role over state and society. Ever since the start of the reforms in 1978, Chinese leaders, administrators, academics and businesspeople have mined societies of the developed world for ideas and models – many of them 'neo-liberal' – that may help the CCP improve its governance and make China a better place. Foreign imports are blended with indigenous socialist and reinvented traditionally Chinese ideas and practices. From a Chinese perspective, state building thus resembles a process of selective borrowing and mixing, producing a unique and evolving governmental rationality that I call *neo-socialism* in reference to both the neo-liberal origin of many of the governmental technologies that are adopted and the new direction that socialist governance is taking.

An intrinsic part of neo-socialist strategy has been the selective, partial and gradual nature of the marketization of state and collective assets and functions. Gradually, markets have been created for a vast range of commodities, resources and services, including labour, capital, insurance, housing, education, health care and land. In none of these cases has the state fully retreated from the markets its own policies have created, retaining a larger or smaller role for governments, state agencies or state-owned enterprises as providers and regulators and, quite often, also as major stakeholders.

Neo-socialism entails more than an old-fashioned Leninist party that puts neo-liberal technologies to familiar uses. Under neo-socialism, innovative neo-liberal and home-grown governmental technologies cut right at the heart of the Party-state itself, serving to support, centralize, modernize and strengthen the Party's leading role in society. Neo-socialism is, however, not an ideology or a logically consistent model of governance but an analytical shorthand for the recombinant and open-ended nature of political and social development. There is neither a blueprint nor are there clearly circumscribed ideological no-go zones. Almost anything can be considered or even tried out, to be judged pragmatically on the contributions it might make to the development and stability of China and CCP rule.

This book describes the changing shape of China's politics, society, economy, nation and globalization through the prism of the neo-socialist experiment and experience, asking questions which start from Chinese realities rather than our own wishes, fears or apprehensions. The title of each chapter consists of a statement that rejects opinions commonly encountered in public debate. In doing so, it is not my intention simply to erect and then knock down straw men but rather to show that perceptions of China are usually based on a misunderstanding or misconstruction of what is happening. This is followed by a discussion of how specialist research helps to frame better questions for debate and research. Each chapter concludes with observations on possible future developments or scenarios.

Chapter 2, 'Why the Communist Party Will Not Fall from Power', starts with an analysis of the nature of socialist party rule. The Party after the reforms has in certain crucial respects become more rather than less Leninist. Under Mao Zedong, Party rule had deteriorated into personal dictatorship and orchestrated revolutionary frenzy. After 1978, Leninist procedures and principles were gradually restored. These included collective leadership, Party discipline imposed on the behaviour of its members and Party control over leadership appointments. The Party also invested heavily in ideological renewal. It changed its mission from revolution to reform, and its political role from exercising the dictatorship of the proletariat to the 'Three Represents' of the progressive forces in society. The ultimate objective of the Party is no longer communism; instead, it promises a united nation, a strong country and a prosperous and harmonious society. Surprisingly, the Party after 1978 retained and, in fact, deepened the highly decentralized structure of the administration that made local governance affordable and adaptable but also very difficult to control. Specifically neo-socialist elements were added gradually, especially after the start of the second phase of reform in 1992. These included the build-up of the central administrative apparatus, marketization of government functions, the rule of law, consultative democracy, and managed political participation of non-state organizations and political actors. After thirty-five years of reform, Party rule is on a much more solid footing than ever before. Despite these successes, not all is well, and the long-term success of the neo-socialist strategy is by no means an established fact. Evidence for this is the apparent need to tighten the reigns over academics, journalists, activists and the Party apparatus under the new Party general secretary Xi Jinping since 2013. Increasingly, Party politics is captured by special interest groups, the private interests of the families of high Party leaders and even organized crime. The fall from power in 2011 of Bo Xilai, at the time Xi Jinping's main rival to take the CCP's top post in 2012, laid bare the deep divisions in the Party leadership and showed that the danger of a return to the devastating factional politics from before the Tian'anmen Movement of 1989 continues to be very real.

Spectacular and sustained economic growth is what is most immediately associated with the Chinese reforms. In chapter 3, 'China's Economy Will Continue to Grow, but Not Forever', I look at one of the most often asked questions, namely how a communist regime and a capitalist economy can exist alongside each other. Despite strong similarities with capitalist countries, China charts its own course of neo-socialist development as much in the economic realm as in other aspects of politics, society and culture. A closer look at the economic reforms shows that the growth of a market economy supports rather than undermines the socialist institutions and strategy of the Party. This is most clearly visible in the massive restructuring of state enterprises. While thousands of state enterprises were let go, a select few were turned into large commercial state-owned conglomerates and spearheads of further economic development and globalization. Neo-socialist industrial policy has thus been highly graded and selective. Whereas markets have been created in which all economic actors have to operate, certain strategic enterprises and sectors of the economy have been protected. The examples of other East Asian developing countries (Japan, Taiwan and South Korea) show that such an approach can work, provided that, at a certain point in time, protectionist measures are dismantled to open up the privileged strategic enterprises and sectors to domestic and international competition. In the absence of any compelling financial or political reasons to do so immediately (and thus possibly prematurely), China can pick the moment to release its state-owned 'national champions' that best serves its own interests rather than those of its international competitors.

Although the legacy of the state-owned sector, tricky as it is, is unlikely to stop economic growth, other challenges might in the longer term be more serious as the current economic slowdown is already beginning to demonstrate. In the second half of chapter 3, I argue that longer-term prosperity has less to do with the further development of a market economy and more with challenges that are generic and global rather than specifically having to do with the socialist legacy of the regime. Among these post-reform challenges, the chapter discusses three: demographic change, innovation-based growth and environmental degradation. If future growth has to be generated by innovation and creativity, solutions will have to be found to the current problems in research, the arts and higher education. The deterioration of the environment and the strictures of environmental protection require a proactive green development strategy. Most importantly, the reduction of the labour force and the ageing of the population are unavoidable. In the coming years, ways must be found for China to get rich not only before it gets older but also before it gets smaller. Although the current model of economic growth will most likely continue to work for some time, there is only a limited window of opportunity to tackle these long-term post-reform challenges. In this period, solutions to the environmental, innovation and demographic problems will have to be found to set China on a structurally different path of economic development.

Chapter 4, 'Freedom without Universal Human Rights', turns our attention to society. Under Mao, Chinese society had been wholly subsumed (albeit never fully controlled) under the Party and the state. This totalitarian ambition was abandoned after the start of the reforms. In the 1990s the autonomy of individuals, families, enterprises and organizations became a cornerstone of the Party's unfolding neo-socialist approach. China has become a society of enterprising strangers who are free, albeit within the political limits imposed by the state, to pursue whatever goals or desires drive them. Just like in capitalist societies, freedom comes at a price: risk, inequality, individual responsibility, alienation. New forms of sociality based on religious beliefs, leisure and pastimes; lifestyles; charitable or political causes; or specific interests have emerged to fill the gap created by freedom and individualization. The increasing complexity and autonomy of society has political consequences. A highly diverse field of political action has grown which is played by a host of state and non-state political actors, including activists, intellectuals, non-governmental organizations, associations and businesses. While this new pattern of state–society relations is unlikely to evolve into a fully democratic political system with universal human rights, politics is no longer limited to what happens within the Party and the state.

In chapter 5, 'From Empire to Nation, or Why Taiwan, Tibet and Xinjiang Will Not Be Given Independence', I argue that under neo-socialism, nation building and nationalism have become even more important than in the past. The CCP is heir to a tradition of reform and revolution going back to China's defeat during the First Opium War in 1842. Until the communist victory in 1949, the concern of countless officials, scholars, students, rebels, activists, writers, scientists and revolutionaries was to 'save the nation' and to overcome the ignominy of 'national humiliation' at the hands of Western and Japanese imperialist aggression. To the Communists, the goal of turning China into a strong and united nation has always been at least on a par with socialism. China as a nation is still very much a work in progress, a project to turn the conquest empire that was the Qing dynasty (1644–1912) into a modern country and nation. Three concepts are at the core of this project: the country of the People's Republic of China, the Chinese nation and the Han Chinese people. Currently, the CCP brings the arsenal of its neo-socialist strategy to bear on the fundamental contradictions inherent to each of these. Strengthening the central state gives greater scope for a unified national school curriculum, infrastructure, language and media and a stronger military, police and intelligence apparatus to bring recalcitrant parts of the country to heel. A national market economy, greater political participation and contestation, social and spatial mobility and individualization turn China from a collection of localities and groups into a connected and integrated society. All these developments combine to enhance the availability and immediacy of a modern way of life for all that revolves around citizenship of the People's Republic of China and Han Chinese culture, history, heritage and identity. Paradoxically, neo-socialist China is on its way to becoming a modern and integrated society in which there is less rather than more space for and tolerance of any form of diversity that challenges the unity of the country, the nation or the people.

Chapter 6 of the book, 'Not Just a Chinese Century', does not simply aim to present a strategic analysis of Chinese diplomatic and military power. Instead, it also tries to gauge the consequences that neo-socialist approaches and developments have on the impact of Chinese people, business, capital and, increasingly, culture in the world that we all live in. Globalization entails the mixing, mingling and creolization of cultures in many specific places. Will China merely be one of globalization's many ingredients and sites? Although I cannot rule out such a minimal outcome, chances are that China's contribution will be a lot more important. Neo-socialist state strengthening, the proactive support for world leading firms, the emergence of an intensely competitive market and society and the aggressive nation-building project are preparing the way for a prominent global influence. In the final analysis, however, even more important might be the fact that China, like the West, sees itself as special: Chinese civilization is superior and should be the norm that all should aspire to. China will become a global power not only because of a deep-seated wish to be independent from Western civilizers. There are also signs that China as an emerging power will not hesitate to become a civilizer in its own right, imposing its modernity on others.

Nobody knows where the journey on which neo-socialist China has embarked will end. The government's policy statements are clear enough about the objectives: a rich and prosperous society, a unified and secure nation and a powerful country that will have to fear no other country in the world. The Communist Party has explicitly made the continuation of its rule conditional on achieving these aims and sees its continued rule also as a necessary condition for success. This book documents the policies and developments that undergird the strategy that make achieving these objectives a strong possibility. Although there is no reason to assume that the Party will no longer be at the helm five, ten or even twenty years from now, it seems unlikely that Chinese society will fully conform to the inane and docile blueprint that the Party seems to have in mind. This book therefore also documents the many developments in politics, society, the economy and the nation that have given Chinese citizens, businesses, organizations and groups a role to play which the Party neither can nor would want to contain. The interplay between the Party and these many actors will take China's future beyond the familiar territory of 'authoritarian resilience' or 'democratic transition'. To get some idea of what that future might look like, I start by looking up close at the largest political arena in the world: the CCP.

2 | Why the Communist Party Will Not Fall from Power

2.1 The CCP and Violence

The rule of the CCP is rooted in terror and violence. This is less special, unusual or evil than it might seem. All modern states are built as much on warfare, conflict and repression as on a social contract between citizens and rulers. The creation and use of conflict and the application and display of violence are normal instruments of rule, even in the most peaceful democracies. A state's monopoly of violence is never a certainty but has to be fought for and defended against external and internal competition, not once but constantly.

The CCP however has been highly unusual in the extent, frequency and scale of the application of violence and the ability to find or create ever new enemies to rally against: in the Party, in the nation or abroad. The CCP and its state were an almost perfect example of mid-twentieth-century totalitarianism, the instrument of the whims of an absolute, deified leader. Totalitarianism is different from ordinary dictatorship or authoritarianism. Totalitarian rule and its ideology enter all institutions of society and reach all individuals, dedicating them to constant mobilization for the relentless application of violence for war and terror on an industrial scale.[1]

[1] My understanding and use of *totalitarianism* takes its cue from Arendt, Hannah. 1951. *The Origins of Totalitarianism*. New York: World. Totalitarianism is a highly charged concept mainly because of its Cold War connotations, when it was used in the West to prove that the current communist enemy and the Nazi and fascist enemies of the Second World War were simply two of a kind. Despite its tainted genealogy, the concept remains useful because it highlights the specificity of twentieth-century applications of absolute power rooted in a high-modern use of science, propaganda, militarism and industrialism. With the possible exception of North Korea, it has become almost extinct in the twenty-first century, although the rise of the Islamic State (IS) shows that at least some of its modalities of rule continue to be a powerful instrument for those who place themselves outside the capitalist global order.

The CCP's defining feature is its absolute dedication to the transformation of society born from the early-twentieth-century Chinese obsession to 'save the nation'. In despair over China's 'national humiliation' at the hands of Western powers and – even more jarring – Japan, students, scholars, activists, politicians and even military leaders explored virtually any idea, ideology or concept that might be the philosopher's stone of modernity, strength and power.

Marxist socialism was just one of these. Certain aspects, such as socialism's stance against nationalism and a revolutionary strategy firmly rooted in an analysis of industrialized Western societies, badly fitted an early-twentieth-century Chinese perspective on progress and modernity. Yet socialism's very root in Western progress and modernity also made it immediately appealing. It claimed scientific status and promised objective truth; condemned traditional rule, religion and established privilege; prescribed a radical overhaul of society and a fundamentally new social order; and legitimated the use of violence against anybody that stood in the way. More important, however, were two crucial non-ideological aspects. The first was the evidence of success provided by the communist victory in Russia in 1917, the second the focus of the Russian Bolshevists and their leader Lenin on a tightly organized revolutionary party and the broad licence given to a small elite of professional revolutionaries.

In many respects, the CCP under Mao Zedong was more nationalist than Marxist. Attaining socialism and saving the nation were conflated from the very start. Socialism would make China modern and strong; opponents and adversaries were as much enemies of the revolution as of the nation. The Marxist pretence of scientific objectivity gave way to Maoist visionary voluntarism that proclaimed that revolutionary victory and socialist transformation can be achieved against all odds by sheer dedication and sacrifice; if you are willing to pay any price, nothing is impossible.

The violence that lies at the core of CCP rule is thus not irrational: Leninist and Maoist organization and ideology inform its objectives and guide its use. The Chinese communist revolution had not been a spontaneous uprising but a succession of protracted and very bloody wars with its enemies, the Nationalist Party (Guomindang, GMD), Japan and rivals within the Party itself. Decades of struggle and several experiences with near-extinction turned the CCP into a tight organization dedicated to the application of military might. The Party's army was the backbone of the revolution, and CCP leaders were first and foremost preoccupied with war and conquest.

Military thinking, speaking and acting quite naturally spilled over both into incessant power struggle within the Party itself and the strategies and tactics aimed at turning military conquest into the revolutionary transformation of Chinese society. Military ways thus undergird the institutionalization of the CCP's rule after its victory in 1949. The organization of society into self-contained urban 'work units' and rural collectives, the adoption of a planned economy and the proliferation and hierarchical nature of the administrative organs of state, Party and army turned rule into a military campaign, emphasizing obedience and subordination, complete dedication to specific tasks and uniformity of structure and action.

Violence was endemic to this system. It served not only to enforce compliance but also to create a constant state of uncertainty and mobilization for change. Maoist–Leninist totalitarianism was therefore very different from ordinary dictatorships. The Party's goal was not merely to stay in power at all costs but a sacred mission of social, political and personal transformation. The Party does not simply rule; it brings deliverance from suffering and injustice and progress towards a better future through revolution that breaks old rules and tests new ideas. The Party's authority and power do not rest on tradition or the impersonal application of rules, laws or procedures but on the heroic 'charisma' ascribed to it. The Party's organizational charisma bestows extraordinary powers and commands extraordinary loyalty and sacrifice: the Party rules because it transcends the personal will or desire of any of its members and followers.

Herein lies totalitarianism's fundamental contradiction. Because the impersonal charisma of the Party trumps established structures, in the end, there is nothing that keeps it in check but the personal power of one or more of its leaders, who must determine what and who is right or wrong, what must be done and what must be avoided. In other words, because of the Party's commitment to transformation, the exercise of its power cannot be tied to traditions, rules, offices or even ideologies but ultimately has to submit itself to whims of individuals. Organizational heroism eventually gives way to individual charisma; totalitarianism becomes total personal power.

This contradiction existed throughout society. It is therefore a mistake to think of the organization of communist totalitarianism in China as a giant bureaucracy smothering all initiative and creativity under a blanket of faceless application of rules and procedures. Rather, it was almost its exact opposite – an 'anti-bureaucracy', as Eddy U has called it.[2] Both at the top and in the individual work units and collectives – the cells that made up Chinese society – rule was highly personalized and often wanton. Decisions about promotions, assignments and much more besides were the unit leader's to make. In this context, it was often impossible to distinguish personal favours from principled dedication to the Party, loyalty to the Party from loyalty to the person of the leader.

Destabilization of established structures was intrinsic to the exercise of power. When structures and rules are only as good as the personalized power that backs them up, destruction becomes an instrument of rule. The discovery of the creative power of destruction lay at the very heart of Mao's political philosophy. During political campaigns, officials, activists and ordinary people were incentivized or even forced to break rules, destroy institutions and arbitrarily persecute others. Like a beast that feeds upon itself, the Party-state's systematic and organized application of violence was aimed at the destruction of its own systems, organizations and people. How leaders, officials and ordinary people negotiated the conflicting demands of this contradiction and how and when they failed lie at the root of all explanations of the twists and turns of post-1949 history.

2.2 Traumas of CCP Rule: The Cultural Revolution and Tian'anmen

The CCP thus derives its strength from the symbiosis and productive tension between the pillars of totalitarian rule: violence, organization and ideology. In the course of a seemingly endless stream of power struggles, wars and political campaigns dating all the way back to his initial victory over his enemies in the Party during the famous Long March in 1934, Mao had mastered the art of total power to such an extent that the administrative apparatus of Party and state could be made to do essentially anything at any human cost. Campaigns in the 1940s and 1950s targeted at specific categories of people, such as rightists, intellectuals, the bourgeoisie or landlords, prepared the way for the

---

[2] U, Eddy. 2007. *Disorganizing China: Counter-bureaucracy and the Decline of Socialism*. Stanford, CA: Stanford University Press.

systematic slaughter and starvation of large segments of the population during the Great Leap Forward (1958–62) and the mass hysteria and civil war of the Cultural Revolution (1966–69).

During the first two years of the Cultural Revolution, the application of arbitrary power finally brought the contradictions of CCP rule to their logical conclusion: the normal administrative functions of the Party-state ceased altogether. China descended into stateless anarchy that pitted innumerable student factions against each other, the remnants of the state and the Party itself and, eventually, the army. The systematic violence and destruction of the Cultural Revolution followed from the logic of CCP politics and administration. It does not suffice to reduce the complexities of struggle between the many local factions to China's social inequalities or pre-existing allegiances: the more immediate logic and demands of violent struggle quickly trumped more predictable interest-based competition for power, resources or opportunities. Participants in the Cultural Revolution actively made choices on the basis of how they interpreted the events around them and their interactions with other participants or groups. Yet the use of violence was neither arbitrary nor simply sadistic: it always served a purpose, no matter how bizarre.

This is not to say that the role of Mao Zedong was unimportant. Much of the objectives, organization, scale and what might be called the aesthetics of violence must be attributed to Mao Zedong's personality and thought. Nevertheless, neither the Cultural Revolution's root causes nor the actions of the participants can simply be ascribed to the aberrations of a crazed leader. Mao worked through and with the organization of CCP politics and millions of its agents and victims. This renders the allocation of ultimate responsibility or blame pointless. In the final analysis, everybody had a choice, no matter how tough, making everybody, and thereby nobody, responsible.

Although very different in many regards, from the point of view of the CCP leadership, the Cultural Revolution shares one crucial characteristic with the Tian'anmen Movement twenty years later in 1989: they were the two periods in post-1949 history when the Party lost its grip. The ordinary application of violence, organization and ideology no longer sufficed; in both cases, the Party's army had to be called in to deploy extraordinary violence to restore normal order. The key difference between the two periods was, of course, that the crisis of the Cultural Revolution ran much deeper than anything before or since. During the Tian'anmen Movement the institutions of the Party and the state remained fully functional, but the Party elite's ability and right to rule China were explicitly questioned and challenged, triggering among the elite memories and fears of events during the Cultural Revolution twenty years earlier.

These two episodes constitute a trauma that cuts to the core of the Party's rule and continues to inform virtually all aspects of CCP politics and policy making. The official silence that continues to surround them is a constant reminder of what the CCP elite wants to avoid at all costs: politics acted out in the streets and their rule subjected to popular mandate. Viewed more positively, the Cultural Revolution and the Tian'anmen Movement opened up a huge and permanent political space within the Party: very few ideological taboos remain, and almost anything that will help to avoid a repetition of these traumatic events can be considered, tried out and, if successful, implemented.

Overall, the CCP elite have not reacted to the traumas of the Cultural Revolution and the Tian'anmen Movement in the way that one might have expected. Rather than ruthlessly suppressing all forms of unlicensed political activity, the CCP has become notably circumspect in its use of violence, opting for a fairly minimal interpretation of the security of the Party's rule. Suppression and persecution are resorted to only when the Party considers its own survival or the integrity of the Chinese nation to be directly at stake. Examples are radical dissident activity (the most famous examples being Nobel laureate Liu Xiaobo and, to a lesser extent, the artist Ai Weiwei), the Falun Gong religious movement and what the CCP labels separatist terrorism in Tibet and Xinjiang.

Restraint and the willingness to experiment extend far beyond dealing with political opposition. They include economic liberalization, poverty alleviation, opening up to the outside world, building a legal system, introducing democratic procedures, strengthening and centralizing the institutions of the state, normalizing the political process and extending social security and welfare to the countryside. These extraordinary developments have only been possible because the Party has gone through a near-death experience not just once but twice. In response, the Party elite have dismantled the totalitarian grip of CCP rule and have allowed the development of a society that is remarkably open, dynamic, diverse and, yes, free. Yet when evaluating the CCP's post-1978 track record, it must be borne in mind that the ultimate intent and purpose of even the most radical policies have never been to make China a democratic and capitalist society but to strengthen and perpetuate the rule of the CCP without subjecting it to the mandate of any other constituency than its own elite. The CCP is still a Leninist organization, more so than under Mao.

Earlier in this chapter, we saw that during the Maoist period, CCP rule all but collapsed under the fundamental contradiction between the organizational charisma of the Party and the personal charisma of its leader, Mao Zedong. To Mao, the Party was merely an instrument to achieve the ultimate aim of communism. Defining exactly what communism was and how to get there was, of course, Mao's own personal prerogative. After Mao's death in 1976, a broad coalition of CCP leaders set out to reverse this logic by returning to Leninist first principles: socialism was the dictatorship of the proletariat led by its vanguard, the Communist Party. The Party's organizational charisma had to be restored and personal charisma and power of individual leaders curtailed. Compared to the Maoist period, means and end in effect swapped positions. The Party no longer existed to serve a master and to achieve a goal larger than itself. Instead, working towards goals (socialism, development, national strength) served to perpetuate the rule of the Party. Party rule itself became the ultimate objective.

2.3 The Sacred Void of Chinese Politics

When the post-Mao leadership resolved the fundamental contradiction of Maoist rule by returning to Leninism, another contradiction emerged. Mao had given the Party a sacred purpose by defining a path towards a communist utopia that transcended Party rule itself. But now that this had been thoroughly discredited, what should take its place? Put differently, could Communist Party rule continue without the ultimate promise of achieving communism?

To answer this question, I look into the nature of CCP politics in some more detail. The CCP is not an electoral machine or vehicle of competition with other political parties. It is also not a platform for political cooperation and competition between like-minded people. The Party is not even an institution, as commonly understood, but only exists in symbiosis with other institutions: the organs of the state, representative government, judiciary and the army, service organizations (hospitals, schools), enterprises, mass organizations, collectives, non-governmental organizations and even other political parties. This symbiosis is always unequal. The CCP acts as the superego of society that guides, inspires, evaluates, coordinates, directs and decides; other institutions will have to follow.

Sometimes this unequal symbiosis is hardly visible; in other places or at other times it is fully institutionalized. As a symbiotic institution, the Party has two faces. At each level of government and in each administrative jurisdiction (the centre, the provinces, the prefectures, the counties and the townships) the Party has its own organizational setup: a Party committee with, under it, several functional departments that supervise and control specific aspects of state and society. It is the Party committee (or the Central Committee, at the central level) that vets all important political decisions and personnel appointments, leaving the implementation and more practical decisions to the responsible organization.

In addition, the Party's eighty million members are organized in cells (called 'branches' or 'committees', depending on their size) existing in the institutions where they live or work. At each level of government the Party committee also serves as the hub for this network of cells of Party members in institutions across its jurisdiction, ensuring the Party's position as the leading force in society. Party members are obliged to organize themselves in cells wherever they work or live. These cells are most in evidence in organs of the state, universities or the army but also exist in, for instance, private enterprises, charitable foundations and other civil society organizations. Rather than treating this aspect of its presence as an antiquated remnant of it revolutionary past, the Party has in recent years stepped up its efforts in building up and activating cells wherever there are Party members.

Two Leninist principles undergird the Party's symbiotic grip over society: democratic centralism and the *nomenklatura* system of political appointments. Democratic centralism means that after a Party committee has made a decision, subordinate Party organizations, cadres and members are bound by Party discipline to implement this decision. Democratic centralism maintains the assumption of the infallibility of the centre regardless of its composition and regardless of any knowledge of the way that a decision has been made.

The nomenklatura system entails that the appointments of individual cadres to key leading positions of the organizations of the Party, state, army, representative government, service organizations and state-owned enterprises are made by the Party committee at a higher administrative level. Nomenklatura appointees serve as the eyes, ears and arms of higher authorities, thus keeping the autonomy of subordinate organizations, local administrations and local cadres in check.

Organizational symbiosis, democratic centralism and nomenklatura allow a Party committee to treat all organizations and institutions under its jurisdiction as pieces on a chessboard. From the perspective of a Party committee, the functional or legal distinctions between a state bureau, an arm of the judiciary, an institution of representative government or a state-owned enterprise matter remarkably little: all are led on a rotating basis by the same body of personnel, and all are subordinate to the common interests as defined by the Party committee.

The Party's omnipresence and hierarchical authority ensure that the whole of society has direction and purpose. This mission justifies its right to rule independently from its actual content; in fact, the mission need not even be revolutionary, transformative or (explicitly) socialist anymore. Under a succession of paramount leaders, the CCP has spawned a dizzying array of ideological innovations, conveniently condensed as the unique contributions of the Party's successive paramount leaders: Deng Xiaoping theory, Jiang Zemin's Important Thought of the 'Three Represents', Hu Jintao's scientific outlook on development and, most recently, Xi Jinping's China Dream. Yet when one goes through the texts that serve as key expressions of these ideological contributions, one is hard-pressed to find something that has anything to do with Marxism, revolution, class struggle, socialism or communism, and this is increasingly so the closer one gets to the present. Instead, modernization, development, national strength and influence, prosperity, stability, order, social harmony and well-being are the defining features of the future that the Party says it is working towards.

Currently, even the commitment to the original core of the CCP's transformative mission has disappeared. Nowadays, little is heard of the establishment of a 'new China' that has thrown off the fetters of Imperial rule and traditional culture. In fact, quite the opposite is happening. In 2013 a new ideological framework of 'core socialist values and pooling positive energy to realize the Chinese dream of national rejuvenation' was presented. These core socialist values include, according to the official version, 'national goals of prosperity, democracy, civility, and harmony; social goals of freedom, equality, justice and the rule of law; and individual values of patriotism, dedication, integrity, and friendship'.[3] Another expression of the new ideological orthodoxy presents the CCP's source of legitimacy as having 'five dimensions'. These include not only popular approval, economic success, a powerful position in the world and the ability to select and borrow policy measures from a variety of sources, both domestic and foreign, but also history and the nature of traditional Chinese society and culture. Gone are revolution and transformation; it is hard to detect anything specifically socialist in the core socialist values or five dimensions of Party rule. Instead, the Party bases its rule on the unity of two opposites: demonstrable pragmatic success and the myth of cultural continuity. Deng Xiaoping and Confucius have been united; the CCP is increasingly explicitly presented as the modern successor to dynastic rule, an issue to which I return in chapter 5.[4]

The expiration of socialism as a goal is commonly said to have created an ideological vacuum threatening the very foundations of CCP rule. A communist party surely must exist to achieve socialism and communism. If a party jettisons its commitment to its core ideology, the argument goes, it also forfeits its right to rule. The Party itself is not immune to this fear either, and speeches and policy documents are routinely filled with empty references to socialism. The post-1978 experience in China, however, shows that matters are not really that straightforward. The argument about the CCP's ideological bankruptcy suffers from an overtly literal interpretation of what socialism in China is. To the CCP, the core referent of socialism is no longer

---

[3] On core socialist values, see e.g. *China Daily*. 2013. China Promotes Core Socialist Values. 24 December, online at http://usa.chinadaily.com.cn/china/2013-12/24/content_17192145.htm, accessed 3 August 2015. For a critical discussion, see *China Policy*. 2015. Anyone for 'Valuism'? 3 July, online at http://policycn.com/15-07-03-anyone-for-valuism/, accessed 3 August 2015.

[4] The information on the 'five dimensions' (*wu ge weidu*) of party legitimacy comes from 'Five Dimensions in Understanding the Communist Party of China', speech of Liu Yunshan, member of the CCP Politburo Standing Committee in charge of party affairs, at a meeting with European China experts in Copenhagen on 11 June 2014; see Li, Eric X. 2014. Emerging Trends in Chinese Studies and the Role of the Party. 7 July 2014, p. 3, online at http://english.cccws.org.cn/archiver/cccwsen/UpFile/Files/Default/20140708162532187779.pdf, accessed 25 August 2015.

Marxist or Maoist emancipatory ideology but Leninist principles of rule with the Party's leading role and transformative mission at their core.

If 'socialism' is no longer an ideology but simply a mission to transform society, no matter into exactly what, the endless stream of conceptual innovations after 1978 should perhaps also be reassessed. Innovation serves not to reinvigorate socialist ideology but rather to engineer its demise without inflicting political damage. In other words, 'ideology' in China is no longer ideological but merely practical. This does not, it has to be emphasized, render ideological innovation unimportant. Although ideology is no longer socialist in content, it is so in practice, as it continues to provide the goals and principles that guide fundamental political choices, whose ultimate aim is not simply to govern but also to change China. Ideology in contemporary China is best thought of as a unique and highly specialized code of political communication that is descriptive and totalitarian at the same time. Capable of flexibly communicating any message and any policy at any time, communist ideology is the constantly evolving fruit of highly specialized creative work that compellingly presents these messages as conveying the only possible correct understanding and evaluation of reality, reducing any logical contradictions that exist to mere threads in a uniform tapestry of declared truth. It is easy to dismiss the highly convoluted world of Chinese ideology as simply living in a lie, but this would not do justice to the strength and depth of Party rule. Those who want to understand what the Party has to say had better suppress their scepticism and learn this language and its referents.

There is a further point. Despite their explicit atheism, Marxism, socialism and communism are often compared to religions. They require conversion and unquestioned belief in dogma and provide a full eschatology that gives sense and purpose to what has to be done here and now. This continues to be an essential insight but misses one crucial point that is particularly salient to contemporary China. Viewing these ideologies as such is predicated on a Western understanding of religion modelled on Christianity. Cross culturally, however, religion is not about dogma and belief or how one expresses this belief. Religion is not even necessarily about the supernatural; rather, it is about the privileging of certain aspects of one's environment, life and experience as sacred, that is, as special and set apart from the normal, profane domains of life. This distinction exists in any society quite independently from what it is exactly that is considered sacred.[5]

If religion is simply about distinguishing the sacred from the profane, it can exist without any dogma and belief, or a material representation and awe of supernatural powers. In his study of the Giriama in Kenya the anthropologist David Parkin has developed this point further. Parkin demonstrates that the Giriama define themselves as a distinct people by reference to a remote, largely uninhabited but nevertheless sacred place of origin called the Kaya. This 'sacred void', as Parkin calls it, is kept pure and sacred through periodic acts of cleansing and purification to ensure the fertility and continuity of the Giriama people.[6]

The concept of a sacred void, I would argue, travels rather well to contemporary China. Leninist principles set the CCP apart from society and represent its rule as a sacred mission regardless of any of the beliefs, dogmas or ideologies that it professes. Just as Giriama elders move secretly in and out of the Kaya, with only the occasional elder identified as having broken some rule, so it is that Party leaders are beyond scrutiny and only occasionally get purged. The sacredness of the CCP is vested, not in its beliefs, but in the mystery of its inscrutable politics, a sacred and secret void at the heart of its rule that has to remain separate and untouched by the profane realities of ordinary politics and that has to be periodically cleansed by political purges such as Xi Jinping's anti-corruption campaign between 2013 and 2015. This is why the workings of the centre of the CCP must remain unknown and unknowable to ordinary outsiders and unsoiled by the profane machinations of power or the representation of special interests.

The sacredness of CCP politics is why the Party maintains an elaborate edifice of largely vacuous ideological innovations and resists the scrutiny of democratic principles and procedures. Jettisoning ideology would turn CCP rule into an ordinary dictatorship that visibly has no other mission than its own perpetuation. Introducing democracy would crowd the sacred void with the profanity of electoral politics that citizens of democratic countries might deplore, yet fully expect and

[5] This view of religion as about the dichotomy between the sacred and the profane was of course long ago formulated by one of the founding fathers of modern sociology and anthropology; see Durkheim, Emile. 1965. *The Elementary Forms of the Religious Life*. New York: Free Press.

[6] Parkin, David. 1991. *Sacred Void: Spatial Images of Work and Ritual among the Giriama of Kenya*. Cambridge: Cambridge University Press.

take for granted: deceitful politicians, greedy interest groups and media theatrics. It is, therefore, too simple to think that the CCP resists democratic elections and accountability only out of fear of losing power to competing parties. Its resistance to democracy runs at a much deeper indeed religious level. Democracy would expose the inner core of CCP politics to the gaze of ordinary people, stripping the Party of the mystery and sacredness that have rendered its rule unquestionable and untouchable for so long.

The sacred void remains essential to CCP unity and rule irrespective of what actually happens at its core. Scholarship, journalism and gossip on CCP politics are rife with reconstructions or speculations about power struggles, purges and factionalism taking place among the Party's elite. Factionalized struggles about the 'correct' Party line continue to be the defining feature of CCP politics from the Party's foundation in 1921 to the purge of Party leader Zhao Ziyang during the Tian'anmen Movement in 1989 and the fall in 2011 of Bo Xilai, rival of Xi Jinping for the Party's highest office. Again and again, the winners of a power struggle have demonized their adversaries and declared their own principles or policies to be the correct ones, saving the integrity of the Party and the survival of its sacred, transformative mission. Factional victory has to be absolute to purge the profanities of politics and to restore the sacredness of the secret void.

In 1989 the Tian'anmen Movement reminded the post-1978 leadership under Deng Xiaoping of the disastrous consequences of such winner-takes-all struggles between different political lines. Henceforth, differences of principle, policy or crude material interests should never again be framed as a struggle of good against evil waged to purge the sacred centre from the polluting presence of the opponents. Despite the occasional lapse (such as the conviction on corruption charges of Beijing mayor Chen Xitong in 1998 or Shanghai Party secretary Chen Liangyu in 2008), fundamental leadership splits and confrontations seemed to have become a thing of the past. The transition to the new leadership of Hu Jintao and Wen Jiabao in 2002 was carefully planned and orderly staged, to be repeated with the transition to the Xi Jinping-Li Keqiang leadership in 2012. CCP politics, so it seemed, was well on the way to becoming institutionalized.

This is why the widely publicized Bo Xilai affair has been so important. The affair exposed that the dynamics of factional politics among the CCP have not fundamentally changed. Unsuccessful in his bid to be anointed as Hu Jintao's future successor at the 2007 Party

Congress and subsequently exiled to the western city of Chongqing, Bo embarked on a maverick campaign all of his own against his rivals Xi Jinping and Li Keqiang. In characteristic CCP political style, Bo used his banishment to his advantage to create a 'Chongqing model' with alternative solutions for the unfairness created by China's rapid development and the estrangement between the Party and the people. Opportunistically tapping into the vast reservoir of 'totalitarian nostalgia',[7] some of these measures borrowed explicitly from Maoist practices, for instance, the requirement for cadres to live, work and eat with the peasants or the collective singing of nostalgic 'red' songs. Other measures were less symbolic. Rural residents were freed from the shackles of the household registration system by giving them urban status; less well-off people were assisted with public rental housing.[8]

Whether Bo Xilai really believed that he actually had a chance to become general secretary at the 2012 Party Congress will probably never be clear, but by going against the grain of the decision made by the top leadership in 2007, he cut right through the restrained factionalism of the post-1989 period. In retrospect, his fall from power seems inevitable: only his purge could restore the purity and unity of the sacred void. However, in light of subsequent events during Xi Jinping's first years in power, it seems clear that this has come at the expense of the informal rules that restrained factional politics after 1989. After having been appointed Party general secretary, Xi embarked on an anticorruption campaign that has ripped through the fabric of CCP policies from top to bottom, targeting, in the words of the campaign, both 'tigers' and 'flies'. The campaign amounts to a purge that the Party had not been subjected to since the aftermath of the suppression of the 1989 demonstrations. Protégés of former Party Secretary Jiang Zemin and security head Zhou Yongkang are prominent among its victims, but the campaign ranges much more widely and deeply to include real or suspected opponents of Xi of many stripes and colours.

---

[7] 'Totalitarian nostalgia' is a concept Geremie Barmé borrowed from post-Soviet studies to describe how 'the image of Mao, long since freed from his stifling aura and the odium of his destructive policies, became a "floating sign", a vehicle for nostalgic reinterpretation, unstated opposition to the status quo, and even satire.' Barmé, Geremie R. 1999. *In the Red: On Contemporary Chinese Culture*. New York: Columbia University Press, p. 320.

[8] For a partisan account of the Chongqing model, see Cui, Zhiyuan. 2011. Partial Intimations of the Coming Whole: The Chongqing Experiment in Light of the Theories of Henry George, James Meade, and Antonio Gramsci. *Modern China* 36,6:646–60.

At a Politburo meeting on 29 December 2014, on the annual report of the Party's Discipline Inspection Committee, the divisions within the Party were addressed explicitly using the language of factions, identifying a 'petroleum gang', a 'secretary gang' and a 'Shanxi gang' as sources of 'landslide-style corruption' and the 'vested interests' of high officials that inhibit urgently needed change. Highly unusually, these observations were openly disseminated through Xinhua News Agency and other channels. Openly admitting to divisions opens up the sacred void of Party politics in a potentially destructive manner. Rather than celebrating diversity and allowing transparent debate, it insists in traditional Leninist fashion that diversity is damaging and that the only possible solution must be to purge dissent and opposition, restore unity and close the sacred void again.[9]

The sacredness of the Party gives its elite a sense of destiny and right to rule even in the absence of absolute ideological imperatives. The CCP is virtually unique in the world in its ability to take a long-term and strategic view that is often sorely lacking in democratic polities or more ordinary authoritarian regimes. The Party is also highly adaptive in its approach to issues, problems or adversity. Its ability and willingness to try, test, discard, improve and try again, often without much regard for short-term consequences or adverse effects, are part of a decades-long legacy of facing extreme adversity and setbacks. The Party's fight with the Guomindang and the Japanese before 1949 and subsequently with the Americans, the Soviet Union and assorted internal enemies has bred what Sebastian Heilmann and Elizabeth Perry have called a Maoist 'guerrilla policy style' that has continued into the reform period.[10]

---

[9] Jing, Li. 2015. China Takes Rare Step of Naming Communist Party Factions Tied to Disgraced Top Cadres. *South China Morning Post*, 5 January, online at www.scmp.com/news/china/article/1674062/fallenofficialsbehindfactionsxinhuasays?page=all, checked 18 August 2015; *China Daily*. 2015. 塌方式腐败 (*tafangshi fubai*): Landslide-Style Corruption. 12 January, online at www.chinadaily.com.cn/opinion/2015-01/12/content_19292028.htm, checked 18 August 2015; Miller, Alice. 2015. The Trouble with Factions. *China Leadership Monitor*, 19 March, online at www.hoover.org/sites/default/files/research/docs/clm46am.pdf, checked 19 August 2015.

[10] Heilmann, Sebastian, Perry, Elizabeth. 2011. Embracing Uncertainty: Guerrilla Policy Style and Adaptive Governance in China. In *Mao's Invisible Hand: The Political Foundations of Adaptive Governance in China*, ed. Sebastian Heilmann, Elizabeth Perry, pp. 1–29. Cambridge, MA: Harvard University Asia Center.

Under Xi's current purge, the Party may seem weak, divided and desperate. However, it is actually CCP politics that has returned to normal after a twenty-year period during which divisions had largely been kept from view. Together with the Party's transformative mission and the sacred void and mystery of its rule, the adaptive capacity of the CCP is a vitally important source of the Party's resilience that runs counter to Western expectations of the brittleness of the rule of the Party now that it is backed up by neither revolutionary socialism nor democratic mandate.

2.4 Fragmentation and Localism

The strength of Party rule also rests in other places where often weakness is thought to reside. The endemic lack of cohesion of the Chinese state is prominent among them. The fragmentation of the state between the domains of different ministries, departments and commissions and the strong localism of sub-national governments are well documented. They undeniably inhibit swift decision making and unified administration and tie the hands of the central authorities. In many policy areas, turf wars between ministries delay policy making, legislation drafting and policy implementation. What makes this issue especially pernicious is that at each level (province, prefecture, county, township) the structure of Party and government mirrors that of the central administration. Central departments thus have functional counterparts in all of China's provinces, prefectures, counties and townships, creating vertically connected 'systems' that have their own agendas and that compete with other such systems.

Arrangements exist to counter the fragmentation between systems. Well known are, for instance, leadership cross-departmental 'small groups' for specific policy areas. Some of these small groups exist merely as occasional meetings of the leaders of several departments of government or the Party that have a stake in a particular policy area or project. Other small groups are fully institutionalized parts of the administration with their own staff, budgetary authority and rules of membership. However, a much more important counterweight to vertical fragmentation between departments is the horizontal integration of local administrations. Vertical systems have as a rule neither the authority nor the budget to enforce compliance of their lower-level counterparts. Unless the higher-level department wishes to allocate funds to pay for its own staff in a lower-level unit, they can merely guide rather than command the personnel of a lower-level department who are on the payroll of their own, local administration.

The strength of and tensions between the branches (vertically connected functional systems) and areas (local administrations) are the source of much frustration for the central leadership. The autonomy of local authorities means that this is anything but a system where the central leadership can impose its wishes without constraint. The totalitarianism of Party rule is thus cushioned by the decentralization and fragmentation of the administrative apparatus. Unpopular or impractical central policies are diluted, adapted or even resisted. Funds allocated for a particular purpose are diverted to others. Local authorities or branch departments set their own agendas or priorities, often in competition with the centre and with each other. Local politics may be captured by special interests, often through organized crime, corruption or the sale of official positions.

It is easy to condemn such practices. Yet the problem is not simple power abuse, greed or stupidity on the part of individual local leaders. Until the early 2000s, local authorities had to rely almost exclusively on their own sources of income to meet their expenditures. This often forced local leaders to engage in predatory behaviour in search of revenue, not only to line their own pockets but also to fund local strategies of development regardless of central priorities or preoccupations. Since then, central policies have seen to it that many of the local sources of revenue have disappeared. State-owned and collective enterprises have largely been privatized, or at least made much more independent. The collection of local taxes has been taken over by the central authorities, and local levies and fees have been banned. Central fund transfers have compensated for some of these losses, but these allocations follow priorities set at the centre, not locally.

Although local authorities in recent years have become very creative in diverting central funds to purposes that they were not intended for, the main source of funds that they continue to have full discretion over is land. Starting in the 1990s, the appropriation of land or homes for development has taken great flight, profiting local authorities, project developers and investors. Ordinary farmers or urban residents who have lost their land or home, however, are often left with only minimal compensation. As a consequence, land appropriation has become the most important source of contention in China, a very visible manifestation not only of the financial crisis of local government but also of the growing gap between rich and poor.

It is easy to take a dim view of local government. The central authorities certainly tend to do so, either because local governments genuinely frustrate their objectives or else more cynically as a convenient way to exonerate the centre from China's many administrative ills. However, the autonomy and intransigence of local authorities are also a great good, and there are excellent reasons why the central authorities hesitate to eliminate them. Local administration in China fulfils many functions reserved for central administrations in developed countries; despite appearances, the central government has only a very limited presence and role beyond the capital Beijing. Even locally stationed army units coordinate their activities with local administrations through their Party committees. Especially county governments are directly responsible for many aspects of economic development, public security, finance, welfare and social security, irrigation, poverty alleviation, education, health care and transportation. The departments of central and provincial authorities therefore hardly have to be directly involved in the implementation and – crucially – the funding of public administration.

Although this makes administering a huge, diverse and, in many places, still undeveloped country practically feasible and financially possible, it does so at the price of creating many unfunded mandates that local authorities either somehow have to find the money for or else simply must neglect. Economic inequality between regions thus also leads to huge differences in public services. More positively, local autonomy allows for much political room to play with. Local authorities often can and do develop their own policies that they think work best for them. If successful, these ideas might even be publicized as 'experiments' or 'models' for emulation elsewhere. In some cases, they might ultimately become incorporated into regional or national policy, especially when such a model had been supported or adopted by a leader at the centre in a bid to demonstrate the efficacy of his ideas in the face of opposition by his political adversaries.

The autonomy of local administrations also serves as an important political buffer. Without institutionalized checks and balances, China's central politics are prone to sudden shifts and changes as certain leaders manage to gain the upper hand. Without the local inertia or intransigence built into the administrative system, policy implementation would swing even more violently than it already does. The viscosity of the system is also why mobilizational or heavy-handed methods – the same totalitarian methods that gave China disasters like the Great Leap Forward – continue to be used even in the post-Maoist period. Fundamental policies such as mandatory family planning (relaxed in 2015 but still not fundamentally abolished), economic development or the fight against corruption continue to require campaign-style politics in which one objective temporarily overrides all others. These methods work insofar as local leaders do indeed fulfil their obligations to the letter (and beyond) in order not to be accused of sabotage or disloyalty, even against their better judgement. However, as soon as the pressure from the higher levels subsides, local concerns and priorities quickly bounce back.

Mobilizational methods are not the only way that the centre can impose its will on independently minded local administrations or departments. Indeed, the relationships between the different parts and levels of the administrative system should not be thought of as a constant tussle for power or influence that produces violent contradictions between centripetal and centrifugal forces, but as a system in which the different elements have been given considerable freedom because there is always a mechanism that keeps their autonomy in check. This mechanism is, of course, the Communist Party itself.

As said earlier in this chapter, the Communist Party does not govern. Instead, it leads, controls and inspires all institutions of government and governance. The Party's continued control over the people who lead and administer the institutions of governance continues to be the most vital feature of China's uniquely socialist mode of governance. Known as cadres in China and other socialist societies, these people should not be thought of simply as bureaucrats or, alternatively, politicians, officials or managers: the concept of cadre includes all of these. Cadres ought to be, in Maoist terms, both 'red' and 'expert': they have to be fully committed to socialist ideology and practice and possess the professional skills and knowledge needed for their job.

The recruitment, training and deployment of cadres are the most important ways in which the Party inserts itself directly into all institutions of state and society and guides and directs the project of socialist transformation. Suffused with 'Party spirit' and bound by the demands of Party discipline and the constraints of the nomenklatura system discussed earlier, the leading cadres who are in charge of the institutions of Party and state are never fully independent, but always have to be mindful of the preferences of higher levels, even if they have not received any direct orders or demands. However, leading cadres are much more than just the faithful servants of their superiors: they are also members of a local ruling elite with their own loyalties, ethos and politics. To understand how cadres navigate these two conflicting aspects of their identity and belonging, I will look at the dynamics of local cadre careers as I encountered them during research in Yunnan province in the Southwest of China.[11]

The career of many leading cadres at the provincial level or below follows a well-established pattern. Initially, cadres are recruited into the administration by the personnel bureau, or 'organization department' in CCP parlance, of a county Party committee as high school or university graduates. If successful enough, these cadres ultimately receive a promotion and their career management is taken over one level higher by the Party committee of the prefecture. For a selected few, this pattern eventually repeats itself with promotion and management by the organization department of the provincial party committee. At each level, a cadre usually serves in several posts of the same rank as they are moved between different functional areas of the administration. Eventually, career progression plateaus at a particular level. Without any further rank promotions, the cadre will continue to receive new postings at the same administrative level in the area under the jurisdiction of their organization department. At some point, an appointment to a post without direct executive responsibility, such as in the local people's congress or people's consultative conference, is usually the signal that they should prepare for retirement.

This career pattern is noteworthy on several counts. First, it shows the lack of separation between party, government and other parts of the administration, despite elaborate institutional arrangements that might give another impression. It is also reveals how cadre management is

---

[11] The following discussion is based on my fieldwork on local cadres and party schools in Yunnan province in 2004 and 2005; see Pieke, Frank N. 2009. *The Good Communist: Elite Training and State Building in Today's China.* Cambridge: Cambridge University Press. A very detailed study on the party's use of the cadre system to strike a balance between decentralization and control is Landry, Pierre. 2008. *Decentralized Authoritarianism in China: The Communist Party's Control of Local Elites in the Post-Mao Era.* Cambridge: Cambridge University Press.

a key manifestation of the Party's exercise of its leading role across all formal institutions of governance, including, of course, the Party itself. However, such career patterns also produce something else that is arguably just as important. Recruitment as a cadre is a highly prized opportunity for upward mobility. As locally recruited personnel, cadres identify very strongly with their locality and its administration and the Party. Being a cadre is more than just a calling, job or career. To them, the local Party committee is not only the concrete manifestation of the Party and its power to discipline, reward and punish, but also the focal point of a local community of cadres of their own rank. This is not only true of cadres working within the central administration of their own area, for instance as head or party secretary of a government bureau. Cadres who have been posted to serve in a subordinate area away from the central administration behave very much like expats. Their spouse and child often continue to live in their flat in the central town or city, with the cadre commuting back and forth on a weekly or sometimes even daily basis.

Cadres are recruited from among the best and brightest in an area. For them, serving the Party includes service to their native place. Furthermore, serving the Party means to work and often live together with other cadres of equal rank and from the same place: from the perspective of cadres, the Party and its administration are not faceless institutions, but a community of peers of equal rank serving in and being largely from the same jurisdiction. Yet this community and jurisdiction are at the same time embedded in a larger jurisdiction: townships are part of a county, counties are part of a prefecture, and prefectures are part of a province. Ambitious local cadres hope and expect that, one day, they will be promoted, leaving their local area and its community of cadres, to become a member of that larger, but otherwise very similar jurisdiction and community.

However, it is important not to oversimplify matters. At each level and locality the cadre corps does not simply consist of people who have all made their careers at lower levels in the same area, eventually earning a promotion to a job at a higher level of the administration. Just as they might at some point receive an outside posting in a subordinate area, so is their local administration supplemented by non-local cadres of senior rank who the organization department at a higher level has put in a handful of key posts. These non-local cadres serve for only a limited, fixed term after which they leave for posts elsewhere and are replaced by fresh appointees. A third group of cadres in a particular locality and level are younger ones who as a rule are better educated and are considered to be more promising. These cadres have been recruited to start their career directly at this level eventually to take them at least one and possibly two or more hierarchical levels higher.

Because a cadre's original area is a part of, and hierarchically subordinated to, this new jurisdiction, cadres who are promoted in a sense never really leave their native area, but simply see the area they belong to expand first to include a county, then a prefecture and ultimately a whole province. The logic of promotion and job rotation expands their loyalties and attachments to more encompassing areas and larger communities of cadre-peers: promotion quite literally expands cadres' horizon of their service to the Party. During my own research at local Party schools I saw this process in action. Cadres who are trained or educated at a Party school are all drawn from the jurisdiction of the administration that the school belongs to. Their stay at the Party school helped them to get to know cadres from other areas in the school's jurisdiction. At the school cadres thus had the opportunity to become part of the much larger community one tier up in the hierarchy and build a range of informal ties that are both the lubricant and glue of the administration. The Party's orchestration of cadre careers on the basis of areas and hierarchical level reinforces and creates the hierarchically nested administrative communities of cadres, creating a powerful fusion of habitual localism and universalism among the people that are the backbone of the Chinese administrative system.

2.5 Bending and Breaking the Rules

There is, of course, a massive price that has to be paid for the fragmented and decentralized nature of the Chinese administration. Local officials are responsible for many more aspects of governance that in most other countries. They are entrepreneurial and adaptive. However, they easily take too many liberties and, if that happens, there are no strong and direct mechanisms to keep their behaviour in check.

One aspect of this has already been mentioned. Local administrations in particular continue to be burdened with huge unfunded mandates (e.g. nine-year compulsory education, pension plans, health insurance, unemployment insurance and welfare) and very few sources of income to pay for them. The diversion of central funds transfers to other purposes, such as land sales and project development, are the most common ways of raising income, but they often violate national regulations.

Such administrative practices are however only one aspect of the monetization of local government. Local officials are responsible for local economic development and many local enterprises were started with the support of (and sometimes by) officials. Local government also controls many of the resources that businesses cannot do without (land, water, electricity, labour, permissions). Although the legal system has been strengthened, it is still not completely independent from political interference and many entrepreneurs seek backing from powerful individuals. The fusion of business and government through a thick network of personal connections and reciprocal support continues to be the norm across China: money and power are often hard to distinguish.

Just as officials are for sale, so are positions. Because jobs in the administration are worth a lot of money, candidates often have to fork out very considerable sums to secure an appointment even – or perhaps especially – in the case of a nomenklatura position that requires Party approval. Paradoxically, the nomenklatura system sometimes encourages these practices. Local Party secretaries are known to cash in on their position just before their transfer to another area through a massive sale of positions that are under the control of the Party committee that they head up.

Corruption and the abuse of power are part of the system, bred by the very localism that also renders it highly flexible, adaptive, resilient and entrepreneurial. It might be the price that China must pay for its unique form of government and economic success. However, localism, corruption and power abuse also mean that officials in China always operate on a very thin line between legal and illegal behaviour. In Chinese local politics there is always more than meets the eye and rules are meant to be broken, but only by a selected few.

Exactly because corruption is so endemic, it is also a very powerful political tool. Allegations and convictions of corruption are frequent, but still relatively rare in light of the fact that most officials are, in one way or another, corrupt. The central authorities routinely pronounce that they will crack down on corruption and will have no mercy on the individuals concerned, no matter who they are. The central leadership thus presents itself as unsoiled by the muck of local politics and the friend of the common man and woman, all very conveniently without any cost to itself. Just as importantly, corruption is a seemingly non-political weapon that victorious politicians can and do use against their foes, and is perhaps best thought of as the post-reform equivalent of accusations of rightism and counter-revolution by Maoists against those who dared to oppose them.

Fortunately, the use of corruption as a tool to finish off a political rival is the exception rather than the rule. Usually, it is limited to cases where a leader either wants to set an example or where his adversary has transgressed the boundaries of normal political competition. At the central level, this pattern is illustrated by three cases mentioned earlier in this chapter, namely Beijing mayor Chen Xitong, Shanghai party secretary Chen Liangyu and Chongqing party secretary Bo Xilai. However, lower down the administrative hierarchy anti-corruption efforts tend to be much less strict than the widely publicized cases of top officials may lead one to believe. Convictions for corruption happen, but are relatively few and punishments are relatively mild, because persecution normally happens through the Party's discipline inspection system rather than through the judicial system. Legal persecutions and tougher sentences only happen during anti-corruption campaigns. While this does boost the legitimacy of the central authorities, it also undermines it. A legal system that needs political pressure to work does not inspire great confidence and reinforces among the Chinese public the conviction that China is still ruled by men rather than by law.

2.6 State Building

The economic success of the reforms has made possible the funding of a massive project of state building that is at the centre of the epochal transformation of China into a modern society and global presence. In the late 1990s, the government under Premier Zhu Rongji carried out a far-reaching restructuring of the government system and a drastic reduction of the number of government departments. In 2003 and again in 2008, further government restructuring was carried out. China has moved away from a government fundamentally predicated on a Stalinist planning ethos to government that limits itself to providing the institutional framework for the facilitation and supervision of the orderly conduct of social and economic life, whose party members are obliged to organize themselves wherever they work or live.

Counter-intuitively, market reform and government restructuring have come with an increase in the strength and size of government, mainly because of the continued expansion of sub-national rather than central state capacity. Compared to the pre-1978 period the government is no longer involved in virtually all aspects of social and economic life, but has much improved its capacity to govern those parts of society that it cares about. Throughout the reform period, public employment has continued to grow from about 1 per cent of total employment in 1978 to 3.1 per cent in 2005, 2.5 per cent of which at sub-national levels. Despite the growth in public employment it would be incorrect to say that China has a bloated bureaucracy: China's public employment remains well below the global mean of 4.7 per cent of total employment with only 1.1 per cent at local levels. In view of these figures, China could probably do with a further expansion of public employment and governing capacity, especially at the central level.[12]

The many facets of government are best illustrated by the state of public finances. Throughout the 1980s, total budgetary revenue declined steadily, something to be expected at a time of decentralization and marketization, bottoming out at 11 per cent of gross domestic product (GDP) in 1996, with central government revenue just being 3 per cent of GDP. In other words, government in general and the central government in particular had ceased to be significant factors in the economy. Tax reform in the mid 1990s strengthened and centralized tax collection. Total budgetary revenue was back to a little over 20 per cent in 2007. Tax receipts continue to rise at 1.5 times the growth of GDP, making government now not only an important but also a steadily growing player in the economy.

Although the improved system of public finances gives the central government control over half the budget, government finances continue to be highly decentralized. After tax reform in 1994, local governments supplemented their much reduced budgetary revenues (mainly local taxes and fees) by further expanding their so-called extra-budgetary revenues (revenues not subject to approval by higher authorities), especially those deriving from the sale of land use rights. With the transition to the Hu Jintao-Wen Jiabao leadership in 2002, the rapid

[12] Figures on public employment are from Ang, Yuen Yuen. 2012. Counting Cadres: A Comparative View of the Size of China's Public Employment. *China Quarterly* 211:676–96.

expansion of government services (welfare, social insurance, pensions, education, and health) and infrastructure investment was largely the responsibility of local governments. This has led to an increase in the share of county and township governments from 28 to 40 per cent of total budgetary expenditures since 1998. Some of this has been funded by local revenue sources, but much has come from central-to-local budgetary transfers, effectively reversing the centralizing trend caused by the 1994 tax reform.[13]

While many aspects of the decentralized nature of public finances might be problematic (at least from the perspective of the central government), the deliberate growth of budgetary transfers and local government responsibilities in the 2000s reveal that this is no accident but a fundamental choice. Sure enough, some of the sharper edges have been removed from local government autonomy. With the abolition of local fees and the agricultural tax in the early and mid 2000s, local governments hardly have any budgetary sources of revenue left, making them more dependent that ever on the transfer of central resources and thus at least in principle more amenable to central guidance.

More importantly, villages and towns and townships – the latter being the lowest level of formal government immediately above villages – lost most of their financial independence in the 2000s. Townships have taken over financial control over villages. Townships in turn have largely been made financially dependent on fiscal transfers from counties; signs are that township governments now operate as mere branches of county governments. County governments themselves have further been strengthened by a reduction of the role of prefectural governments immediately above them and increasingly deal directly with the provincial authorities. China is thus moving from a five-tier government structure (centre-province-prefecture-county-township) to a de facto three-tier structure (centre-province-county). This amounts to a certain degree of centralization with powers clustered in fewer places and levels lower down the administrative hierarchy, but overall

[13] Information on China's public finances here has been taken from Wong, Christine. 2009. Rebuilding Government for the 21st Century: Can China Incrementally Reform the Public Sector? *China Quarterly* 200:929–52, and Wong, Christine. 2013. Reforming China's Public Finances for Long-Term Growth. In *China: A New Model for Growth and Development*, ed. Ross Garnaut, Fang Cai, Ligang Song, pp. 199–219. Melbourne: ANU Press.

does not change the fundamentally decentralized nature of the system. The central government is richer and in some regards more powerful than before, but still deals with society almost exclusively in an indirect fashion through lower-level governments.

2.7 The Rule of Law

The emphasis on the rule of law is perhaps the most emblematic aspect of China's evolving system of governance. Strengthening the 'socialist legal system' was a feature of the reforms virtually from the word go, starting with the promulgation of the criminal law in 1979 and a new constitution in 1982. As an explicit corrective to the arbitrary use of power during the Cultural Revolution, the rhetoric of the rule of law was an important aspect of the rejection of Maoism at the time. Building a legal system and the rule of law were the antonyms of and antidotes to 'politics', 'ideology' and the 'rule by man' of the Maoist period. More pragmatically, building a legal system was also considered important to accommodate the emerging market economy, and especially foreign investment and trade, establishing universal rules to trump personal power and connections. Together with law-making, the construction of a socialist legal system also included the building of an entire legal profession and judicial infrastructure, including a system of courts and public persecutors, law schools and law degrees, lawyers' practices, and professional associations. However, only at the Fourteenth Party Congress in 1994 was the rule of law adopted as the basic principle of governance.

Clearly, the rule of law jars with the leading role of the CCP. Although the principle has been adopted that all organizations and people in society ought to be subject to the law, the Party's pre-eminence continues to be guaranteed by a special provision in the preamble to the constitution that states '[u]nder the leadership of the Communist Party of China...the Chinese people of all nationalities will continue to adhere to the people's democratic dictatorship and the socialist road'. The constitution itself, however, remains silent on the role of the CCP. Instead, in its first two articles the constitution defines the people's democratic dictatorship as 'led by the working class and based on the alliance of workers and peasants' and identifies not the CCP but the National People's Congress and the local people's congresses at various levels as 'the organs through which the people

exercise state power'. In 2014, the Fourth Plenary Session of the CCP
Central Committee was devoted to the theme of the rule of law. The
Plenum put forward five principles by which the rule of law has to be
based on 'China's realities'. The first of these principles was the leadership of the CCP.[14]

This contradiction of principles is reflected in the rule of law in
practice. Many laws do indeed constitute the foundations and the principles of governance in a particular domain and are the basic documents defining the scope and nature of the work of the administrative
department(s) responsible for that domain. However, a thicket of often
secret or 'internal' government or Party regulations, documents, opinions and guidelines informs policy making and implementation. Laws
are indeed promulgated by national or local people's congresses, not
the Party. However, the Party committees of people's congresses are
very powerful. Law-making by people's congresses is therefore only
partially independent from the Party and laws are to a very large extent
instruments to serve Party rule. The promulgation of a law often signals
the final resolution of political disagreement foreshadowed in earlier
policy documents, temporary regulations or trial laws. Laws are therefore often best described as aspirational: statements of policy intentions and objectives rather than standards of current behaviour. The
political weight of laws means that much is at stake in the passing of a
law. Drafting or revising of laws often takes many years, long debates
and many versions before final promulgation by a people's congress.

Yet the law matters a great deal to companies, individuals and even
government departments. The legal profession in China is thriving and
tens of thousands of domestic and foreign law firms do brisk business.
The law also provides the basis for protest, petitions or even full litiga-
tion against decisions of government. Activist lawyers or activists with
legal expertise take on cases of citizens who seek redress or compensation for wrongs suffered or as a way to expose corruption, misman-
agement or power abuse.

---

[14] For the full text of the constitution and preamble as revised in 2004, see
www.npc.gov.cn/englishnpc/Constitution/node_2824.htm. On the Fourth
Plenum's Decisions on Major Issues Concerning Comprehensively Advancing
the Rule of Law, see Zhang Hengshan, 'Interpretation of the 4th Plenum of the
18th CPC Central Committee', at Briefing on the Fourth Plenary Session of the
Eighteenth CPC Central Committee (for Foreign Businesses in China),
International Department of the CPC Central Committee, 3 November 2014.

Although courts have considerable freedom in adjudicating cases brought before them, the CCP exercises supervision over the legal system through its Party committees. The Party has little or no interest in the vast majority of court cases, but in politically sensitive cases CCP supervision or meddling by individual Party leaders may encroach upon the independence of judges or public persecutors. It would, however, be a mistake to dismiss the rule of law as incomplete and therefore useless, a legal facade hiding hard-nosed dictatorship. The rule of law caters pragmatically to the needs and nature of Chinese society with both a robust market economy and rights-conscious citizens and an administrative system led by the Communist Party. Indeed, in the CCP's mind's eye the rule of law and Party leadership cannot do without each other. Without the rule of law, Party leadership could once again deteriorate into personal dictatorship; without Party leadership, the rule of law would be under constant threat by special interests and unprincipled political usurpers. Under the rule of law, rights and freedoms of citizens are guaranteed. Citizens have and do use the power to sue their government and each other. The CCP in turn continues to reserve its right to override the rule of law, usually through administrative procedure but sometimes also by directly interfering in the adjudication by courts. In practice, this has created a system of very considerable, but not absolute rule of law that appears flawed when held up against the standard of Western democratic countries, but serves the need for justice and accountability of many without threatening the Party's supremacy.

2.8 Marketization as Governance

Market reform is usually interpreted as the encouragement of the growth of a market economy outside the state. Yet the market-state dichotomy that this implies is misleading. Despite reform, the state is still intimately involved in the economy, not only as a regulator but also as a player and stakeholder, an issue that I will return to in chapter 3. Furthermore, marketization has also become a vitally important strategy of governance that in many ways is very similar to (and has extensively borrowed from) neo-liberal deregulation, commercialization and privatization of state functions and assets in many Western countries since the late 1970s. Coming most immediately to mind here are public services (health care, education, housing, transportation) and social security and welfare (retirement, unemployment) where reforms have forced the state to retreat and allowed competition and privatization.

Counter-intuitive perhaps is the fact that marketization has also cut right to the heart of the CCP itself, deployed as a tool to improve the Party's capacity to guide and lead the administration and society. In my own work on CCP schools I found that marketization had become a key strategy for the modernization of the training, education and management of party cadres.[15]

Perhaps the best example of the marketization of CCP core functions is provided by propaganda. Propaganda in contemporary China aims at guiding and forming public opinion only on certain important matters and has moved a long way from the often coercive methods of the Maoist period used to impose ideological uniformity. Chinese propaganda officials have, for one, carefully studied the way the Blair government in the UK and the Bush administration in the US managed the media and spun the government's messages, one of many examples of the incorporation in China's neo-socialism of Western neo-liberal governmental techniques.

There should be no mistaking that propaganda continues to be a core task of the Party. Propaganda work has adopted the ideas and methods of Western mass communication, media techniques, public relations and advertising. It includes all means of communication, both conventional ones such as mass media (TV, radio, print media), education, culture (literature, film, theatre, music, art), and internet-based means of communication (e-government, web-based publishing and broadcasting, social media).

Direct censorship is only a small part of propaganda work. Self-censorship and positive guidance on topics, approaches and wordings create a broad uniformity in the messages across all media. Commercialization has been an essential component in this new approach. Commercialization makes maintaining an extensive propaganda apparatus more affordable and has enabled the growth of a remarkably diverse media landscape comparable in many regards to democratic countries, although it is by no means free of Party influence or in extreme cases even repression. Commercialization means that the

---

[15] See, Pieke, Frank N. 2009. *The Good Communist: Elite Training and State Building in Today's China*. Cambridge: Cambridge University Press, chapter 5.

form and content of communicative products must be such that people would like to consume them. So, newspapers or TV programmes routinely carry items critical of social and political trends. Even more important is the fact that commercialization itself sells: Chinese readers have been found more readily to believe a newspaper they think to be commercially produced and thus more independent from the authorities. Lastly, commercialized mass communication helps keep the government and the Party informed of events, trends, opinions, moods or ideas that otherwise do not easily percolate upwards through the administrative hierarchy. Such a 'responsive authoritarianism' helps the regime to adapt or change policy in a timely fashion, thus enabling political change without requiring the political pluralism of a democratic system.

2.9 Consultation, Participation and Democratization

The political system of the People's Republic of China has from the outset been adorned with an extensive democratic and consultative edifice. As discussed earlier in the section on the rule of law, at each level of government the people's congress whose delegates are directly or indirectly elected is the formal legislative body and highest authority. Under the tutelage of the CCP, at each level of government, eight 'democratic' parties are represented in the people's consultative conferences. Originally part of the CCP's strategy to forge a broad coalition of forces in its struggle against the Japanese and later after the Second World War with the Guomindang, the CCP has deliberately nurtured the role of the democratic parties since the start of the reforms. Cadres from the democratic parties are appointed to government posts, recently even including a minister at the central level.

   Although the CCP is firmly committed to this structure, it also realizes that the people's conferences and people's congresses alone are not enough to ensure the transparency and accountability needed for a stable and legitimate political system equipped to deal with the diversity of interests created by a market economy. Other institutions and mechanisms have also been brought into play. One of these is the complaints system. Each level and branch of government includes a 'letters and visits' office to receive complaints and petitions from members of the public, but until the 1990s these were rarely heard from. By taking their case to such an office, complainants avoid the costs, complexities and risks of legal action: the government itself is asked to remedy its own incorrect actions or decisions. Complainants can be very tenacious, taking their case if needed to ever higher levels of government, including the centre in Beijing. In 2005, the central government received 603 000 petitions; a year earlier in 2004, petitions to governments at county level and above had reached 13.73 million. Since 2008, the central government has taken a stricter attitude; as a result, taking a petition to Beijing as a protest tactic has gradually waned. Complaints often lead to open protest. Since the early 1990s, demonstrations, sit-downs and blockades by aggrieved petitioners became increasingly widespread not only to seek redress for individual grievances, but also as a normal part of collective action and bargaining over a wide array of issues, including jobs, facilities for the handicapped, cadre power abuse and corruption, house demolition or land appropriation, pensions, and environmental pollution.

Perhaps the most widely known aspect of reform of the political system is the introduction of formal elections for the appointment of local-level officials. Although democratic elections were held for rural team leaders throughout the Maoist period, in the mid 1980s the CCP embarked on the much more ambitious introduction of village committee elections. Village elections became a legal requirement in 1998 and are now routinely held across the country. Subsequently, several places in Sichuan province held experimental elections for township heads. Although only a relatively small number of people were allowed to vote in these elections, some of these elections included non-Party members. Unlike village leaders, township heads are full state cadres normally appointed by the Party through the nomenklatura system. Such elections therefore cut right to the heart of the CCP's grip over the administrative system, and it should therefore not come as a surprise that these initial experiments were not followed through. The Party opted instead for the further development of the appointment system with an open registration and examination of candidates, after which the Party committee makes the final selection.

It is tempting to speculate that the introduction of consultative, participatory or democratic mechanisms are the start of a gradual process of democratization, seeds that eventually will germinate and grow because of the inherent superiority or desirability of democracy. This is not, however, how the Party sees things. Democracy, consultation and participation are mechanisms to make the political system, including the Party itself, work better. They introduce greater transparency in appointments, prevent power abuse and corruption, forestall the growth of entrenched power bases, strengthen the legitimacy of office holders and enhance receptiveness to public demands and interests. Democracy, participation and consultation are part of the arsenal of neo-socialism, not weapons against it.

2.10 Social Management and Social Governance

Since 1998, macro-economic control, the provision of public services and social management have been defined as the three basic functions of government. While the first two are in line with what governments all over the world say they do, the latter seems opaque. In the concept of social management – since the Third Plenum of the Eighteenth Party Congress in November 2013 rebranded as 'social governance' to emphasize the role of the government and the party – Leninist party leadership over society and neo-liberal ideas about the autonomy of society come together. According to the Party, state–society relations are increasingly a matter of facilitation and supervision. China's social structure has created new social contradictions and differences of interest. Only by strengthening and improving social management can these interests be coordinated and planned as a whole, social contradictions be resolved, social stability and order be guaranteed, and the social base of the rule of the Party be consolidated.

Social management and social governance are umbrella terms that cover a broad range of approaches to governance with the overall aim to improve social stability, to strengthen the leadership of the party, and at the same time to enable autonomy and self-rule in society, including democratic institutions and procedures, grassroots government, civil society social organizations, and the use of volunteers. Social governance is also shorthand for discussions and negotiations between citizens who protest or otherwise create a disturbance, and local authorities. Special 'stability maintenance funds' have been created that enable local cadres to pay off demonstrators, either directly in cash or by funding solutions to their demands. However social governance also has another, harsh face. This includes 'striking hard' against crime, management of the internet by restricting its autonomy and using digital technologies for propaganda and social control, building a rapid response force for disasters and disturbances, and even the establishment of a Council of State Security to coordinate Party control over all aspects of security work in combating terrorism, religious extremism

and separatism.[16] Social governance builds selective and unequal partnerships with organizations and individuals outside the government
and Party. It allows social forces a voice and role in the governance of
their own affairs, but always on the condition that social stability is
maintained and Party rule guaranteed.

Despite the efforts to manage society, the Party is no longer completely in the driver's seat. As the Party gets better at management and
governance rather than simply controlling society, society in turn gains
increasing room and leverage to manage the Party and government.
The Chinese political system has always been highly decentralized and
fragmented, and neo-socialist governmental techniques have added to
the space that already exists. New voices make themselves heard that
officials have to take into account when making or implementing policy, an issue that I will return to in Chapter 4.

2.11 Which Paths Can the CCP Take?

Since coming to power in 2012, CCP Party General Secretary Xi Jinping has given a new face to Chinese politics. Eating dumplings with
the masses, appearing on TV to explain policy in a language that
everyone can understand, and impressing the world's leaders with an
easy demeanour that projects both accessibility and powerful self-
confidence, Xi could not be more different from his bland and aloof
predecessor Hu Jintao. But will this also change the nature of the Chinese political system?

Xi Jinping is not all smiles. Civil rights activists and lawyers, journalists, bloggers and academics find their freedom curbed in ways not
seen since the period immediately following the suppression of the
Tian'anmen protests in 1989. Xi's anti-corruption campaign claims
one high-profile victim after another, exposing not only ordinary graft
but also the vast fortunes amassed by Chinese leaders. The case of
tycoon Liu Han, executed in 2015 for 'organizing and leading mafia-
style crime and murder', also revealed something else: the infiltration
of powerful criminal networks into the political system.

---

[16] An example of the use of information technology to serve the party's purposes
is the recent anti-corruption whistle-blowing website and social media apps
administered directly by the CCP Central Discipline Inspection Committee.

The muffling of critical voices and the anti-corruption campaign are not as much of a watershed as they might seem. Targets of the anti-corruption campaign do indeed extend to the highest level, but seem to be limited to Xi's main rivals and their allies; the most prominent victim has been Zhou Yongkang, Party security supremo until 2012 and protégé of former Party Secretary Jiang Zemin. This is party politics as usual, with the deep rifts caused by the Bo Xilai affair (sentenced to imprisonment on corruption charges in 2013) explaining much of the unusual ferocity of the campaign. As has been the case during past campaigns, intense factional infighting comes with a temporary clampdown on intellectuals and the media, especially those associated with the fallen leaders, to avoid factional conflict spilling out into the public domain. These events reveal that divisions within the CCP elite continue to be a source of regime instability which is much more worrisome to the leadership than any of the threats from the outside: separatists, dissidents, religious extremists. Rivalry among top leaders rips apart the appearance of Party unity and undermines the myth of the CCP's omniscience and sacred right to rule.

If Xi Jinping's anti-corruption campaign were really to clean up Chinese politics, very different questions ought to be asked. The real point about corruption is not the illegal use of political position for self-enrichment, which is pretty much universal, but how corruption infiltrates the political process itself. How do bribe-taking or, even more worrying, the business interests of billionaire Party leaders themselves influence policy making and implementation? In other words, has the CCP become the vehicle of a power elite that rules the country only to serve its own interests? Answers to these questions would tell much about the extent to which the fusion of power, money and organized crime has progressed, how this has changed the CCP and the political system through which it rules, and how wide the gulf really is that separates theory from fact in Chinese politics.

3 | *China's Economy Will Continue to Grow, but Not Forever*

3.1 The Politics of Growth

China's economic growth since the onset of the reforms in 1978 has been unprecedented. Beyond this minimal consensus, economists inside and outside China disagree on just about any aspect of China's developmental trajectory. Has economic development principally been driven by the inexorable rise of the private sector, the marketization of the state sector, the opening to the world market, or more generally by sagacious policy making of the CCP? Is reform a linear process that started modestly and gradually deepened and radicalized, or has reform at certain junctures taken abrupt changes of direction, perhaps even rolling back earlier, more radical policies?

Debates on China among economists are generally wrapped in assumptions on how an economy ought to work, leading to conclusions about what is wrong or missing and what still needs to be changed or put in place before the economy can be proclaimed fully reformed. Doing so might come at the risk of losing sight of how the economy actually functions. Each economy, and most definitely the Chinese one, is a unique configuration that only imperfectly fits the moulds of economics. In this chapter I will try to avoid what the economist Ronald Coase called the 'blackboard economics' of models and assumptions and stay as close as possible to the reality on the ground. I will draw on the research of economists, sociologists and political scientists on the politics of the complexities and contradictions that shape the economy. I will then gauge the seriousness of the main challenges and opportunities for continued development that depart from Chinese realities instead of wishing to prescribe a particular cure.

We will have to start by questioning several common assumptions. The first such assumption is that Chinese modernization and development started with the announcement of reform at the Third Plenum of the Eleventh Party Congress in 1978. The Third Plenum's most important contribution was that it created and publicly signalled a consensus among the Party leadership that old Maoist ideas no longer worked, but had led to disaster after the first few 'golden years' immediately after the communist victory in 1949. The initial reforms drew directly on earlier periods of reform, especially the years immediately after the Great Leap Forward (1962–65) and after the fall and death of top military man Lin Biao in 1971. Initially at least, the reforms in 1979 were more like just another step in a long-standing debate and power struggle between moderates and radicals within the CCP leadership rather than a complete break with the past. The crucial difference in 1979 was, of course, that Mao was no longer around to throw a spanner in the works.

Furthermore, at the onset of reform China was by no stretch of the imagination simply an undeveloped economy, a blank slate on which the most beautiful policies could be written. High economic growth, development and modernization did not start in 1979, but merely entered a new phase in the period after 1979. Like other East Asian economies (Japan, South Korea, Taiwan, Hong Kong) during the Cold War period, China in 1949 had protected its domestic economy from foreign competition, reformed the rural sector, encouraged import substitution and embarked on an active industrial policy in which the state coordinated and sometimes even led the strategic development of modern industrial sectors. The difference in China's case was that this took place in the politicized context of high socialism, causing a much more extreme and much longer drawn-out isolation from the world economy. The next phase of development entailed export processing and the development of an industrial sector that built on the comparative advantages of an East Asian society, chiefly cheap, relatively well-educated and disciplined labour and a strong, pro-development and non-predatory state. Although this phase only happened very late with the reforms, it ultimately followed from the same logic of economic development as elsewhere in East Asia. Despite the ideological grandstanding and the many wasted years and pointless human sacrifices, in the final analysis the Maoist period is part of a distorted but still recognizable trajectory of long-term economic development and modernization in which the reforms constituted a phase instead of a fresh start.

The second common assumption about the reforms that has to be questioned is that the replacement of a planned economy by a market economy must entail the substitution of capitalism for socialism or, more concretely, the ascendancy of the private sector and the demise of the state-owned sector.[1] In this analysis, the state sector is usually presented as a drag on the reforms: the CCP's obsession with the state-owned sector continues to get in the way of a full market transition and the happy hunting grounds of full-blown capitalist prosperity. Protectionism and an extremely high level of investment in the state-owned sector nevertheless continues to spearhead the leadership's approach to China's economic growth and structural transformation. Like it or not, the state-owned sector rather than the private or foreign-invested sector constitutes the core of the CCP's strategic vision and objectives, and this is a reality that any analysis of China's economic present and future will have to come to terms with instead of dismissing it as misguided, irrational, wasteful or simply ignorant of the objective laws of economic science.

The third common assumption is that it should be possible to generalize about the Chinese economy as a whole. Obviously, China is a very large country with a great deal of variation in the level of economic development and prosperity, and this at least is commonly acknowledged. However, the complexities of China's development trajectory have had outcomes that are very different not only across different parts of the country, but also for different sectors of the economy. Policies for specific sectors such as telecommunications, banking or aviation, not only vary greatly, but have also not necessarily been consistent over the years. Moreover, these differences only partially overlap with the policy regimes that apply to specific forms of ownership (state-owned, private, and foreign-invested). From a political economy perspective, one is hard put to speak of one economy, and this is as a rule insufficiently factored in as part of discussions on China's economic state and prospects.

---

[1] Over the years the most consistent advocate of the 'market transition' theory and primacy of the private sector has been the sociologist Victor Nee, see Nee, Victor. 1989. A Theory of Market Transition: From Redistribution to Markets in State Socialism. *American Sociological Review* 54,5:663–81, Nee, Victor, Opper, Sonja. 2012. *Capitalism from Below: Markets and Institutional Change in China*. Cambridge, MA: Harvard University Press. In China, too, several economists take neoliberal positions, including Mao Yushi, winner of the 2012 Milton Friedman Prize for Advancing Liberty, and Wu Jinglian, advisor of former premier Zhu Rongji.

Together, these three assumptions that tend to colour perceptions of China's economic development (reforms as a fresh start, capitalism replacing socialism, unified political economy) add up to a linear narrative connecting past, present and future which undergirds almost all of the popular and many of the academic analyses. In this narrative, reforms started modestly with the introduction in the late 1970s and early 1980s of limited market reforms in the rural areas and the creation of special economic zones for foreign investment. In the second half of the 1980s this was followed by the introduction of contract responsibility systems in the urban areas. Thanks to these reforms, the market became more and more important and in the first half of the 1990s the plan gradually became obsolete. This in turn paved the way for the deepening of reform in the second half of the 1990s that targeted the state sector and fully integrated China into the world economy, culminating in its accession to the World Trade Organization in 2001. At this point the narrative runs into problems, because after about 2003, progress seems to have stalled. Further reforms with more room for the private sector and foreign investments were either shelved, not completed, or simply never saw the light of day. Instead, the central government reemphasized the importance of the state-owned sector and chose for a more generous distribution of the fruits of economic growth. The narrative thus asserts that the reform project is by no means finished. More radical reform policies are required to guarantee long-term economic development. From the perspective of our narrative, the package of policies announced by the new Xi-Li regime seems to have taken this message to heart as more and deeper market reforms are promised, although doubts exist, especially about the continued emphasis on the state-owned sector or the lack of 'genuine' reform of the financial sector.

To say that this narrative is wrong would be missing the point. Much of it is in fact absolutely right in its description of some of the key developments in the last 35 years. However, it gets things wrong when it thinks that market reform itself is the objective of policy making. This assumes that China's policymakers are neo-liberal economic thinkers who cannot make sense of events or developments that run counter to the market transition logic, except by invoking vested interests of powerful players (state-owned enterprises, corrupt politicians) or a lack of sophistication, irrationality or plain stupidity of 'neo-Maoist' leaders and 'leftist' economists who want China to return to the Dark Ages of high socialism. Developments that run counter to the neo-liberal narrative are thus dismissed as aberrations or setbacks that will eventually have to be overcome.

In this chapter, I will try to make sense of these aberrations and setbacks by emphasizing the political economy that informs and shapes policy making and implementation. It would be foolish to assume that the logic of economic development and market transition play no role whatsoever, that it is all a matter of interests and policy making. Yet it would be equally foolish to dismiss human agency altogether. Despite broad and powerful similarities with other developing and developed capitalist countries, China charts its own course of development as much in the economic realm as in other aspects of politics, society and culture.

3.2 The Market and the State

Statistics are often invoked to prove that the rise of the private sector has been inexorable. From virtually nothing on the eve of reform, the private sector nowadays makes up anywhere between one-half to almost two-thirds of the economy. In 2012, the private sector was reported to contribute over 60 per cent of GDP.[2] Conversely, the GDP share of state-owned enterprises has fallen to below 30 per cent.[3] In terms of employment a similar picture emerges. In 2011, total urban employment amounted to 359 million of which 121 million (34 per cent) in private employment and only 45 million (13 per cent) in public enterprises. If employment is included in enterprises with other forms of ownership (collective, shareholding, limited liability) that are nevertheless substantially privately controlled, the picture is even clearer: the private sector's share surges to 183 million or 51 per cent of total urban employment. These figures stand in stark contrast even to those of just ten years earlier. In 2001, private sector urban employment stood at 37 million or just 15 per cent of a total of 241 million. Moreover,

---

[2] See *CCTV Online English*. 2013. Private Sector Contributes over 60% to GDP. 2 June, online at http://english.cntv.cn/program/bizasia/20130206/105751 .shtml, checked 17 November 2014.

[3] OECD Working Group on Privatisation and Corporate Governance of State Owned Assets. 2009. State-Owned Enterprises in China: Reviewing the Evidence. OECD occasional paper, online at www.oecd.org/corporate/ca/ corporategovernanceofstate-ownedenterprises/42095493.pdf, checked 17 November 2014.

employment growth is not simply caused by the success and growth of established private enterprises. Each year, millions of new enterprises add to the depth and reach of the private sector: between 2001 and 2011 the number of private firms and individual businesses rose from 26.4 to 47.3 million.[4]

These figures seem to confirm the story of a linear progression from state socialism to market capitalism. But is it really all that simple? At many points since 1978, political decisions have interfered with the neat logic of market transition, sometimes blocking it, at other times spurring it on at a forced speed, and at yet other times reversing it. To illustrate this it might be useful to go back to the origin, growth and demise of celebrated township and village enterprises (TVEs) in the 1980s and 1990s. TVEs emerged seemingly out of nowhere in the early 1980s. Local governments and farmers started often very modest enterprises that produced basic consumer goods or inputs for larger state factories that the planned economy did not supply. Suddenly, the countryside and not the cities were the cutting edge of market reforms. When the growth of TVEs became known in the second half of the 1980s, a debate ensued on the causes and consequences of their success. One group of scholars insisted that this was indeed driven by the entrepreneurship of private individuals and firms who were the sharp edge of a transition to a fully private market economy that eventually would make state socialism obsolete. Other scholars pointed out the fact that many TVEs in rural China (and slightly later and more hesitantly state-sector-affiliated 'income generating' enterprises in urban China as well) were funded and initiated, or at the very least facilitated by local governments.

This debate was never really resolved, although both sides acknowledged that the nature of TVEs and private enterprises varied greatly across China. In the more prosperous areas of the Yangzi River Delta near Shanghai and Nanjing and in parts of the North China Plain, TVEs built on a strong tradition of collective agriculture, proactive local government, and privileged access to national or international markets and state-sector partners. In this context, local governments were often conspicuously present in the TVE sector. In the Pearl River Delta around Guangzhou (Canton), foreign investment,

---

[4] Figures are from Lardy, Nicholas R. 2014. *Markets over Mao: The Rise of Private Business in China*, pp. 70, 83 and 139–40.

especially from Hong Kong, kick-started local industrialization that eventually would make this part of China the world's workshop. In other, poorer and more remote parts of China, most famously the area around the city of Wenzhou, TVEs from the onset were often little more than private enterprises simply condoned by poor and weak local governments.

Events in rural China in the 1990s made this debate largely obsolete. In the mid 1990s, many of the celebrated TVEs across the country were suddenly privatized or liquidated. This often happened out of necessity. Many TVEs had capitalized on their advantage of being a first mover in sectors traditionally ignored by the state plan. By the 1990s competition had become intense; at the same time, collectively owned TVEs started showing many of the signs of privilege and state protection that had already bogged down state enterprises for much longer. However, dismantling the TVE sector happened suddenly and universally so that political factors clearly were also at play.

I have witnessed the dismantling of the TVE sector with my own eyes. In 1996, I conducted research on a very successful village-owned enterprise near Shanghai that produced slippers for export to Japan, where it had a market share just shy of 30 per cent. The company employed virtually everybody in the village and started to expand to achieve greater vertical integration, buying up other enterprises that supplied it with materials and goods that it needed for its production. When I returned a year later, the ebullient mood of the year before had disappeared. The enterprise was in the midst of turning itself into a joint-stock firm owned by workers and management, a move that was ordained from above and made little sense to anybody I spoke to in the village. Other factories in the area were simply sold off, merged, trimmed or stripped or simply bankrupted. In certain cases, even allegations of corruption were used to force local officials-turned-entrepreneurs to cooperate. TVEs had suddenly fallen out of favour and were subjected to a much harsher policy regime that insisted on separating government from enterprises and hard budget constraints. This political decision was only partially informed by the logic of the market and was carried out as a political campaign in time-honoured CCP fashion.

The rollback of TVEs in the mid and late 1990s led political scientist Yasheng Huang to an important reassessment of market reform. In 2008, after a decade of silence on the TVEs, he argued that the TVEs of the 1980s had in fact not been collective firms at all. They were mostly private enterprises that paraded as collective enterprises to circumvent legislation against larger private enterprises at the time. According to Huang, the 1980s represent not just the beginning of market reform, but were in fact the high tide of indigenous private sector capitalism, whose development was stunted and rolled back in the 1990s to make room for the marketization of large state-sector and foreign-invested enterprises.[5]

Huang's assessment of the 1990s, as not a deepening but a reversal of capitalist market reform, provided an important corrective to received opinion. The story of the TVEs' fall from favour is just a small part of the much larger story of the restructuring of the state sector in which Premier Zhu Rongji was not the unqualified neo-liberal hero he was made out to be. Reform has not been a matter of simple progress and deepening because of the inescapable force and superiority of market capitalism. The power of politics trumped economic logic and made reform take a much more tortuous and unpredictable course.

Until the mid 1990s, the state sector was highly fragmented. Despite the appearance of central planning, state enterprises were controlled by specific (local or central) governments and ministries and their departments who energetically defended their turf against others. State enterprises were not seen as assets whose return ought to be maximized, but as tools to serve a range of policy objectives, including employment, welfare, social security and the production of specific goods or services. Under the economic plan, the state sector had been the source of most government revenue, but many state enterprises started to become loss-making in the 1980s. This worsened rapidly in the 1990s. State enterprises faced ever more competition in an unfamiliar market environment that now not only included other state and collective enterprises, but also a growing number of private and foreign-invested competitors. Radical reform became increasingly urgent if not downright unavoidable.

An important preparatory change to reform was the promulgation of the Company Law of 1994, which separated ownership of state assets from political control. In principle, state enterprises could now be freed from their original socialist policy mandates (lifelong

[5] Huang, Yasheng. 2008. *Capitalism with Chinese Characteristics: Entrepreneurship and the State*. Cambridge: Cambridge University Press.

employment, pension obligations, health care, housing, social security) and be turned into state-owned commercial undertakings. This paved the way for the 'hold on to the large and release the small' policy of 1997 associated with Zhu Rongji, which presented a strategic view of the reform of the state sector and laid the axe to the waste and sloth of state enterprises. Tens of millions lost their jobs and security as a result. Yet Zhu's goal was not the privatization, but the corporatization of the state sector, i.e. turning state enterprises into independent firms that would have to fend for themselves in the socialist market economy regardless of their form of ownership.

Tens of thousands of state and collective enterprises were slimmed down, bankrupted or turned into joint-stock companies or privately owned firms. However, the methods and timing of doing so varied enormously. Immediate and outright sale to domestic or foreign investors was relatively rare. Some enterprises were allowed to spin off or merge their most commercially viable parts. Like the TVE near Shanghai which I discussed above, most state enterprises first issued shares to their employees, in effect partially monetizing the latter's state socialist entitlements to social security and welfare. Subsequently, the employees were often given the option to sell their shares back to the firm, severing their ties with the firm and exchanging their residual claims for immediate cash. Finally, the firm would be fully privatized by means of a management buyout or sale to a third party, although the owners were often required to retain a large share of the workers, at least initially.

The logic that drove this process was less an economic than a political one. Local governments, who were the owners of the vast majority of state enterprises, were responsible for the implementation of enterprise reform. In most places a gradual approach that started with a shareholding system jarred less with state socialist ideology and practices than outright and immediate privatization. It also bought time to find and fund settlements and for retraining and reemployment of redundant workers, limiting the likelihood of widespread social unrest which local governments in particular were sensitive to.

Certain parts of the state sector, however, were not jettisoned at all, especially but not exclusively at the central level. Selected state enterprises were turned into commercial state-owned enterprises, the backbone of a new national or regional industry. At the central level, a team of 'national champions' was created to compete with domestic private or foreign-invested firms. In the longer term, these companies would also have to operate internationally and become a match for the largest companies from the US, Europe and Japan. With this, the language shifted from the need to reform state socialism to nationalism. Reform and economic development were not only about a better life for the Chinese, but also about undoing the one hundred years of national humiliation at the hands of imperialist aggressors before 1949 and regaining China's rightful place among the most powerful and affluent countries in the world. China's new state-owned companies were modelled on the Korean *chaebol* and Japanese *keiretsu*: highly diversified and internally integrated conglomerates of enterprises closely linked with government. The key thought behind this was that China's new national industry would only be able to be competitive if it adopted the characteristics and strategies of international capitalist firms.

One of the main drivers behind the new approach to reform was the competitive pressure from foreign-invested firms. China has been very different from other rapidly developing East Asian countries in the timing and extent of foreign investment. Japan, South Korea and Taiwan all initially kept a very tight lid on foreign investment to give room to domestic firms to develop and become internationally competitive. China, however, opened itself up to foreign investment early on, selectively at first in the 1980s, but more generally (albeit never completely) in the 1990s. This is explained in part by the fact that the reforms were not the beginning of industrialization in China, but merely a new phase. It is therefore a mistake to treat the start of the Chinese reforms as the equivalent of the start of industrialization in South Korea or Taiwan in the 1950s and 1960s.

Another explanation of China's early opening up was the different international context: China was not a US ally and did not have access to the American market to the extent that Japan, Korea and Taiwan did. The 1980s was also the time of the spread of neo-liberal theory and practice which prescribed free trade as the best development strategy, although it is doubtful whether the CCP leadership in the early 1980s had much knowledge of or interest in neoliberalism. Instead, the leadership shared a belief that China had cut itself off from the world for too long and that foreign things must be better. Also important was the demonstration effect of Hong Kong's wealth and the effective lobbying by a handful of Hong Kong business tycoons which translated in the approval of the first industrial investment zone just across the Hong

Kong border in 1979. Once word of its success spread, other places started lobbying for their own special economic zone (later broadened into the concept of the open city).

Whereas most foreign investment in the 1980s and early 1990s had largely come from Hong Kong, Taiwan and Southeast Asian overseas Chinese, after the announcement of further reform in 1992, foreign investment diversified and dramatically increased, ultimately making China the world's largest recipient of foreign investment. Foreign capital was courted in a highly fragmented way: each area and local government had its own policies to attract and accommodate foreign investment on top of national policies that privileged foreign-invested firms over domestic private firms. In certain places such as Shanghai, foreign investment almost completely crowded out the local private sector; in most other places, foreign-invested firms were seen at the very least as posing unfair competition to domestic private and state enterprises. Unfair or not, the foreign-invested sector also set the example of capitalist business practices and human resource management that domestic private and state firms would have to follow to become competitive. The rapid rise in foreign investment in the 1990s therefore made further and much more radical reform of the economy urgent. State enterprises and many of the earlier TVEs and private enterprises would have to follow suit and adopt similar capitalist practices, even if this meant large-scale redundancies of workers and the restructuring, slimming down, privatization or even bankruptcy of the firms involved.

But it was not just foreign competition which paved the way for a new national industrial policy. What made the creation of the national champions even more interesting was that it was inspired and enabled by some of the most powerful players in international finance. Carl Walter and Fraser Howie in their book on China's financial system show how the creation of China Mobile, China's most successful telecom company which in 2014 ranked no. 55 on Fortune's Global 500 list, was created in preparation for its international initial public offering (IPO) in 1997. To be able to present a credible company on the New York and Hong Kong stock exchanges where the IPO was to take place, Goldman Sachs investment bank lobbied Beijing to merge the fragmented provincial telecom providers into one truly national company. Earlier in the 1990s, several rounds of unreformed state-owned enterprise IPOs had raised disappointing sums in the range of several tens or hundreds of millions of dollars. The China Mobile IPO was different, raking in US$4.5 billion. The spectacular success of this IPO paved the way for similar IPOs, finally including in 2005 and 2006 even the largest banks. The creation and success of the now-famous state-owned national champions of the world's largest communist country was thus made possible by the institutions of world capitalism. The bottom line, so it seems, quite simply was that everybody – or at least those in the right places in Beijing and New York – got (much) richer in the process.[6]

The state-owned national industry is thus a neo-socialist hybrid. Part state enterprises and part spawned by the world's capitalist system, they fit neither the prescriptions of neo-liberal free-trade theory nor those of socialist state monopoly. Moreover, the state chose to be selective and strategic in deregulating the economy. Allowing competition from international firms and domestic private enterprises was limited to certain sectors of the economy. Other sectors were in fact *reregulated* in the 1990s through the creation of giant state-owned enterprises. In these sectors, the protective umbrella of the central government has got stronger rather than weaker, although this served nationalist rather than socialist goals. Under this umbrella, oligopolistic competition between firms or different branches of a single firm was encouraged and often became intense. One important consequence is that it is impossible to generalize too much about the state-owned sector as a whole. Despite all the talk about national champions and the emphasis on state-owned enterprises, the development of each sector is different, depending on the shifts and changes in the strategic view that the central government has taken in each individual case and the balance of power between the central and local governments. A disaggregated view is therefore needed that also takes into account the specific history of each sector and the path dependencies that this has created.

Sarah Eaton's work on the aviation industry illustrates this very well. In 1984, the central government ended the monopoly of the Civil Aviation Administration of China (CAAC), opening the airline market not to private business (which hardly existed at that point), but to local governments and individual government departments. Although many

---

[6] Walter, Carl E., Howie, Fraser J. T. 2012. *Red Capitalism: The Fragile Financial Foundation of China's Extraordinary Rise*. Singapore: John Wiley, pp. 178–182.

new airlines were quickly set up, competition only became fierce in the early 1990s when controls on ticket prices were lifted. In the course of the 1990s, deregulation and competition led to predictable outcomes: falling ticket prices, over-investment, profits that turned into losses, rising debts, dropping safety standards and a rising number of accidents. Yet all this was not enough for an industry shake-out. Airlines were owned by local governments or departments which protected them from bankruptcy. Spurred on by the economic downturn caused by the 1997 Asian financial crisis, the central authorities stepped in in 1998. Using CAAC's leverage as the industry's regulator and supervisor they restructured the industry, forcing all airlines under the umbrella of one of the three airlines affiliated with CAAC itself: Air China, China Eastern and China Southern. An oligopoly was thus created from which foreign and domestic private entrants continued to be barred and in which only three commercialized national champion companies competed. Subsequently in 2003, CAAC's responsibility for the asset management of the three airline groups was transferred to the CCP's Organization Department and the State-Owned Assets Supervision and Administration Commission (SASAC). Ultimately, the outcome of reform has thus been an airline industry that is both commercially viable and autonomous and a direct instrument to achieve the central Party-state's strategy objectives.[7]

This example shows that a neo-socialist economic strategy can be more than a collusion of central government strategy and global capitalism. As I have shown in chapter 2, the fragmentation of the state makes China different from other East Asian countries. Creating national champions means wrestling away from different departments and local (provincial or sub-provincial) governments the monopolies or assets that are often essential to their financial survival. Nevertheless, local governments continue to pursue their own strategies of economic development. In part this relies on the state-owned assets that continue to be under their control, sometimes copying the model of the central government in setting up their own champions. Mostly, however, local governments encourage the private and foreign-invested sectors that have been much more important than for the central government anyway.

---

[7] Eaton, Sarah. 2013. Political Economy of the Advancing State: The Case of China's Airlines Reform. *China Journal* 69:64–86.

Overall, the following pattern emerges. Policy making enabled foreign direct investment and, to a lesser extent, the growth of the private sector especially after the start of the second phase of reform in 1992. This in turn started fundamentally to reshape the economy, challenging state enterprises in ways that they were ill-equipped to counter. To meet these challenges, the central government decided to focus on certain strategic sectors, consolidating assets that were fragmented across departments and local governments and constructing in these sectors regulated markets that kept private and foreign-invested companies out, but allowing (often vigorous) competition between a selected few state-owned enterprises. Other sectors deemed less strategically important were intentionally left to foreign-invested or private enterprises, often as part of developmental strategies of local governments.

Within the reformed state-owned sector, politics and the economy are still (and perhaps even more so than in the past) intertwined. The Party controls appointments to the highest positions in state-owned enterprises. Leaders rotate between state-owned enterprises or between state-owned enterprises and organs of the Party, the state or representative government. Conversely, the highest leaders of state-owned enterprises also figure prominently as members of the CCP's Central Committee. The question is, of course, who is in charge? Formally speaking, the state has the final say as the owner of state-owned enterprises. In 2003, the State-Owned Assets Supervision and Administration Commission (SASAC) was set up as the state's instrument to supervise and control central state-owned enterprises. It is, however, unclear how much real supervision the SASAC can exercise and thus to what extent the state as a whole actually has a grip on what nominally are its assets. Control over the appointment of the leaders of state-owned enterprises gives the CCP at least a firm stick to enforce Party discipline. This is probably enough for now but may no longer be so in the not-too-distant future.

An even greater problem is the long-term financial unsustainability of the system. State-owned enterprises continue to be given huge injections of cash, either by issuing shares or as loans from state-owned banks. Since the global financial crisis in 2008, the government has mandated even higher levels of investment to avoid an economic downturn which has become a lasting feature of the economy instead of its return to the level before the crisis. Since 2009, investment constitutes fully 48 per cent of total GDP. The investment spree has saddled state-owned enterprises, financial institutions and especially local governments with very high levels of debt and massive assets without clear business models to earn back all that money.[8]

China is probably the only country that has both the financial wherewithal and the political system to make such an investment drive possible. Loans and debt are financed from historically high foreign currency reserves and the famously high savings rate of households. Leaving the banking system unreformed and the currency non-convertible ensures that most of that money can only end up where the state allows it to go. In addition, state-owned enterprises have divested themselves from many of the liabilities of the past, such as pensions, and are under no real pressure to repay the debts that they continue to incur. Instead, old debts tend to be refinanced by extending new loans: an endless and politically mandated spiral of borrowing and investment. This is reminiscent of the old planned-economy problem of soft budget constraints and reveals some of the same habits. The difference is of course that this is now happening in an ebullient market rather than a struggling planned economy. Under these conditions, state-owned enterprises and those who control them have immeasurably greater opportunities for waste and self-enrichment.

With all that money going to state-mandated projects and to a selected few state-owned enterprises, the economy is in effect being mortgaged largely to support the central state-owned sector. This is not necessarily a bad thing as long as it is part of a clear strategy of economic development. The question is therefore where a sound protectionist industrial policy ends and wasteful catering to special interests begins, those of the state-owned sector being the most prominent among them. Actual as opposed to wished-for economic development is not a matter of choosing between the principle of the capitalist market and the power of the socialist state. Indeed, all historical experiences of successful development, from eighteenth-century Britain and the nineteenth-century US to the East Asian miracle economies of the twentieth century, have been the product of policies that were a mix of these two.[9] Moreover, in economic development many things can

---

[8] Naughton, Barry. 2014. China's Economy: Complacency, Crisis & the Challenge of Reform. *Daedalus* 143,2:14–25.

[9] Chang, Ha-Joon. 2007. *Bad Samaritans: The Guilty Secrets of Rich Nations and the Threat to Global Prosperity*. London: Random House.

and do happen at the same time regardless of the principled contradictions that might exist between them. At some point, liberalizing the banking system, making the currency fully convertible and creating a level playing field for state-owned, private and foreign-invested firms will have to happen. If the leadership gives in to foreign pressure and acts too soon, it will kill off sectors of the economy that still need to be nurtured. If it waits too long, many sectors of the economy might become dangerous liabilities for China's economic future.

The interlocking of economic and political power in the context of a market economy could lead to some seriously worrying outcomes. China's developmental state could either collapse under its mountain of debt or deteriorate into a kleptocracy. Many of China's state-owned enterprises have now developed well beyond the point where monopolistic state protection ought to have been lifted. Although they could continue as publicly owned enterprises, the time has come to let them prove their viability in the face of full market competition, both domestically and abroad. Undoubtedly some will fail, and so it should be. To make this happen, the debt mountain will have to be restructured, budget constraints hardened and the currency made fully convertible. The financial system will have to be opened up and banks turned into independent and genuinely profit-oriented enterprises. China's economic growth will no longer have to be driven by state-inflated investment, but will need to transition to a more balanced composition with more room for private investment and domestic consumption.[10]

However, such a cure of more neo-liberal medicine alone, necessary though it might be, ignores the political dimension of the problems and is for the Chinese government therefore, not enough. Following up on the general promises made at the CCP's Third Plenum in 2013, in May 2015 the government announced a new package allowing a mixed-ownership system of state-owned enterprises. Private investors are allowed to take a minority ownership share. Despite appearances this is anything but a first step to privatization. External partners will

---

[10] The challenges to China's long-term development and the policy shifts that are needed to face these challenges have been clearly described in a high-profile joint report of the World Bank and China's State Council, published shortly before the transition to the new Xi-Li regime in 2012, see World Bank, State Council of the People's Republic of China. 2012. *China 2030: Building a Modern, Harmonious and Creative High-Income Society*. Washington, DC: The World Bank.

only be allowed to take a small share and will not get any control over the enterprise. Many equity partners moreover may in fact be state-owned financial institutions. Furthermore, the government has explicitly reaffirmed the principle that strategic sectors of the economy will be reserved for state-owned enterprises. Private-public partnerships are part of a broader policy package that aims at creating even larger conglomerates of state-owned enterprises under new holding companies. Creating mega-monopolies is thus presented as the way to create truly globally competitive companies. The state is still in the driving seat, and the main impact of the new policies might be that the grip over large state-owned enterprises is strengthened by reducing the fragmentation of state control. To this purpose, a small new central coordinating group has been set up that brings together the main players, including the SASAC, the Ministry of Finance, the National Commission for Development and Reform and the Central Bank.[11]

However, it would be a mistake to focus too much on the problems of the state-owned sector. The economy continues to grow, albeit at a slower rate. Prolonged inaction would indeed be disastrous, but there are no acute problems that require an immediate and fundamental change of course. The total level of debt of China at 236 per cent of GDP is about the same as Australia's or Korea's, and still well below that of the US or almost all of the EU countries with the exception of Germany. What is worrying however is the rapid growth of the level of debt which is much higher than that of any country except some of the EU's peripheral economies and Japan. Most of China's debt is corporate (and 60 per cent of corporate debt is owed by state-owned enterprises), with public and especially household debt being relatively small. Particularly the central government is in good shape with a current (2014) debt level of just 21 per cent of GDP. In this sense the situation now is fundamentally different from the 1990s, when state enterprises were running up massive losses that required immediate

---

[11] See 'Circular on Opinions Regarding Key Point Work on Deepening Economic System Reform', online at www.gov.cn/zhengce/content/2015-05/18/content_9779.htm, accessed 28 July 2015; for an excellent discussion, see Mirjam Meissner, Lea Shih, Luisa Kinzius, Sandra Heep, *Like a Phoenix from the Ashes: Reforms Are to Bolster China's State-Owned Enterprises*. Berlin: Mercator Institute of Chinese Studies (MERICS), 2015, online at www.merics.org/en/merics-analyses/web-specials/like-a-phoenix-from-the-ashes-reforms-are-to-bolster-chinas-state-owned-enterprises.html, accessed 28 July 2015.

and drastic action. The state-owned sector's growth is indeed dependent on government-mandated investment and debt, which is a strategy that must run out at some point, but not immediately. Current monetary policies prudently aim at stabilizing and then gradually reducing the level of debt to pre-2008 economic crisis levels.[12]

Moreover, as discussed at the start of this section, the fate of the economy no longer hinges on the state-owned sector. Thanks to the growth of the private sector, the state-owned sector has continued to shrink in relative terms during this period, despite the many privileges that have been showered upon it. Despite an allegedly hostile policy environment, the private sector has continued to grow fast during the 1990s, 2000s and beyond. Even during the decade after 2002 when government policies reemphasized the state-owned sector and market reform is said to have stalled, the private sector managed to grow robustly, doubling its size and share in employment.

The neo-liberal explanation would be that this simply proves the inherent superiority of capitalist private entrepreneurship. Be that as it may, such an explanation fails to scrutinize state policies in detail, and particularly the differences between localities and how policies impact on specific sectors of the economy. When the central government cherry-picked the best state assets back in the 1990s, local governments had little option but to become much more invested in the private and foreign-invested sectors. Unwittingly, the central government's focus on the crown jewels has given China's economic development a massive private sector asset at the local level. This is in fact somewhat similar to the TVEs of the 1980s that emerged because of central government neglect rather than proactive policy making. Just like when TVEs spearheaded the development of a market economy, a scenario now opens up for China's economy gradually growing out of the stranglehold of the state-owned sector through local-level policies that create and increasingly level playing field for all economic actors, regardless of form of ownership. In the past, China's highly decentralized political system often served as a hedge or buffer against one-sided or extreme policy at the centre. This time round, decentralization by

[12] The analysis and assessment of China's debt draws on Aidan Yao, *China's Debt: From Diagnosis to Treatment*. Investment Research. Axa Investment Managers, 17 April 2015, online at www.axa-im.com/en/research-news-archives/-/news/research-research-and-strategy-weekly-china-s-debt-2/41825838/maximized/CNp9, accessed 28 July 2015.

enabling the growth of a highly diverse economic structure may very well save the day again.[13]

3.3 Beyond Reform

Despite the professions of the importance of continuing reforms, China's future economic development depends only in part on the ability of the CCP to eradicate the legacy of state socialism and put in place a level playing field for all economic actors. In many ways, China has already entered a post-reform phase and the reform of the state-owned sector maybe one of the last (and admittedly the toughest) legacies of the socialist economy. Achieving longer-term prosperity will increasingly depend on other things. At the dawn of the current post-reform era, many of the economic challenges that China is facing are generic and global rather than specifically post-socialist: they are confronted by many rapidly developing economies. While acknowledging the seriousness of the many problems and issues that the Chinese economy is facing, more and more of these have little to do with the socialist legacy of the regime. Past policies and the nature of the political system often give them a specific twist, both in terms of the problems that they present and solutions that are possible, and as such they cannot be separated from the broader neo-socialist project that the Party has embarked on. However, such problems should not be cast in terms of fundamental weaknesses or strengths of socialism and the CCP regime. Instead, they should be considered specific responses and solutions the emerging institutions of neo-socialist rule are predisposed to come up with, and to what extent these might be different from other types of political systems.

Below, I will discuss the main long-term post-reform challenges under three broad and interconnected categories: demographic transition, structural transformation from a labour-intensive to a knowledge-intensive economy and environmental degradation. Of these three, demography is the most fundamental, ultimately determining the

---

[13] This observation does not mean that there aren't any serious problems with China's local governments. Budgetary discipline, for instance, is notoriously lax, and the central government continues to look for ways to exercise greater control, see Wong, Christine. 2013. Reforming China's Public Finances for Long-Term Growth. In *China: A New Model for Growth and Development*, ed. Ross Garnaut, Fang Cai, Ligang Song, pp. 199–219. Melbourne, Australia: ANU Press.

scale and impact of the other challenges. The environmental crisis and transforming the economy are challenging enough, but can in principle be solved by sound policy making and investment. Population trends are fundamentally different. The consequences of events and decisions of often decades ago (more or less people of certain ages and sexes) are absolute and cannot be undone by policy making in the present or future.

3.4 Demographic Transition

China is currently on the brink of a demographic transition that will fundamentally change its society and economy. In all economically developing societies, rapid population growth caused by falling mortality rates gradually comes to an end as society becomes more affluent and fertility starts to decline, often ultimately below replacement level. Urbanization, higher living standards, better sanitation and health care, general availability of contraception, greatly expanded costs of raising and educating children, social security, salaried employment, greater equality between the sexes and female labour participation, individualism and consumerism all conspire to make having more than one or two children decidedly less attractive, if not downright impossible.

In China, all these changes have also taken place and fertility rates already started to decline in the 1970s. Since the late 1970s, this largely natural transition has been condensed into an artificially short period of time because of long-term mandatory family planning, often (and strictly speaking incorrectly) referred to as the one-child policy. In mandatory family planning state power is used in a way that is strongly reminiscent of the campaigns of the high socialist period. What is characteristic of the reform period, however, is that political mobilization is backed up by scientific expertise rather than revolutionary rhetoric. The need for family planning policy is presented as a necessary result of scientific modelling of the population: an objective, undeniable and non-political truth that can only be ignored at China's peril. The family planning policy thus illustrates on a massive scale what can go wrong if the full force of an authoritarian state is harnessed to back up a scientistic tunnel vision. Couples in need of a son to continue the family line and as security for old age are often obliged to abort, abandon or at the very least not register a baby daughter. As a result, China's sex ratio is now dangerously skewed with in some places 120 or so men for every 100 women. Tens of millions of children and young adults, many more of them women than men, were born illegally and have none or very few rights. Recent modifications of policy may soften its impact but are too little and especially much too late to change its human costs and demographic impact.

China's demographic challenges are often presented as the danger that the country will get old before it gets rich. However, the problems are much more severe than simply a rapid ageing of the population caused by modernization and increased health and wealth. The severe distortions of China's demographic structure caused by the one-child policy will have a deep and lasting impact on China's society, economy and possibly even politics. At some point between 2011 and 2015 (individual demographers and labour economists differ on this point) China entered a phase in which the population of working age (sixteen to sixty years) started to shrink – very slowly at first but gaining momentum especially after 2025 – although the total population will continue to grow, most likely until at least 2030. In wealthier parts of China having one or no children has now become the norm with very few couples wishing or feeling capable of raising more than just one child. In part, this has happened because in the 1990s the ambitions of the Party-state expanded from merely controlling the size of China's population to also improving its 'quality' to build a unified and strong nation. The discourse on quality deliberately conflates many different dimensions and explanations of success (education, wealth, health, genetic makeup, occupation, residence to name just a few), in effect telling poor peasants, migrants, the unemployed, the uneducated and the handicapped to catch up or else be permanently left behind. With small families and a full focus of all family resources on just one 'quality' child having become the norm, any relaxation of the one-child policy is therefore unlikely to have much impact, and would at any rate take a full generation to have any effect on the size of the working population.

The forced pace of the demographic transition will have many consequences, many of which are already underway. It will turn the long-term demographic dividend of a relatively large working-age population that adds to economic growth into a demographic deficit that will increasingly become a drag on the economy. More economically inactive people will have to be supported by less people who work, putting pressure on pensions, social security, health care and education, sectors for which funding is anything but secure.

China will no longer be a country with an abundant and cheap labour force. Cities will no longer be able to profit from the influx of cheap migrant labourers from the countryside to boost their economies. Labour-intensive industry, both domestic and foreign-invested, will have to move from coastal to inland areas where there still is a relatively large labour force, or move abroad to other low-wage countries. Industry that stays will have to invest more to raise labour productivity and shift to capital and ultimately knowledge-intensive production. A shortage of women is more likely turn women into a scarce commodity for marriage, sex or work than to correct for gender inequality.

While it is impossible to predict the exact consequences that this will have, smuggling and trafficking of women, commercialization of gender roles and relations, and increasing bachelorhood especially of poorer men, will surely be among them. China will become a country of immigration rather than emigration, starting with enticing highly skilled labour from the developed world to help upgrade the economy, followed by the importation of unskilled labour from developing countries – principally in South and Southeast Asia – for services and manufacturing.

3.5 Structural Transformation

The issue of highly skilled immigration leads to the second long-term challenge, namely the move towards innovation-based economic growth. The structural transformation of China's economy is often described as the need to avoid the so-called 'middle income trap' which several other developing countries in Asia, the Middle East or Latin America are said to have got stuck in. Some of the very factors that drove their success, such as low wages or easy adoption of low-end technologies, disappeared as these countries started to develop. It is however incorrect to present this as just a problem. China is not stuck in a middle income trap, but has successfully positioned itself for the next stage of economic development. In the 2000s, China has made great strides in creating employment for its population, despite state industry layoffs which occurred in the 1990s amidst a still growing labour force. The days of an endless supply of unemployed or under-employed rural labour are gone. As a result, the country has witnessed rapidly rising wages across the board and a nationally integrated labour market has emerged: the official minimum wage has increased by on average 12.8 per cent annually between 2008 and 2012 with the exception of the recession year of 2009.[14] As the labour economists Albert Park, Cai Fang and Du Yang write, 'the end of surplus labor in China can be viewed as a tremendous economic achievement.' Rising wages and labour scarcity are evidence that China is ready to upgrade its economy and produce higher-value goods and services.[15]

The price for this has been the widespread informalization of employment, especially among migrant workers. Many workers lack stable or secure employment, do not have a written agreement or contract, and are not provide with social security or health insurance. Because of their weak legal position, workers often get paid in arrears and employers frequently fail to pay wages due at all or pay only a part. Working conditions are often abysmal and a danger to workers' health and safety. Labour relations have come to resemble those in other developing countries and in the informal sector of developed economies. Even state-owned enterprises have restructured their employment by retaining only a core of permanent and formally employed workers and a large number who are only temporary and informally employed. Efforts of the authorities to regulate the labour market and strengthen the legal position of workers have had some effect, in particular the 2008 Labour Contract Law. Implementation, however, is often patchy as it runs up against the vested interests of employers in collusion with local governments that are competing for investments.

The challenge is not to preserve China's status as a low-wage, export-processing haven. Finding qualitatively different competitive advantages that will propel the development of a high-income advanced economy means developing sectors of the economy that are knowledge and capital-intensive, which in turn points to investment in education, innovation, science and technology. Since the 1990s, the Chinese leadership has gone about pursuing this agenda in a characteristically neo-socialist fashion, mixing marketization with centralization of core elements, decentralization with privatization of non-essential

---

[14] Chan, Jenny, Selden, Mark. 2014. China's Rural Migrant Workers, the State, and Labor Politics. *Critical Asian Studies* 46,4:605.

[15] Park, Albert, Cai, Fang, Du, Yang. 2010. Can China Meet Her Employment Challenges? In *Growing Pains: Tensions and Opportunities in China's Transformation*, ed. Jean Oi, Scott Rozelle, Xueguang Zhou, pp. 27–55. Stanford, CA: Stanford Asia-Pacific Research Center.

aspects, and globalization with a strong leading hand of the central state.

Policy makers acknowledge that innovation cannot simply be achieved through government planning. Initiative and creativity of individuals, enterprises, universities and research institutions drive the development of new technologies, products and economic sectors. This is true for all sectors of the economy, but is especially clear in knowledge-intensive sectors, such as information technology or biotechnology, and in the creative and entertainment industries. A knowledge-intensive society needs well-educated people. Higher education can therefore no longer be restricted to a small elite. The number and scale of universities have increased, but except for a small number of key institutions, responsibility for universities has been devolved to lower-level governments. Private universities have been set up as have a few Chinese campuses of foreign universities, such as the University of Nottingham Ningbo China or New York University Shanghai. Universities have also been required to become financially self-supporting by charging tuition fees, raising research grant income, offering bespoke professional courses and setting up partnerships with business. Universities and individual researchers have also been encouraged to develop foreign partnerships in teaching, research and publishing. Finally, foreign students are actively encouraged to come to China as much as Chinese students are encouraged to spend time abroad. Consequently, China has become integrated into the international academic world in ways that would have been unimaginable a few decades ago.

China's higher education sector has grown enormously. In 1991, the enrolment rate in higher education stood at 3.5 per cent of all 18 to 22 year olds; in 2006, this had risen to 22 per cent, caused by the happy confluence of the state's expansion of higher education and the rising 'educational desire' among the one-child-policy generation and their parents. According to the 2010 *Outline of the National Plan for Medium- and Long-Term Educational Reform and Development (2010–2020)*, enrolment should reach 40 per cent by 2020, on a par with many developed countries. Rapid expansion has come at a price: the quality of the education offered at literally thousands of universities and higher vocational schools varies greatly. Although there are now a lot more university graduates, many of these turn out to be unemployable: in the first half of 2000s the unemployment rate of those with an upper-high school education remained roughly the same at 12 to 13 per cent, while the unemployment rate of those with lower levels of education dropped sharply to between 5.9 and 7.7 per cent. Graduate unemployment or employment at a level below their formal qualifications has become such a widespread phenomenon that a Peking University researcher coined the term 'ant tribe' to describe their plight: 'They share every similarity with ants. They live in colonies in cramped areas. They're intelligent and hardworking, yet anonymous and underpaid.'[16] Despite the rising unemployment of graduates, there is in fact a robust demand in the economy for those with a good education, as evidenced by the fact that the private return on college education has increased sharply from 12 per cent in 1988 to 37 per cent in 2001.[17]

The central government seems to contribute to these problems. Its policies single out a small number of top universities and research institutions for special funding with the aim of turning them into world-class research universities, whereas government funding per student has actually dropped since the 1990s. The original plan to boost the quality of the top nine universities (the 'C9 project') started in 1998. In 2015 it was succeeded by the 'World Class 2.0 scheme'. Focusing in particular on internationalization by creating separate hubs for international collaboration with top universities, the scheme intends to propel some of these universities to the top fifteen in global rankings.[18] The main focus of policy is thus not on raising the quality and relevance of teaching across the board, but enhancing top-notch research and innovation. Such research is expected to make a significant contribution to escaping the middle income trap and making China a prosperous and developed country by mid 2020. Naturally, as with the 'national champions' state-owned enterprises discussed earlier in this chapter, nationalist and strategic considerations weigh in heavily. Having world-class universities is also constructed as an important measure of national greatness. Beating the developed world at its own

[16] On the 'ant tribe', see 'China's "Ant Tribe" Still Struggling', *China Daily*, 14 December 2010, online at www.china.org.cn/china/2010-12/14/content_21536966.htm, accessed 1 August 2015.

[17] Figures have been taken from Simon, Denis Fred, Cao, Cong. 2009. *China's Emerging Technological Edge: Assessing the Role of High-End Talent.* Cambridge: Cambridge University Press, and Park, Albert, Cai, Fang, Du, Yang. 2010. Can China Meet Her Employment Challenges? In *Growing Pains: Tensions and Opportunities in China's Transformation*, ed. Jean Oi, Scott Rozelle, Xueguang Zhou, pp. 27–55. Stanford, CA: Stanford Asia-Pacific Research Center.

[18] Sharma, Yojana. 2015. Hubs to Take Elite Universities into World-Class Club. *University World News* 286, 16 October, online at www.universityworldnews.com/article.php?story=20151015211423407, accessed 30 December 2015.

game of advancement through science, technology and innovation is a seductive goal in its own right, as are the military uses of technological innovation.

The country is thus facing two contradictory problems at the same time: the economy's need for large numbers of employable highly educated graduates and the thwarted hopes of unemployable highly educated single children. Although the government does not seem to spend much time on the latter problem, it certainly has been active in developing solutions to the former, usually phrased as the need to train, develop, retain and attract 'talent', i.e. people who possess the strategic abilities and skills needed for China's further modernization. Programmes for fostering talent started in the 1990s. Since 2002 it became significantly more of a priority when the new Party general secretary Hu Jintao made the central Party organization responsible for talent development.

Talent development programmes usually consist of awards, stipends or other incentives given to a select number of outstanding individuals in the hope and expectation that they will become leaders in their field. A prominent consideration in talent programmes is the global competition for outstanding researchers, innovators, investors and entrepreneurs. Increasingly in the 1990s, the flow of students and scholars to developed foreign countries was framed as a brain drain on China. Although there has never been any serious talk of putting restrictions on foreign study, talent programmes target prominent Chinese individuals abroad with a view to attracting them back to China for employment, either permanently or temporarily. More recently, non-Chinese foreign talents have also been targeted. As a result, top Chinese universities and research institutes no longer employ non-Chinese only as short-term foreign experts, but also as regular members of academic staff. Although China's talent programmes are insignificant in demographic terms, the flow of educated Chinese back to China is not. The cumulative total number of returned students since 1978 in 2010 was 630 000, or about one-third of the total of 1.92 million who left China in that period. Returnees are heavily concentrated in Beijing and Shanghai, where they constitute a sizeable part of the highly educated segments of the work force.[19]

[19] Zweig, David, Wang, Huiyao. 2013. Can China Bring Back the Best? The Communist Party Organizes China's Search for Talent. *China Quarterly* 215:590–615.

An innovative society does not just need better science and technology, but also arts, entertainment, media, marketing and fashion that turn new ideas and technologies into things that make life better, or at least more interesting or gratifying. The creative or culture industry is a linchpin in changing China from the 'workshop of the world' into a leading creator of goods and services. This is a message that has not been wasted on either the leadership or private entrepreneurs. Private and public investment in the creative industries has risen sharply (28 per cent in 2012 alone, for a total of RMB 1.96 trillion). In 2013, the government announced that China's cultural and creative industries ought to contribute 5 per cent to the total GDP in 2015, up from 3.48 in 2012.[20]

To the CCP leadership, culture is directly connected to the drive to strengthen China's 'soft power', which might be glossed as 'globalization on the party's terms'. At least equally important are culture's domestic applications. Like science, culture has always been intimately connected to politics. Under Mao, cultural production was to serve the revolution plain and simple, while under Deng in the 1980s, greater artistic freedom was carefully monitored to ensure that artists would not be enlisted for political change. Although these attitudes have not gone away, a discernible neo-socialist model of 'managing rather than running' cultural production has emerged. In the next chapter I will discuss in more detail how commercialization of the media has become a tool to guide and fund government propaganda and how the internet and social media have blossomed and have become an integral part of the lives of hundreds of millions of people, but always with the limits set and enforced by the state.[21]

Culture has been recognized as an industry. Markets for cultural products have emerged in which commercial enterprises, both public and private, compete, innovate and grow. This includes not only popular or mass culture (fashion, games, literature etc.), but also high culture. Across the country, creative clusters have sprung up where

---

[20] Figures are from Jing Bartz, 'What Are China's Creative Industries – Really?', *Buchmesse Blog*, 28 May 2014, online at ablog.book-fair.com/2014/05/28/china-creative-industries/.

[21] An outline of this approach to cultural production is given in Section XI of the 'Decision of the Central Committee of the Communist Party of China on Some Major Issues Concerning Comprehensively Deepening the Reform' adopted at the Third Plenary Session of the Central Committee of the Communist Party of China, 12 November 2013.

artists produce, exhibit and sell their work. Some of these have grown very large and famous, becoming major touristic attractions, such as Factory 798 and Songzhuang town in Beijing or Dafen Art Village in Shenzhen. Creative clusters are usually set up in cooperation with local governments to whom art is simply a way of making money and developing their area. The central government condones and even encourages such creative clusters, but at the same time ensures that the activities do not step across the 'red line' of criticism of the Party or individual leaders.

3.6 Environment

China's environmental degradation is the political and economic challenge that perhaps most captures the imagination of audiences across the world. The spectre of one-fifth of humanity poisoning itself and with it the rest of the world for the sake of economic development resonates deeply with the environmentalism that has become part of the political mainstream in many countries. The ecological wreckage caused by China's growth-at-all-costs approach has inspired books with apocalyptic titles like *The Bad Earth* and *The River Runs Black*.[22] Undeniably, air, water and soil pollution from industries is a danger to health, directly to people in the immediate vicinity and more insidiously to populations far and wide. Beyond pollution, land erosion, mining, desertification, urbanization, industrialization, and the construction of water reservoirs and hydroelectric dams destroy fertile land and squeeze the population and agriculture onto a diminishing territory. Dust storms and critically high levels of air pollution in Beijing are widely reported and greatly vex the local and resident expatriate population. More dangerous to health are the effects of toxic products and waste of highly polluting enterprises across rural China. China's carbon dioxide emissions are the largest in the world and any serious solution to global climate change will need to engage the Chinese government.[23]

[22] Economy, Elizabeth. 2004. *The River Runs Black: The Environmental Challenge to China's Future*. Ithaca, NY: Cornell University Press, Smil, Vaclav. 1984. *The Bad Earth: Environmental Degradation in China*. Armonk, NY: M. E. Sharpe.

[23] One the most extreme examples is Guiyu in Guangdong province, which specializes in the recycling of electronic waste; see www.greenpeace.org/eastasia/campaigns/toxics/problems/e-waste/guiyu/.

International organizations and foreign governments, non-governmental organizations (NGOs) and the media put increasing pressure on the Chinese government. This has been more successful than is often thought. International donors have groomed a cadre of local environmental activists and organizations, and their efforts are having an important impact, especially as long as funding from abroad continues to be forthcoming. Although there is often a mismatch between the principled environmentalism of international donors and the more practical concerns of local governments and people, the central government has proven to be much more willing to adopt an environmentalist agenda. Environmental protection within the government has evolved from just a leadership group in the 1970s to an inter-agency bureau (the Environmental Protection Bureau) in the 1980s to a ministry-level agency (the State Environmental Protection Administration) in the late 1990s to a full ministry (the Ministry of Environmental Protection) in 2008 with subordinate environmental protection bureaus at each administrative level. To back up environmental protection work, laws and regulations have been duly promulgated, principally the *Environmental Protection Law* (1989), the *Decision of the State Council Concerning Certain Environmental Protection Issues* (1993) and the *Environmental Impact Assessment Law* (2002).

'Sustainable development', the buzzword of international agencies, has become commonplace in China. In the 2000s, environmental protection activities both by the state and civil society have become very prominent. In 2004, national environmental groups rallied to prevent the construction of a string of hydroelectric dams in the Nu (Salween) river in Western Yunnan province. In 2005, the State Environmental Protection Administration halted thirty large-scale industrial projects. The 2014 revision of the Environmental Protection Law promises to tighten the noose on polluters even further, with Premier Li Keqiang at the 2014 National People's Congress going as far as 'declaring war on pollution'.[24]

---

[24] On the thirty industrial projects, see Tilt, Bryan. 2010. *Struggling for Sustainability in Rural China: Environmental Values and Civil Society*. New York: Columbia University Press, p. 79; on the Nu River, see Yang, Guobin, Calhoun, Craig. 2007. Media, Civil Society, and the Rise of a Green Public Sphere in China. *China Information* 21,2:211–36, and Tilt, Bryan. 2015. *Dams and Development in China: The Moral Economy of Water and Power*. New York: Columbia University Press.

The problem is, however, not simply one of legislation, regulation and enforcement. Sustained development often continues to trump sustainable development. Moreover, environmental protection unequally distributes gains and burdens. In the 1990s the central government continued the construction of the Three Gorges Dam despite widespread concerns and protest. The interests of industry and cities in North China for which most of the diverted Yangzi River water was intended and more generally the national demand for electric power trumped concerns over more localized environmental and human costs. Similarly, the government continues to encourage private car ownership as part of its dream of well-off middle-class living. Although China is also at the forefront of popularizing electric car use, traffic congestion and car emissions continue to be very serious problems in the cities.

More important than the conflicting policy objectives of the central government itself is the mismatch between central and local governments. Whereas the central government has most to gain and relatively little to lose from stricter environmental standards, many localities and their governments depend on the employment and revenue generated by often highly polluting industry. Moreover, in many localities the imposition of stricter environmental standards and their associated costs (factory closures, erosion of profit margins and reduced employment opportunities) is often imposed on those places or enterprises that are the lowest in the political pecking order.

The result is a political economy of environmental protection in which the costs have to be borne by those who are powerless and poor, while others who can curry favour with the local leadership continue to pollute and develop. Rural communities that in the 1980s and 1990s managed to develop on the back of polluting industries now sometimes find themselves back to square one with just agriculture to rely on. Their environment may be cleaner, but they are also a lot poorer again. This is not to say that people in backward areas are unable to understand that pollution is bad for them, or that environmentalism is a luxury that only developed places can afford. People who directly profit from highly polluting activities because of employment or compensation paid to them by polluting factories do indeed often deny the hazards that they face. Other people in their communities, however, are keenly aware that their crops, food and health suffer, and are often prepared to lodge complaints, involve the media, stage protests or even file lawsuits, which sometimes do indeed tip the balance of a government decision. The privatization of many rural industries in the second half of the 1990s has sometimes made this easier: protesting against a polluting factory is no longer necessarily the same as protesting against the government.

China's decentralized administrative system is both part of the problem and part of the solution. Environmental standards are the responsibility of local environmental protection bureaus and have been built into the performance evaluation of local cadres who are therefore under pressure to show tangible results. Rolling out stricter environmental policies in this way is relatively simple as it does not require nationwide funding and organizations for implementation: the environment has become just another unfunded mandate imposed upon local governments. Environmental protection can thus be done swiftly and cheaply, but local cadres are largely on their own to find ways and means to meet their targets. The good part of this is that they are free to find local solutions to local problems; the bad part is that they are also free to exercise their discretion about who to spare and on whom the axe should fall.

Environmental protection reveals all the strengths and weaknesses of China's neo-socialism. The central government weighs in heavily with legislation and regulation that bear the imprint of both foreign and domestic priorities and approaches. The role of civil society is prominent and in certain respects even encouraged by the central government as whistle-blowers on polluters and in assisting the government in rolling out its policies. The central government relies for much of the implementation of its environmental agenda on local governments that bear the lion's share of the financial burden, but in return are given the room to adapt policies to local circumstances and to distribute the gains and losses of environmental protection as they see fit.

In the longer term the challenge is not simply to legislate, regulate and punish environmental pollution, but to incentivize the market economy to create solutions. Environmental protection does not simply mandate limits to growth, but also provides opportunities for sustained and sustainable development. As mentioned earlier, China is at the forefront of the development and introduction of electric cars and for some time now has been the world's largest producer of solar panels. These aspects of green development chime very well with the government's agenda of transitioning to a qualitatively different, innovation-driven economic growth model. Environmental regulation, if designed and implemented prudently, creates opportunities for enterprises to develop commercially viable products and services to reduce the environmental footprint of economic growth. In this sense, the seriousness of the deterioration of the environment puts the responsibility on the government to create the conditions for the further development of the market economy by being at the forefront of green development.

3.7 Conclusion: A Window of Opportunity and Limits to Growth

Two types of economic challenges will have to be met in the years to come: restarting and completing market reform and long-term post-reform structural transformation. The Xi-Li regime has chosen to meet these challenges by reigniting the mixed and pragmatic approach that has been a feature of policy making since the start of the 1978 reform. Market reform prescriptions are selectively and gradually accepted, but not with the intention of ending the role of the state in the economy. The government accepts the argument that there has to be distance between the market and the state. Nevertheless, it sees itself as much more than a neo-liberal regulator and facilitator of market forces. China will continue to chart a course between being a neo-liberal regulatory state and an East Asian developmental state with its fusion between business conglomerates and the state bureaucracy. This course is unique and distinctly neo-socialist due to continued CCP control over key enterprises and sectors. Top-down strategic direction will continue to be given not only through old-school state ownership and control over key enterprises and the financial sector, but also through proactive leadership over the post-reform economic strategy on issues such as innovation, labour supply and the environment.

The reform of the vestiges of the planned economy and the completion of a full market economy remain highly contested. The dismantling of the planned economy in the late 1990s created a fundamentally new political economy that not only generated many years of continued high economic growth, but also hugely influential vested interests. The Xi-Li regime has admitted the need to break through these vested interests for further reform to be successful, yet it has also made it clear that the state sector will remain central to the economy. It will not turn the national champions into fully private firms and the central government's financial health means that there is no immediate and compelling need to do so. To roll back the capture of these firms by individuals and their families, the state's nebulous and residual ownership of these firms must first be clarified and shored up before there can be any talk of future privatization. China could moreover still continue with a select number of state-owned enterprises but only if these firms serve the interests of the state and nation instead of their own or those of their de facto private owners. State ownership should, in other words, no longer mean soft access to capital from loans or shares and unconditional protection against private and international competitors, but ought to be a way for the state to make and target strategic investments that serve long-term national goals.

Deferral of reform of the state-owned sector is directly connected with the issue of rising public-sector debts of governments, state-owned enterprises and state-owned banks. Although public debt has risen since 2008, the public sector's assets still easily cover public debt and there is no reason for immediate alarm. In the short term, the state of China's public finances thus gives the government the leeway to continue for some time along the path of high, debt-fuelled economic growth, especially since the private sector also continues to grow in size and in proportion to the economy.[25]

Growth induced by debt, government spending and the private sector should buy the necessary time for a gradual structural transformation of the economy to meet the long-term post-reform challenges of demographic change, innovation-based growth, and environment degradation. Put negatively, these post-reform challenges set a time limit on the current model of economic growth: they define the window of opportunity that the economy has before long-term adverse developments become immediate. If future growth has to be generated by innovation and creativity, solutions will have to be found to the current problems in the higher education sector, including the low overall quality of graduates, the creeping re-politicization of academic and creative life, and the continuing foreign drain on the country's best and brightest. To avoid further deterioration of the environment and overzealous environmental protection from becoming serious impediments to further growth, a proactive green development strategy will have to

---

[25] For a summary of two Chinese reports on the rising public debt, see Arthur R. Kroeber. 2014. *After the NPC: Xi Jinping's Roadmap for China*, Washington, DC: Brookings Institute, online at www.brookings.edu/research/opinions/2014/03/11-after-npc-xi-jinping-roadmap-for-china-kroeber.

supplement regulation and enforcement. Most importantly, the reduction of the labour force and the ageing of the population are unavoidable. While the size of China means that it will, and indeed must become the largest economy in the world, demographic trends will make achieving and especially maintaining that position a lot harder than it may seem at present. Immigration, education, innovation, globalization and investment are all part of the solution, but it remains an open question whether they will be enough. In the next ten to fifteen years the country must not only get rich before it gets older, but also before it gets smaller. If it doesn't, it is unlikely that there will ever again be another opportunity.

4 | *Freedom without Universal Human Rights*

4.1 Perspectives on Freedom and Human Rights

Human rights are alien to totalitarian systems. This is not simply because such systems cannot allow unchecked freedom for fear of instability. The contradiction is much more fundamental than that. Totalitarianism doesn't even need human rights, because a society independent from the Party, the state, the military and the economic plan simply does not exist. Society is part of the totalitarian organism: there is nothing beyond the system that rights can or should protect.

In China this changed with reform. Organizations, families and people have gained interests and identities that they pursue and protect from the state and from each other. Political protection, informal support and interpersonal loyalties and obligations – practices carried over from totalitarian times and enhanced by the greater leeway created under reform – are commonly used to fill this gap. However, as the economy and society become more complex, the need is felt for uniformity and predictability in social relations and economic exchanges that only the rule of law and a rights-based legal system can provide. However, such rights are a gift of the Party and the state, instruments for the correct conduct of human relations and conditional on their proper use. But have these rights opened a Pandora's Box of the introduction of universal human rights that can be asserted independently from and, if necessary, against the Party and the state?

This question cuts right to the heart of the many prejudices, misperceptions and deliberate misconstructions in Western debates on China and the future world order and in Chinese debates on the dominance of the West and China's modernization. Understanding the development and reach of human rights is therefore essential to understand what contemporary China is and where it is going.

The Chinese government views human rights principally as an international relations issue. The 1989 Tian'anmen crackdown made the People's Republic of China the target for serious and systematic allegations of human rights abuses for the first time since joining the United Nations in 1972. In countering these allegations the government has taken a two-pronged approach. First, convinced that human rights are merely a Western stick with which to beat China, the government has sought a prominent role in international human rights forums and entered into a multitude of multilateral and bilateral discussions on human rights issues. China uses these forums and discussions to try as much as possible to reduce criticism of itself and more generally to emphasize that it is states that must first keep their own house in order. However, China has also worked gradually to change the international human rights regime to make in more amenable to its own agenda. In 2006, it scored an important victory with the establishment of the UN Human Rights Council to take over from the UN Commission on Human Rights. The Council is less inclined than the Commission to take human rights as a universal yardstick for the performance of individual countries, taking the view that it is more a responsibility of individual states to evaluate their own human rights conduct.

Second, the Chinese government has acknowledged the importance and recently even the universality of human rights, but prefers to present this as an aspiration rather than a binding norm for the present. Since 1991, China has issued no less than eleven white papers and at least two national action plans on human rights. The 2004 revision of the constitution even added to article 33 the sentence that '[t]he State respects and preserves human rights.'[1] The state's commitment to human rights is predicated on China's developing country status, the need to take care of basic survival, development and social and economic rights first and political rights later, and the good work done and progress already made regarding many, if not all aspects of human rights. The government funds an elaborate infrastructure of human rights research to provide the evidence and arguments on human rights progress. Researchers also include some of the more liberally minded 'establishment intellectuals' working in Party and government think

---

[1] For the full text of the 2004 constitution, see www.npc.gov.cn/englishnpc/ Constitution/node_2825.htm, accessed 3 August 2015.

tanks, creating room for at least some genuine debate, albeit within the limits set by the government.

In sum, the government is stalling, and quite successfully so. Western statements on politics and society in China are routinely couched in terms of the level of their compliance to the international norms of full and universal human rights. Against this standard, human rights are judged to be insufficient, incomplete, violated or threatened, leaving the government in effect no other legitimate choice than to surrender its sovereign power over its population and territory and fully comply with the demands of foreign governments and organizations. This approach is a sure-fire way of forestalling any genuine discussion with the Chinese authorities. Measuring China's human rights 'progress' against international yardsticks is therefore counterproductive no matter how universal one believes these rights to be. Such an exercise is based on the conviction that progress can only take one direction, namely towards the kind of society Westerners usually think they have. It serves more as a form of self-congratulation than to help people in China finds realistic ways to work towards better lives given the possibilities and constraints of their society and political system.

Rather than assuming that Westerners know what is best for China, I will explore in this chapter empirically what freedoms and rights Chinese people have, and how these are distributed and used. First, I will look at the more ordinary freedoms beyond the political framework of human rights when people make decisions about residence, jobs, money, education, marriage, travel or leisure. Second, I will look in more detail at the practical implications of the regime's use of democracy, human rights and the rule of law. Third, I will investigate how and to what extent the international discourse on human rights and democracy has or has not taken root and to which local uses it is put, and by whom.

4.2 A New Society

Although the post-1978 reforms were spearheaded by the creation of a market economy, they were about much more than economic growth and rising living standards. The reforms did something really fundamental: they liberated – or even created – society from the totalitarian structures of the state socialist system.

Before the reforms, individuals and households were first and foremost members of socialist units: rural collectives in the countryside and work units in the cities. Membership of these socialist units meant not only secure employment and income (a job in a work unit in the cities or work on collective land in the countryside), but also entitlement to the services, goods, social security and welfare that their collective unit was able to distribute. This included housing or land to build a house on, medical care, schooling and consumer items. The collectives and work units were the point of contact with the Party and the state; they governed, cared for and disciplined the population. In fact, from the perspective of most ordinary Chinese, they *were* the Party and the state.

The abolition of economic planning teased state and society apart. A society has developed that consists of organizations, enterprises, households, citizens and other social actors who pursue their goals in ways and places of their own choosing. Simultaneously – and this is only infrequently explicitly acknowledged – the reforms also created the state as a separate entity that takes society as an external object of care, management, development and control. For the first time, speaking of state–society relations therefore made sense. Individual citizens and other members of society were given the right and responsibility to act on their own accord. As they seek to assert their autonomy, the state has become an external actor that is a source from which to obtain entitlements, services, infrastructure, spoils, justice, law and order or, conversely, a force of repression and control that they seek to avoid.

The social effects of reform have not stopped at the liberation of society formerly subsumed in the totalitarian system. Society itself started changing virtually from the moment it was created. The greater freedoms and prosperity of the 1990s and especially the 2000s gradually loosened the grip of families, households, villages, employers, neighbourhoods, schools and other social organizations over their members. Survival no longer depends on membership or long-term reciprocal relations and support. Opportunities, services and security can be bought or otherwise obtained. Social relations, exchanges and commitments are becoming contractual, time-limited and circumscribed.

As a consequence of reform, Chinese society was first created and then transformed, a time-warped modernization that is not yet complete but whose contours are nevertheless clearly visible. From the cosy – or suffocating – lifelong familiarity and mutual dependence of rural collectives and urban work units, China is evolving into a society of enterprising strangers, individuals who come and go in pursuit of whatever goals or desires that drive them.

Chinese society has also become immeasurably wealthier. Yet some real problems have emerged that in the long term threaten to undo many of the gains of reform. China has become a society of, at times, stupendous self-enrichment and crass display of wealth, but also one where many ordinary people struggle in the face of unrelenting and harsh competition. Yet others have altogether been left by the wayside: poor, powerless or simply unlucky. Air, water and soil in many areas are now so polluted that they have become virtually unusable. The environment is just one aspect of the rising concerns about health, well-being and safety. In the last fifteen years, highly publicized incidents have occurred, such as the SARS crisis of 2002, the extensive damage and death toll of the 2008 Wenchuan earthquake and scandals with tampered baby formula in 2006 and 2008.

These issues and events have alerted the population to the many uncertainties, risks and dangers of living in a modernizing society and globalizing market economy. Like anywhere else in the world, freedom and private choice have come at the price of individual responsibility, alienation and the dissolution of the social and moral fabric of simpler but also safer times. New, individualistic norms and expectations not only come with a stronger sense of both individual rights and meritocracy, where winners are free to reap the rewards of success and losers must accept the consequences of failure. They also include the often distressing insecurities, risks and lack of moral compass that are part of living in an environment inhabited by potentially predatory and immoral others.

Modernization and individualization are not only anonymous social processes, but also contested ideas and ideals. In China, individualization is often linked to the decline of social norms and a lack of social responsibility. Individualization is perceived as being at odds with both socialist ideology and traditional Chinese culture that emphasize group membership, solidarity and the relatedness of the social person. Individuals in China thus have to negotiate different moralities: those of the capitalist market, the (neo-)socialist state and local ideas about social relations, community and fairness. The new generation of single children is said to be utterly focussed on personal life and professional success, but many single children also carry the burden of excessive expectations from ambitious parents and the prospect of becoming the sole caregiver for their aged parents.

Freedom and individualism are about more than risk, insecurity and the breakdown of social responsibility. New norms of behaviour and morality are emerging that take society as a whole as their object rather than specific people, groups or relationships. Some of these are based on religious ethics and charitable practices; others are explicitly secular and based on nationalist convictions or a belief in global citizenship. A countervailing trend is emerging of socially responsible behaviour towards strangers, volunteer work and charity, and the importance of morality in guiding one's behaviour not only towards the people that are close, but also to society in general. The large numbers of volunteer relief workers during the 2008 Wenchuan earthquake, in particular, created a perception, especially among younger Chinese, that society was changing for the better.

There is also a completely different corrective to the social atomization caused by greater freedom and the rise of individualism. Independent individuals become free to establish relationships with whomever they like and for whatever reasons they want. The cultivation and manipulation of connections was already widespread in the latter part of the collective period. It became ubiquitous in the 1980s and 1990s when the state still controlled large chunks of the economy and no business could be conducted without the consent of officials. In the absence of a functioning rule of law, the 'art of using connections' brought plan and market together and served as an essential lubricant in the operation of economic transactions and a hedge against political risks.

The nature of economic transactions started to change with the final dismantling of the planned economy in the mid 1990s. Much less is now heard about gift-giving and petty corruption to curry favour or obtain goods. The rule of law is established well enough to back up normal contractual claims and obligations. Most things have become readily available on the market and access to them can no longer be monopolized by officials or other gatekeepers. The state itself plays a much less significant role in the economy, owns fewer businesses and controls the distribution of far fewer commodities.

But it would be a mistake to think that the growth of a market economy and associated individualism must lead to a simple decline in the use of connections or the role of officialdom in the economy. If nothing else, the revelations during Xi Jinping's anti-corruption campaign show that the abuse of power for personal gain runs further and wider than ever. The state has stepped up its regulatory power and spends lavishly on all sorts of public projects. Business therefore still needs access to officials for permits, permissions and information on new opportunities, regulations or potential threats. Officials are no longer satisfied simply to fleece the market but have gone into business themselves. Official positions, especially those at lower levels in the bureaucracy, are now for sale. As a result, personal wealth seems to have become an increasingly important determinant of one's official career.

The use of connections and corruption has gradually changed but has not become less important. In the past, connections were inclusive in the sense that they opened up the state to those who were traditionally excluded from it. They facilitated the emergence of a market economy by bringing state and market together, giving a new class of entrepreneurs access to the state's power to distribute and decide. As power and money since the mid 1990s have started to fuse, this phase of opening up and inclusion gradually seems to have come to an end. Although it is too early to draw any definite conclusions, connections increasingly serve to exclude as much as to include, defining the boundaries of a new power elite in which business and officialdom have merged.

4.3 Spatial Mobility

The freedom of movement is probably the most basic and visible of freedoms that was severely restricted in the period before the reforms. Decisions about residence and employment were made only to serve the needs of the planned economy. Industrialization, the fetish of state socialist planning, was believed only to be possible in modern cities where people were assigned jobs for life. The countryside served as a source of food, raw materials and labour for city-based industrialization. A strict household registration system was created to lock the population into place and to insulate the cities from the backwardness, poverty and overpopulation of the villages.

It has been one of the great achievements of the reforms to reduce many of these divisions and restrictions. In the past thirty years, hundreds of millions of rural dwellers have migrated to the cities. Yet some stubborn vestiges of the household registration system remain that make it impossible for the vast majority of these migrants to settle permanently. They therefore either remain circulatory migrants with one foot in the village or else settle for second-rate citizenship of their city of residence without many of the rights to housing, health care, schooling and security that permanent urban residents enjoy. This often forces migrant families to split with parents working in the city and 'left-behind' children staying back in the village either to be cared for by grandparents or to fend for themselves.

Because of their uncertain or inferior legal status, rural migrants, both men and women, often find themselves in a situation not unlike that of international migrants in many parts of the world. Thanks to the largely decentralized nature of the administration, household registration has evolved into an internal passport system, in which each municipality acts as a semi-independent state that exercises considerable discretion in designing and enforcing its own individual immigration regime regardless of the objectives of the central government. Some measures have been directly copied from international migration. The best-known example is the creation of so-called 'blue seal' permanent residency permits, which cities give out to rich or deserving applicants much like certain Western countries give permanent residency to people who invest a certain minimum sum or have educational qualifications that are in short supply.

Migrants tend to be concentrated in specific areas, often poorer neighbourhoods or rural enclaves within or at the margin of a city that do not require urban household registration. Other migrants live in dormitories or rooms provided by their employer or gangmaster. Migrants are often looked down upon as uncultured rural bumpkins who compete with the established population for public services, jobs and space. Again, comparisons with attitudes towards immigrants from the developing world in Europe or North America are not hard to make.

Migration is by no means limited to rich areas along the coast. Especially after the start of the central government's 'Go West' investment drive in 1999, cities in the interior and Western parts of the country also receive large numbers of migrant workers, traders and entrepreneurs, either from rural areas nearby or from elsewhere in China. If a destination city happens to be in an area dominated by ethnic minorities, relations between Han Chinese migrants and the local population can grow quite tense and can even spark outright conflict and riots.

Especially for women, migration has provided a way to become socially and financially independent from parents, husbands or parents-in-law. However, their independence also makes them more vulnerable. Many women who have left their native place find themselves in very exploitative situations as live-in domestic help, in sweatshops or in the sex industry. However, despite the difficulties that many women experience, for the majority it is not victimhood but a sense of agency that predominates. They take pride in their independence away from home and satisfaction from a modern lifestyle with money to spend.

As was mentioned briefly in the previous chapter, the wealth, social inequality and scarcity of women generated by the reforms and the one-child policy have led to many forms of commercialization and commodification of women and female sexuality, including interregional marriage, smuggling, concubinage and de facto polygamy, divorce and remarriage, and prostitution. This is rapidly developing a transnational dimension. The whole of East and Southeast Asia has become connected by a dense web of (often commercially facilitated) transnational marriages and sexuality. Women from poorer areas and countries relocate to richer countries to work in the sex industry or to marry (generally rural lower-class) men. China is both a source and a destination of women in this network. So, women from North Korea or Southeast Asia come to China to marry Chinese men. Taiwan and South Korea – where just like in China son preference has led to a highly skewed sex ratio – attract women from mainland China and Southeast Asia. Finally, married men from Taiwan or Hong Kong maintain a mistress or even a second family in Shanghai or the Pearl River Delta.

Migration is not always voluntary, even without raising the spectre of China's forced labour camps. Disasters (floods, earthquakes), environmental degradation and government high-modernist projects (dams, cities, roads, railways, airports or more generally 'development') have forced large numbers of rural people off their land. Resettlement often marginalizes these people when they end up without enough land or without a job in a place they don't know.

Roughly since the start of the new millennium, a next generation of 'new migrants' turns out to be less interested in retaining links with their village. They move to the cities without the intention to return. They are more inclined to give up their agricultural land rights and switch their household registration to a city. Many are the children of first-generation rural migrants who have grown up and were educated at least in part in a city environment. Their motivations and aspirations are very similar to those of urban youth, despite the fact that as rural migrant children they were often educated at lesser schools than their fully urban peers and continue to suffer discrimination in the job market and daily life. Many of these rural and urban youth are highly mobile, often moving in quick succession from one job or city to another in search of a higher income, better prospects, or simply a more interesting lifestyle: rural-urban migration becomes urbanization and more generally an aspect of social and spatial mobility, social stratification and the formation of working, middle and upper classes.

4.4 Inequality, Social Mobility and Class

Maoist China was a society with a relatively equal distribution of income, although it was never a haven for socialist egalitarianism. In fact, during the first two decades after 1978, important aspects of the reforms reduced some of the inequalities of Maoist society. For 25 years after the introduction of mandatory state grain purchasing in 1954, prices of agricultural products had been kept artificially low, forcing the countryside to subsidize urban industrialization. After 1978, not the farmers' enthusiasm for family farming, but the simple act of raising procurement prices for grain reduced these 'price scissors' between urban and rural areas and raised rural incomes. Subsequently in the 1990s, the abolition of many privileges in urban work units reduced the regressive income subsidies to urban state-sector workers of the planned economy. Finally, general economic growth has massively reduced absolute poverty by 'lifting all boats', although large pockets of poverty continue to exist, especially in remote areas and among the urban unemployed.

Despite these egalitarian developments during the first years of reform, the processes of marketization, globalization, individualization and social and spatial mobility have changed the pattern and degree of social inequality, most noticeably after the year 2000. Chinese society is much more unequal than it was in the pre-reform past and unequal in ways that are fundamentally different. The accumulation of capital assets has generated differences in wealth that are much more unequal than the differences in income. Opinions are strongly divided as to the nature and implications of this transition. Will the contradictions of capitalist exploitation turn China into an arena of Marxian class struggle, or is it becoming a country where classes are better understood in a Weberian sense as a hierarchy of social strata defined by occupation, life chances and status? Will the old pattern of inequality, based on differences in political power and status, continue to be important? What are the implications of rising inequality for popular perceptions of fairness, political stability and regime legitimacy?

As a start it might be useful to remind ourselves that inequality is not simply a matter of status, income or standard of living, but also of expectations. China is a highly aspirational society. A belief in the opportunities to move up in the world by dint of hard work, thrift and ability is widely shared among the population, even among disadvantaged groups and in the absence of a level playing field. Although China is now one of the most unequal countries in the world, the widening gap between the rich and the poor is not a cause of social unrest or political instability, a 'social volcano' waiting erupt. Freedom and aspiration, it seems, trump fairness and poverty.

One arena of such competitive aspiration is education. Rising standards of living and the marketization of education have impelled hundreds of millions of middle-class families to invest virtually all their resources in the education of their one child, a bottomless pit in which they will continue to throw money regardless of the expected return on the education received. The aim is for the child to score high enough in the nationwide college entrance examination for admission into a good university and beyond that perhaps to get the opportunity to study abroad. This near-universal 'educational desire', as Andrew Kipnis calls it, is one of the main channels of social mobility in Chinese society.

Perhaps the most visible dimension of inequality is housing. Rural Chinese have always owned their homes. Money in the countryside could therefore immediately be translated into housing: in the countryside building a new and luxurious house is the principal way to keep up with the Jones's. In the 1990s when I conducted research in China's richest rural area between the cities of Shanghai and Suzhou, local residents could readily identify five 'generations' of private homes starting from the collective period. Each generation was larger, higher and built with more expensive and ostentatious materials without necessarily being more comfortable to live in.

In the second half of the 1990s, urban Chinese also became owners of their own home when work units started selling their rental housing to the tenants. Although work units continue to be heavily involved in providing apartments for their members, a bustling property market has developed. Many urban residents no longer think of their home as just the place where they live, but also as property, and increasing numbers of people own one or more apartments for investment and rental income. Particularly in the booming large coastal cities house prices continue to increase. For several years there has been persistent speculation among experts and policy makers of a property 'bubble' that might burst at any time, triggering an economic downturn like the one that put an end to the Japanese miracle in the 1980s, but this has not yet happened.

Residence now reflects choice, wealth, power and status, leading to a spatial sorting of the population in different types of neighbourhoods that looks more and more like capitalist societies. This is in part still a product of the work units that commission or purchase housing from developers and sell on the individual flats or houses to their employees, usually at a subsidy. However, most properties are bought and sold directly on the market, available to anybody who can pay the price and has a local residence permit, including rural migrant workers in poorer areas and foreign residents in richer ones. Many other properties are rented out, again to anybody a landlord chooses. Paradoxically, as Chinese neighbourhoods become arguably more homogeneous in terms of standard of living, they have also become socially more diverse and fragmented. As a consequence, neighbourhoods are no longer communities, but have become co-residential areas of strangers who have nothing else in common other than their socio-economic status.

In a rapidly growing economy the freedom to realize one's aspirations often meets with success, but not for everyone. This brings me to class. China is becoming a society that is increasingly split between winners and losers, pitting rapidly growing and increasingly wealthy and self-conscious middle and upper classes against an array of working and lower-middle-class groups. This is by no means a straightforward transition from inequality based on rank, status and privilege associated with a planned economy to one based on achievement in a market economy. The coexistence of the successors of institutions inherited from state socialism and a market economy mean that there continue to be two separate dimensions of inequality. The elaborate hierarchy of authority and status of the Party-state continues to create ruling elites at each administrative jurisdiction, most prominently at the centre. Beyond these elites, the Party-state still has the power to enforce administrative statuses that unequally distribute residence, job opportunities, welfare, education, housing, health care and social security. Laid-off state-sector employees, rural residents and migrants find themselves at the bottom of this hierarchy. Alongside the inequalities of the state socialist system, the market economy has created groups of upper and middle-class entrepreneurs, professionals and white-collar workers and lower-class wage labourers, farmers and the self-employed.

What complicates matters is the fact that although state and market hierarchies are separate, they largely involve the same people. One's place in one hierarchy therefore also influences the likelihood of success or failure in the other. The fact that migrants and laid-off state-sector workers are excluded from many of the privileges of the socialist state system makes it likely that they end up in the most menial and lowest paying jobs in the market economy, despite that fact that they have been excluded from the perks of the state socialist system in very different ways. As discussed earlier, at the other end of the spectrum wealthy entrepreneurs have gained access to the power of the state informally through the use of connections or formally through privileged access to Party membership and an increasingly prominent role in the political and social affairs of the CCP. Members of the CCP elites, in turn, cash in on their power and connections. Their families are busy amassing large fortunes and head up significant business conglomerates in China and abroad.[2]

State and market inequalities therefore interact. At some points they amplify each other or have started to merge; at other points they maintain a greater distance. *With marketization, the distributive hierarchy of the state has not disappeared, as conventional market transition theory predicts, but is transformed into ways of inclusion and exclusion from the opportunities and spoils of the market economy.* Perhaps the best way to make some sense of this is to look at the evolution and

---

[2] The most systematic exposé of the wealth of China's political elite to date has been the ChinaLeaks report in January 2014, see www.icij.org/offshore/leaked-records-reveal-offshore-holdings-chinas-elite.

distribution of property rights, as Andrew Walder, Tianjie Luo and Dan Wang have done. Market transition theory assumes that a fully private economy is the only possible end-point of the dismantling of state socialist economies; anything else is simply incomplete and in-between. In reality, market transition in China entailed many different ways that control over productive assets was restructured and redis-tributed, a 'recombinant' reallocation of property rights that ranges from full privatization to the retention of such rights by managers, workers or political elites.

Walder and his co-authors illustrate this through the highly divergent trajectories of ownership in three sectors. In agriculture, final owner-ship of land was retained by rural collectives; farmers were only given time-limited and non-transferable use rights. The result was an agri-cultural sector consisting of innumerable smallholders without antag-onistic classes of landlords and a landless proletariat. In the state steel sector, by contrast, reform turned state enterprises into large compet-itive firms owned by the state and (minority) shareholders and con-trolled by state-appointed managers. While they reaped the benefit of the property rights that they had obtained, large numbers of former workers were simply shed. They were left without any claims to owner-ship or rights to income or benefits, a highly unequal and combustible outcome. A third sector, real estate, did not exist in the pre-reform period but was created as an outcome of reform. Non-agricultural land became a commodity controlled by local governments who allocated or sold transferable use rights to individuals or newly established enter-prises, making the development of a highly profitable real estate sector possible. As a new growth sector, real estate has high levels of private, mixed or even foreign ownership, enabling the accumulation of vast private wealth.

Marketization thus means very different things across the economy. It reallocates property rights in specific ways, each with different impli-cations for the distribution of power, income and wealth or, in other words, social stratification and class formation. When applying this insight, and at the risk of gross simplification, the following class/status groups can be identified, none of which is as yet fully formed and whose further evolution remains uncertain. At the very top, a power elite is emerging composed of the leaders of the Party, state and busi-ness, the latter including both private and state-owned corporations. In the formation of this elite, the resonance between state and market inequality is the strongest. In the further evolution of this elite the most important questions are the extent to which private and state-sector elites will continue to merge and reproduce (for instance through co-residence, intermarriage or by copying each other's lifestyle) and to what extent the new power elite will close itself off from aspiring members of middle-class and upper-middle-class groups of professionals, businesspeople or white-collar employees.

These middle-class groups themselves are likely to follow a similar trajectory of evolution. Some are already extremely mixed to begin with. Businesspeople may be former cadres and other state-sector employees, farmers or recent graduates. Professionals and white-collar employees are for the time being more uniform, mainly because they are predominantly urban and relatively well-educated. In the longer term, strategies of upward mobility are likely to homogenize these groups. Education for children, home ownership in middle-class residential areas, and a consumer lifestyle will make these groups not only look more alike, but may very well also make them socially more compatible. The main question is to what extent the merging of the middle classes will also cross the rural-urban divide. Will successful rural entrepreneurs or their better-educated children continue to suffer from the stigma of their rural origin or the barriers erected by the household registration system?

The interaction between state and market hierarchies creates the toughest obstacles for upward mobility at the lowest rungs of the ladder. Rust-belt state-sector employees or the unemployed, farmers in still largely agricultural areas, and farmers evicted from their land are groups whose distinctive state-sector statuses are reflected in clearly separate privileges (or the lack thereof) and identities. Among these groups at the bottom, migrant workers occupy an ambiguous but highly significant place. Drawn mostly from underprivileged rural groups, they are among those who have been able and willing to buy into the 'Chinese dream' of upward social mobility. At least some succeed. They start a business or find longer-term employment in a city or return home with money to invest or to build a house. They also remind others of what could have been. This is one of the reasons why lower-class urban residents take great care to distinguish themselves from rural migrant workers, even those who live in their own neighbourhood. The urban poor not only look down upon rural upstarts, but often feel more than a little threatened by their hard work, entrepreneurship and aspirations of upward mobility that they themselves seem to lack.

The fluidity of society and rapid social mobility of the early reforms are gradually beginning to give way to more permanent patterns of inequality without as yet filling into models such as Marxist class analysis or other sociological models of stratification. Many scholars in China moreover hesitate to use Marxist class analysis because of its sensitivity in a still nominally communist country. In itself, it is not particularly interesting to try to determine whether this means that China is becoming a class or a status society, exactly which classes or status groups China already does or doesn't have, or what 'class' may mean in the Chinese context. More important is to acknowledge that inequality as an objective and subjective fact continues to evolve, including the formation of classes and status groups. What is certain, however, is that the freedoms gained by many Chinese to unleash their ambitions and aspirations not only leads to highly unequal outcomes. The opportunities to do so in the first place, have and continue to be highly unequally distributed, and this is at least in part due to the effects of interaction between the state socialist system and the market economy. Inequality in itself is much less of a source of discontent than the perception that access to opportunities is unequal and unfair. Large groups at the lowest rungs of society find themselves permanently excluded; in time they may blame themselves less and the government and society more for this unfairness. When that happens, they might no longer accept the 'Chinese dream' that promises that prosperity for a few will eventually translate into affluence for all, a future challenge that the regime's neo-socialist strategy of governance might be ill-equipped to counter.

4.5 Consumption and Lifestyle

Life in contemporary China contains many contradictions. The new freedom, upward social mobility and individualism brought about by the market economy are conditioned by status differences imposed by the state and personal relations and obligations. Inequality is hardening and the contours of more permanent status groups are beginning to emerge that put a ceiling on the aspirations of ambitious individuals and families. Nowhere are the contradictions of freedom more visible than in the way that people shape their sense of self and personhood in their choice of lifestyle and patterns of consumption.

Let me begin with the elite. In chapter 2, I argued that corruption is systemic and inherent to the way that the CCP and its administration are organized and run. I am now at a point to take this argument one step further: corruption is also part of an elite culture of connections which defines a way of life and a moral system based on reciprocity, masculinity, (quasi-)kinship and honour. These elite networks include businesspeople and officials as well as criminal societies and underground brotherhoods that further serve to protect the private interests of this elite and even do some of the dirty work of the state, by force if necessary. Corruption follows logically from the culture and opportunities arising from the networks of officials, businesspeople and criminals. For corrupt officials, belonging to these networks in turn demands a certain lifestyle that only corruption can sustain.

During his ethnographic research among the new rich in Chengdu city, John Osburg often heard his informants complain that the endless entertainment they had to endure prevented them from using their wealth to develop their own, private lifestyle away from business associates and contacts. To them entertainment and consumption was work, not leisure. The lifestyle of China's nouveau riche – crass and decadent in the eyes of many – is therefore more than simply a matter of men and women behaving badly in a society that has become excessively individualized and has lost its moral compass. Excess is an inescapable way of life associated with moral obligations to a network of other powerful and wealthy people. As a result, there is a surprising conformity in the patterns of consumption and lifestyle among local elites of businesspeople, officials and criminal bosses. China does not have a leisured old elite whose lifestyle the new elite can emulate. Banquets, massage parlours and paid sex have become part of an inescapable culture of abandon that has its roots in the art of personal connections of the 1980s that cemented the trading of favours for money. At the time, private wealth could not be invested and could only be spent on food, drink, sex and presents. The materialism and hedonism of officials and entrepreneurs also signalled their explicit flouting of Maoism's prescription of selfless dedication to the revolution, frugality and restraint: a post-Maoist counter-culture of the rich and powerful.[3]

---

[3] Osburg, John. 2013. *Anxious Wealth: Money and Morality among China's New Rich*. Stanford, CA: Stanford University Press.

For most of the elite it is the price and not the quality, rarity or refinement of what they buy that distinguishes them from ordinary people. With the possible exception of a very small group of the truly rich and powerful in Beijing or Shanghai, being rich in China means doing and buying the same things as everyone else, just more of it and much more expensively. Yet the superficial uniformity in conspicuous consumption belies real and important dimensions of distinction and individualism. Like in all other consumer societies, where one shops, what and which brands one buys and at what price is connected to income and perceived social status. Fads and fashions follow each other in quick succession with elite preferences often trickling down to lower income groups.

It is not just China's new rich who have the freedom to explore new ways of life. One of the great changes since the early 1990s has been the expansion of free time: weekends are now off from work and three annual one-week long holidays have been created. People not only have more disposable income, but also more time to spend it. The implications of freedom and leisure reach far beyond the superficial pleasures of consumption and consumerism. Earlier on in this chapter I showed that in the 1990s and 2000s, society emerged as a domain of activity separate from the state. In response, individual Chinese have become what Lisa Rofel has called 'desiring subjects'. Without the state telling them what to do, think, want or where they belong, people must shape their sense of self from their own aspirations, hopes, needs and passions. The freedom or even necessity to shape one's life is not hard-won in battle against the state, but an artefact of state policy that in the final analysis is always conditional upon its proper and responsible use. In other words, freedom is a gift that signals the state's rejection of the Maoist intrusion of all aspects of life and the preoccupation with work and production. The state may be out of sight, but it still watches closely from below the horizon.

China's new desiring individuals are free to seek fulfilment and purpose from a seemingly endless range of options. Highly sophisticated markets have arisen for virtually every aspect of life, from fashions to foodways, healing practices, sports, hobbies, travel, entertainment, art, sexualities, ideologies and beliefs. Through their lifestyle, the Chinese participate in online or real-life communities or networks of those who have made like-minded choices. However, with the retreat of the state and politics from giving direction and meaning to all aspects of life, such choices and connections are often felt to be fleeting, if not ephemeral. As pop artist Shen Lihui sings in one of his songs, 'every day I am someone else.'[4].

4.6 The Proliferation of Religious Life

Among the bewildering array of lifestyle choices religion stands out, because it is here that the lingering concerns and apprehensions of the state arguably remain the strongest. It is here therefore that the limits of personal freedom are tested the most. The CCP's formal stance on religion is based on a compromise between the CCP's adherence to Marxist atheism and the recognition that religion is a normal (or at least unavoidable) aspect of a modern society. In addition, the CCP has been particularly wary of Christianity, because of its association with foreign imperialism during China's one hundred years of 'national humiliation' before 1949. Religion should be allowed, but kept under close watch to avoid its potentially baleful consequences. To do this, policy distinguishes between religion – normal, modern and allowed – and superstition – backward, dangerous and forbidden. The CCP recognizes only five religions (Daoism, Buddhism, Islam, Protestantism and Catholicism) which are managed through an elaborate system of institutions controlled by the Party's own United Front department. Everything else that does not fit into these categories, or is simply not considered important enough, is either philosophy (most notably Confucianism) or simply tradition or culture.

Underneath this seemingly simple classification lurks the much older distinction dating back to the Qing dynasty – if not earlier – between healthy orthodox and subversive heterodox sects and practices. The main concern of the state both then and now has nothing to do with what is believed or even what is modern or backward, but whether religious activity and organization are seen as a threat to the state. Freedom of religion is not a right, but a matter of the state which sets the limits of the permissible in the interest of self-preservation. It is for this reason that although in contemporary China orthodoxy is equated

---

[4] Shen Lihui quote from De Kloet, Jeroen. 2010. *China with a Cut: Globalisation, Urban Youth and Popular Music*. Amsterdam: Amsterdam University Press, p. 23.

with the five recognized religions, their practitioners nevertheless have to be constantly on their guard not to trigger the suspicions of the state. This is especially true for attempts to recruit, proselytize and organize outside of officially sanctioned religious institutions, particularly with the aid of foreign organizations, believers or missionaries, or when religion is associated with separatism and terrorism, most notably Islam among Xinjiang Uighurs and Buddhism among Tibetans.

Apart from Uighur Islam or Tibetan Buddhism, heterodoxy resides most of all in China's many syncretic sects, millenarian movements, and local cults. Evil 'associations, teachings and lodges' are vigorously persecuted and their leaders routinely sentenced to death or given very long jail sentences. However, as Timothy Brook observed in an article on Qing religious policy, tolerance or repression of religious organizations and practices was often directly connected to the realities of local administration and the competition for authority between members of local elites.[5] This continues to be the case in contemporary China. During rural research in 1996, I was taken to the site of a village temple, where I was surprised to find only a makeshift and very modest structure. I needed only to ask a few questions to learn that the actual temple had recently been torn down during an anti-superstition campaign, as had happened many times before. It was a public secret that during a campaign the villagers temporarily buried the bricks and other building materials of the temple under the floor of their houses to be dug up again after the campaign. County public security officials later readily confirmed that they very well knew what was going on, adding that they and the villagers were all getting tired of the sudden shifts and changes of central policy which forced them to enter the villages to ensure such token compliance to campaigns.

The local embeddedness of heterodox religion even extends to some of the organizations that are routinely brandished as counterrevolutionary or a danger to state security. During fieldwork in rural Hebei province near Tianjin and Beijing, Thomas DuBois found that many of China's most notorious secret sects, such as the Heaven and

[5] Brook, Timothy. 2009. The Politics of Religion: Late-Imperial Origins of the Regulatory State. In *Making Religion, Making the State: The Politics of Religion in Modern China*, ed. Yoshiko Ashiwa, David L. Wank, pp. 22–42. Stanford, CA: Stanford University Press.

Earth Teaching and the Teaching of the Most Supreme, actually operated in broad daylight, providing essential ritual and healing services to
their local communities.[6] There is therefore a very considerable bright
side to the undetermined nature of state policy. Folk religious institutions and practices have again firmly become part of what Prasenjit
Duara calls the 'cultural nexus of power' that linked the local elite,
other classes and the state in late Imperial and Republican China.[7]
This nexus also includes kinship organizations, schools and institutions associated with the five recognized religions, such as churches or
mosques. During the reform period, the cultural nexus of power has
deepened the localization of the Chinese state. Many village officials
double up as functionaries of temples, churches or kinship organizations. In this way, these institutions shore up state governance but do so
in local terms and conditions, strengthening the position of local elites
both within their own community and in their relations with the state.
In order not to ruffle any feathers higher up the administration, promotion of tourism or the preservation of local cultural heritage are often
used as a pretext to restore temples, shrines or other material representations of local communities, an issue to which we return in the next
chapter.[8] In other cases, popular religious temples are registered as Buddhist or Daoist. As the scope of informal religious orthodoxy broadens,
state rule and village governance become ever more enmeshed.

In urban areas, the proliferation of religious life is associated less
with local communities and more with individual choice and a private search for belonging and meaning in life. Nevertheless, the informal extension of the scope of orthodoxy and the complicity of the
local political elite is by no means an exclusively rural phenomenon.
A highly diverse market of religious services and organizations has
arisen which caters to China's desiring individuals seeking to sculpt
their sense of personhood and lifestyle. Religious proliferation constantly tests the boundaries of the permissible, especially at the level
where religions dare to organize and proselytize. Much less of an issue
seems to be the potential heterodoxy of the beliefs that they preach: it is
what they do rather than what they say that mostly triggers suspicion.

---

[6] DuBois, Thomas David. 2005. *The Sacred Village: Social Change and Religious Life in Rural North China*. Honolulu: University of Hawai'i Press.

[7] Duara, Prasenjit. 1988. *Culture, Power, and the State: Rural North China, 1900–1942*. Stanford, CA: Stanford University Press.

[8] I return to the issue of cultural heritage and local identity in chapter 5.

Most successful are therefore those religions that rely less on formal institutionalization and more on charismatic religious entrepreneurs who attract a following through personal contacts and word of mouth, such as Pentecostal Protestantism and especially the many forms of Buddhism that have proliferated in recent years. Organized religions that insist on their formal independence invite hostile responses from the state, as is illustrated by the suppression of the Falun Gong after 1999 or the continuing troubles of the Roman Catholic Church.

The CCP is beginning to respond to the expansion and localization of religious life beyond the sanctioned institutions of the five recognized religions. Since 2005, registration of other religions has become possible in principle and the State Administration of Religious Affairs established a new division for popular religion and new religions. In practice, religious policy is left largely to local authorities and their local bureaus of religious affairs and public security. In many places, this leaves an ambiguous grey zone where specific religions are neither forbidden nor fully recognized, but are allowed to exist and proliferate, sometimes even with the support of foreign missionaries. Nanlai Cao's study of Protestant churches in the capitalist capital of China, Wenzhou city in Zhejiang province, provides a particularly good example. Although many churches in the city are 'house churches' that have not been formally registered, they operate in full view of the authorities. Rich and powerful 'boss Christians' provide backing for their church through their connections or position in the local administration. The local authorities in turn welcome the contribution that churches make to social stability and public morality. In addition to the culture of connections, conspicuous consumption and organized crime mentioned earlier in this chapter, religion thus seems well on its way to become a further component in local governance and elite formation, not only in rural areas but in China's cities as well.[9]

4.7 Protest

In the previous sections I have explored the personal freedoms that Chinese citizens have gained in the reform era. These have on the

[9] Cao, Nanlai. 2011. *Constructing China's Jerusalem: Christians, Power, and Place in Contemporary Wenzhou*. Stanford, CA: Stanford University Press.

whole been very considerable as the Chinese experience few real constraints in the choices they make on how they lead their life. Human
rights, democracy and the rule of law are part of life, business and politics. They are enshrined in the constitution and other laws and given
a prominent place in the running of the Party, government, the legal
system and the organs of representative government. More broadly,
they are part of the CCP's strategy of social governance that seeks a
greater autonomy for society under the tutelage and supervision of
the Party and the state. A further understanding of human rights in
China should therefore also include the implications of these aspects
of the political system. How these rights have been taken up by Chinese
citizens and activists operating at the fringe of or even in opposition
to the state is what the next three sections of this chapter will look
into.

Individuals or groups of citizens use the means that the political system puts at their disposal to defend rights and interests infringed on by
the government or business and to seek redress for unjust government
action. While doing so, they constantly test and push the boundaries
of the permissible which they must be careful not to transgress. The
most common issues are land appropriation, house demolition, forced
resettlement, pollution, redundancy, wages, work conditions and work
safety. Demands for structural political change, criticism of the CCP
and its leaders and calls for the independence for Tibet, Xinjiang or
Taiwan are obviously not permitted and in fact not even contemplated.
Methods include perfectly legal actions such as petitioning local or
central government agencies, appealing to representatives of a people's congress, contacting newspapers, TV programmes or individual
journalists, and filing lawsuits, but also 'disruptive' methods, such as
demonstrations, sit-ins, blockades, attacks on state agencies or strikes.
Sometimes, such actions escalate, turning into full-fledged riots. Collective actions are local and the vast majority are small, involving a few
dozen to a few hundred people. Some, however, are much larger, involving up to tens of thousands of people and posing an immediate threat to
public order. Putting a number on actions that violate the law or regulations is notoriously difficult and arbitrary. Throughout the 1990s
and 2000s figures in the tens of thousands were given, usually based
on public security sources. However, in 2012 the famous Tsinghua University sociologist Sun Liping went public with an estimate of 180 000

protests, riots and other mass incidents in 2010, or three times the number in 2003.[10]

Resistance and protest are not without risk. Protesting power abuse or exploitation by local government or businesses easily incurs the wrath of the powers-that-be. Protesters are often wantonly beaten up by police or local thugs; alternatively, they can be detained, charged and sentenced to jail. One common tactic of protesters is to try to find safety in numbers (despite the fact that this makes a protest action even more threatening and often explicitly illegal): petitions, for instance, are submitted collectively rather than individually. Leaders of protests or lawyers taking up a case therefore take a special risk: they stand out and the authorities often prefer to crack down on a handful of notorious troublemakers rather than full-on repression of a whole protest movement.

Protest is usually explicitly phrased in terms of rights or a breach of the law, coupled with more general claims of the immorality of the actions of government agencies, individual officials or businesses. Such 'rightful resistance', as Lianjiang Li and Kevin O'Brien have called it, should not be construed as evidence of the decline of state control, the brittleness of the political system, or even the inevitability of political change, although the CCP itself certainly seems worried about the unstoppable increase in their number each year, which is one of the main reasons for stepping up 'social management' and 'social governance' of civil society in recent years.

Petitions, protests, and collective actions have increased because of the larger space given to autonomous political action and the prominence of the Party and state's rhetoric on the rule of law and clean government. Another important factor is the different agendas of central and local authorities and between specific government agencies: the fragmentation and decentralization of the Chinese administration facilitates protest. For the central authorities, protest is often a useful indicator of problems across China and leverage to keep local officials in check. The central authorities also don't have to deal with the consequences of protest. They can afford to be tolerant and critical of

---

[10] See Feng Shu, 'A National Conundrum', *Global Times*, 10 February 2012, online at http://english.peopledaily.com.cn/90882/7725198.html, accessed 29 August 2014.

local authorities. While the central authorities safely occupy the moral high ground, local officials have to solve the issues, address injustices and deal with the disruption and threat to their career prospects caused by protests. Protest is a right tacitly given to Chinese citizens, not to challenge the political system, but as a check on local government and more broadly local businesses and elites.

4.8 Civil Society

The 1980s witnessed the emergence of a host of clubs, associations and organizations serving specific interests, professions or tasks. They were seen by many as the sprouts of civil society that would challenge the CCP's political monopoly and foster demands for a more democratic political system. In the 1990s some of these organizations took on a more explicit political form by advocating a particular cause or problem.

Pioneered in the 1990s by the Ford Foundation, some organizations began to be actively nurtured by foreign donors. Foreign NGOs, such as the World Wildlife Fund and Greenpeace also set up shop in China. Funding from abroad continues to be pivotal for many of China's civil society organizations and catering to the priorities of these donors is the cornerstone of their survival and growth. These organizations do not, on the whole, show any signs of working towards a political transformation in China. Civil society in China currently consists of hundreds of thousands of organizations, clubs and associations. Instead of asserting their independence from the Party and the state, the vast majority actively cooperates with the authorities in their area.

To ensure that civil society organizations remain fragmented and local, they are explicitly forbidden to establish subsidiaries in other parts of China. Civil society organizations have to register with the Ministry of Civil Affairs and, until a very recent relaxation of this requirement, could do so only if they had a formal association with a state or Party organization that assumes responsibility for the organization. Many 'social organizations' (the world civil society in usually avoided in China itself because of its liberal political charge) have in fact been set up by a state or Party organization to assist that organization in carrying out its tasks or to create employment for members of staff made redundant. An unknown but large number of civil society organizations has chosen not to or has been unable to register, but these organizations find it much more difficult to raise funds and carry out their chosen mission, rendering them on the whole small and ineffectual.

The grip of the Party-state in China is such that it has been able to mould a civil society sector in its own image, unable to and largely uninterested in engineering a transformation of the political system. As part of its 'small state, big society' strategy, the state has shed the ambition to carry out the increasingly complex and demanding governing tasks that have to be done in society. These include a range of welfare issues and needs (addiction, HIV/AIDS, schooling and training, housing, poverty alleviation, the environment to name a few), as well as the promotion of specific interests, such as business sectors, homeowners, people evicted from their house or land or those who have suffered from environmental damage.

The state even reaches out to potentially dangerous groups such as workers. Blue-collar state-sector and migrant workers are among those groups that suffer the most in China's globalized capitalist economy. Both the official unions and labour NGOs are active in raising rights' awareness among workers, fighting or mediating cases against employers and helping with health and other issues. Workers also frequently fight for their rights and interests on their own, including when necessary by organizing protests and even strikes. Skilled and better-educated workers, gangmasters or team leaders and dormitory-based networks play an important role in this. Workers' activism is of course ideologically threatening to a party that still defines itself as socialist and the state is very sensitive to organization or cooperation beyond a localized issue.

The official unions and labour NGOs have to be very circumspect in what they do: helping workers to fight for their rights as employees is fine and part of the state's social governance strategy to strengthen social stability. Asserting labour rights that involve collective bargaining and independent unions are seen as competing with state power and thus a threat to stability, so organizing workers for class-based action is most definitely not allowed. Labour organizations funded from abroad also have to be careful not to be accused of 'foreign meddling'. Organizations that represent workers' rights in the Pearl River Delta and Beijing, have recently been invited to tender for specific projects from local government organizations. In return, they have to cooperate with the official trade unions of the CCP, which thus gets a grip over groups of workers that have traditionally fallen beyond their grasp: laid-off unemployed workers, migrant workers, and the self-employed.

Like civil society organizations across the world, Chinese social organizations and their leaders work to address particular issues to make their city or their neighbourhood a better place to live in. In China, that means working together with and not against the state. Civil society organizations in China and elsewhere are largely practical in navigating the cliffs of suppression, co-optation and commercialization: they submit to the agenda of their donors, work together with the authorities and serve the ambitions of their leaders. Their job is not to start a revolution, but to improve the society they are part of. As such, they work with, add to and change Chinese politics in interesting and important ways, but it is not realistic to expect a more fundamental transformation of the political system to come from their efforts.

4.9 Public Intellectuals, Artists and Dissidents

Human rights and democracy were important political issues for critical intellectuals, artists and dissidents in the 1980s who hoped to engineer genuine change to China's political system. Many of them operated at the interface of the Party and society at universities or research institutes such as the Chinese Academy of Social Sciences. The influence of people like Yan Jiaqi, Su Shaozhi or Fang Lizhi during that period was in large part based on the patronage of one or more top Party leaders, particularly party general secretary Hu Yaobang until his fall from power in 1987. Other critical voices were raised by individuals such as Wang Xizhe, Wei Jingsheng, Wang Dan and Liu Xiaobo, leaders or participants of the many protest movements of the 1970s and 1980s that culminated in the 1989 demonstrations.

The opposition of all these individuals has been successfully quelled. After 1989, the CCP leadership concluded that the main reason why the demonstrations in that year had escalated was that Zhao Ziyang and his supporters had allowed this to happen, hoping to use popular unrest for their own political gain. It appears that the leadership has sworn never again to allow divisions among themselves to spill over into society. Subsequent dissident activity, such as the establishment of the China Democracy Party in 1998, could therefore never develop any real traction and was relatively easily suppressed. Even Charter 08, a manifesto calling for freedom, democracy and the rule of law written in 2008 by veteran dissident Liu Xiaobo and signed by intellectuals, lawyers, and officials, failed to split the leadership and ultimately fizzled out. Liu himself was later arrested and given another long jail sentence before receiving the Nobel Peace Prize in 2010.

In recent years, China's most famous activist has been Ai Weiwei, whose background and activities are conspicuously different from Liu Xiaobo. Liu's ideas and activities are comparable to those of famous twentieth-century dissidents from the Soviet bloc, such as Vaclav Havel or Andrei Sacharov. Ai is an avant-garde artist without a clearly articulated ideology or political agenda. Ai behaves like a court jester, mocking and challenging the powers-that-be through his art and actions. He achieved his greatest fame (especially outside China) as the artistic consultant to the design of the 'birds nest' Olympic stadium in Beijing, which he subsequently criticized as China's fake smile towards the West. Caught up in the tightening political situation in China after the 2007 Seventeenth Party Congress and the 2008 Olympic Games, Ai started to become more confrontational, perhaps in the belief that his background (his father Ai Qing had been a famous communist writer and poet) would continue to protect him. Eventually he was arrested in 2011. After his release from jail, Ai has been systematically censured just like other more conventional dissidents, and his voice has become much less prominent in China (although not abroad) since.

4.10 The New Face of Chinese Politics

All meaningful political opponents of the regime are either in jail, abroad, dead or have turned to more private pursuits. Human rights and democracy are no longer issues that any opposition dares to openly make its own. Instead, specific rights or specific issues have become the focus of opposition or criticism: land, housing, work, health, the environment, sexuality. The political system as a whole is no longer the target as it was in the 1980s and or even the 1990s. The greater freedoms earned or given in the 2000s to pursue specific interests or issues therefore translate not into less but rather into more regime stability, which is, one suspects, exactly how it was intended.

Traditional state socialist political systems do not allow independently organized political activity: all political processes take place within the confines of the Party-state. This is diametrically opposed to liberal political theory in which democracy and a vigorous civil society of independent political actors are considered essential to keep the state at arm's length from business, religion, culture and private life. At present, the relationship between state and society in China clearly fits neither of these categories as it is shaped by the unique structure of the fragmented neo-socialist state. Society is no longer simply part of the Party-state but it is not fully independent, let alone antagonistic. Citizens enjoy very substantial rights and freedoms, but these are neither inalienable nor innate to the individual. After 35 years of reform this can no longer be explained as simply a long drawn-out transitional phase to liberal democracy. China has settled into a pattern that is a complex hybrid of many elements, yet is also something altogether new.

Viewed from the perspective of society, the crucial components of this change are marketization and individualization. In first half of this chapter I have shown how these have reshaped economic, social, cultural and religious life. Building on the discussion of contentious politics, civil society and dissidence in the second half of this chapter, I would like to suggest that marketization and individualization also have an impact on the nature of politics itself. Despite the efforts to manage society, the Party is no longer completely in the driver's seat. As the Party and government get better at management and governance rather than simply controlling society, society in turn gains increasing room and leverage to manage the state. Leaders of protests and petitions, NGOs, public intellectuals, business lobbyists and other political entrepreneurs have not only made politics much more complex and diverse, but have also created something that is beginning to resemble a market for political influence and highly individualized career opportunities at the interface of society and the Party-state. Below I will briefly look at the evolution of and players in this new political field.

Despite appearances, NGOs are often weak institutions that exist mainly as a vehicle for an ambitious, vocal individual leader. What many of these individual NGO leaders have in common is good personal relationships with one or more officials, usually in the local administration, who support the cause of the leader and her or his NGO. Much of the energy of the leader and resources of the NGO are devoted to cultivating this relationship instead of strengthening the NGO's own organization: the NGO therefore remains caught in a vicious cycle of structural weakness and dependence on official backing. From the perspective of the authorities, NGOs themselves matter much less than the individuals that lead them, who are their real partners or opponents in their particular policy area.

Research on activist lawyers and leaders of home-owner committees brings out the individualization of the political field even more clearly. Activist lawyers deliberately defend cases that allow them to contest officials or government agencies to enhance their own reputation and influence. Early on in their career, they are often celebrated by the central authorities, receiving prizes for their efforts to help in the fight against corruption and power abuse. However, ambitious lawyers seek out ever more contentious cases, even including the defence of dissidents, because only working close to the 'high voltage line' of official disapproval ensures them the fame and exposure they need to effect more structural change rather than just the settlement of an individual case of injustice. Activist lawyers talk and act like politicians. They seek to influence public opinion, policy making and reform by publicizing their cases in the media, submitting petitions to the National People's Congress, or organizing debates. They use the tools of the legal system for extra-legal purposes operating in the ill-defined and shifting grey zone between the state and society.

Activist lawyers also include what Susanne Brandtstädter terms 'rural law activists' who have learnt to use the law in their fights against injustice in their own local area. While they often remain in their own village and continue to identify with a rural way of life, the more successful among them take on cases or otherwise advise clients from many other places. Such rural law activists change the political game not only through their application of the law but also because their work transcends the boundaries between the backwardness of rural areas and the modernity of urban China. Often against considerable odds and at great personal risk, their work contributes to the emergence of a common citizenship and a public sphere based on the rule of law that transcends the old divisions of socialist China.

Somewhat more mundanely, many leaders of China's rapidly proliferating homeowners committees are also becoming more like politicians. In recent years, home-owner committees have linked up in larger networks that enable them more effectively to pursue the interests of homeowners against real estate management companies or the local authorities. Leaders of the committees are often highly educated, professionally employed and effectively networked individuals. They take the lead in petitioning the government or seeking internet or media publicity. Some act out of idealism hoping to improve Chinese society and administration, others are more calculating, yet others are a bit of both. Like activist lawyers, the more daring and effective leaders tend to radicalize, seeking out more contentious issues and using increasingly radical means, such as sit-ins, rallies or demonstrations. Effective leaders may be co-opted by the authorities. They may be offered a seat on the local people's congress, which in turn presents further opportunities to cultivate relationships with officials that can be used for private business, more effectively promoting the interests of homeowners, or perhaps even to start a formal political career.

Unlike the 1980s, intellectuals no longer only seek influence through the patronage of a top Party leader, but have redefined themselves as scientists and professionals. While some have set themselves up as public figures, the majority have taken on the role of professionals whose expert knowledge and skills may be deployed in the course of the policy-making process, but who are no longer pawns or players in the CCP's internal political game. Prominent contemporary artists formerly critical of the government, too, have been co-opted into the mainstream as professional artists with the creation of the Chinese Academy of Contemporary Arts in 2009.

Some intellectuals have consciously built up a public presence in China and abroad through their academic and popular writings, TV appearances and on the internet. Opinions and debate are aired openly and span a considerable range from neo-conservative nationalism to free market internationalism. Some among them are home-grown, others have been trained in Europe or the US, usually as economists or political scientists, returning to China in the hope of making a difference. Yet others have stayed abroad, using the greater autonomy (and perhaps academic authority) that this brings as both leverage and political insurance in case things turn sour. Some specialize in one particular policy field; others volunteer their opinions and advice in many fields, including those beyond their own core competence.

One of the most distinctive aspects of neo-socialism is a fundamental retooling of the relationship between the CCP and the country's intellectual elite that took shape after 1989. The CCP has created more distance between the factional power politics within the leadership and debates and conflicting interests in society. Policy making, as a result, has become more a matter of weighing external interests and opinions and less a way of defeating one's opponents. With this, the social position of artists and intellectuals also has been redefined: no longer are they both the conscience of the nation and at the same time deeply connected to the factional politics of their patrons within the leadership.

If the Chinese leadership wishes to continue to develop science and technology as part of its overall strategy of achieving an affluent and advanced society, it is paramount that scientific professionals and public intellectuals remain dissociated from CCP power politics. Only then will they have the space and freedom to take their research and teaching in directions that move the frontiers of knowledge and technology further, without constantly having to look over their shoulder to ensure that there is sufficient political backing for their work. It is exactly in this regard that the long-term effect of the clampdown on the freedom of academics, journalists and lawyers and political activists and the re-politicization of the media, art and academic research in 2014 and 2015 might be severe.[11] If the expression of certain opinions is again associated with support for certain leaders who have fallen out of favour (Bo Xilai, Zhou Yongkang) instead of as contributions to public debate, it will be very hard to convince these professionals that they can continue to do their work properly under CCP rule. This will not only directly threaten the Party's strategy for innovation and economic upgrading, but in the longer term may also have an adverse impact on the whole neo-socialist edifice so carefully constructed in the past 25 years.

Public intellectuals, NGO activists, lawyers or other civil society actors operate largely 'outside the system' of the Party and the state. Other kinds of political entrepreneurs seek to influence the policy-making process itself. Such new political players exploit and add to the

---

[11] The sternest policy document of the Party Centre and the State Council on strengthening party control on higher education is *Opinion Concerning Further Strengthening and Improving Propaganda and Ideology Work in Higher Education under New Circumstances* (Guanyu jin yi bu jiaqiang he gaijin xin xingshi xia gaoxiao xuanchuan sixiang gongzuo yijian). Only a summary of the document has been made public on Xinhua Web on 19 January 2015, online at http://news.xinhuanet.com/2015-01/19/c_ 1114051345.htm, accessed 1 August 2015, which has been translated on *China Copyright and Media*, 16 February 2015, online at https://china copyrightandmedia.wordpress.com/2015/01/19/opinions-concerning-further-strengthening-and-improving-propaganda-and-ideology-work-in-higher-education-under-new-circumstances/, accessed 1 August 2015.

many fissures and gaps in the system between different levels and agencies within the administration. The growth in China of local associations of farmers and businesses in the 1980s prefigured the emergence of a wide range of business associations at the national and local levels as central planning of the large state sector was dismantled in the 1990s. The ministries that used to plan and supervise a particular sector of the economy were turned into business associations to assist with the regulation of industry and to provide channels to insert the views and interests of their sector into public policy making. The equivalent of what is termed interest representation or lobbying in democratic systems is therefore at least in part the direct descendant of the planned economy in China, predicated not on a separation or even opposition between state and society, but on their organic connection.

These changes run much deeper than the ubiquitous and widely publicized use of personal relations and corruption discussed earlier. The latter are endemic and often massive sums are at stake, and no anti-corruption campaign, not matter how severe, will be able to root them out. However, personal connections and corruption are mainly tools to secure cooperation on specific issues relevant to just one specific party. Influencing more general policy decisions in favour of a particular constituency, however, requires a more systematic approach. NGOs, business associations, networks of home-owner organizations, but also large individual businesses have developed a range of methods to further their cause. These include formal methods such as conferences, media coverage, research, policy briefs or expert opinions, but also informal meetings with selected leaders. Confrontation rather than deference has become increasingly common, with organizations, firms or individuals publicly or privately expressing their dissatisfaction with a particular decision.

The Party-state in turn has developed its own ways of informing its policy making through research, expert opinions or opinion polls. Indeed, the Party now likes to refer to itself as a 'learning' Party. Think tanks associated with individual leaders emerged in the 1980s, and now each self-respecting government or Party department has its own bureau, section or institute for policy research. Party schools, school of administration and regular universities are frequently asked to carry out specific policy-related projects. The Politburo of the Party itself holds regular 'study sessions' to be informed of expert research and opinion in specific policy areas. Especially since the early 1990s, increasing numbers of very highly educated experts have chosen to work within or with the Party-state apparatus in the belief that their influence on policy from within the system would be greater than agitating against the system from without as activists, dissidents or exiles.

Beijing increasingly comes to resemble large Western political centres such as Washington or Brussels that are filled with research institutions, think tanks, lobbying organizations, lawyers' offices, and foundations that broker influence, knowledge and power. There are of course still definite political no-go zones and policy making ultimately still takes place inside the sacred void of the leadership small groups, committees and departments of the central Party and government apparatus, but these no longer operate in splendid isolation. Policy is influenced through a variety of channels, some of which have emerged organically, while others have been quite deliberately put in place. No matter what happens in the next ten years or so, the Party seems sure to want to retain its power mystique and central position, while at the same time creating more distance from society and opening itself up to a wide range of influences on the policy-making process.

4.11 Conclusion: Viewing China's Future beyond the Human Rights Discourse

Today, the presence of the state in Chinese society is different from what it has ever been. It is both more powerful and resourceful and less direct and invasive. Gone are the days of closed work units, neighbourhoods and rural collectives as the foundation of governance. At the same time marketization and individualization have made society much more complex and fluid. High levels of social, occupational and residential mobility, social and economic stratification, and cultural, religious and social diversity have created new freedoms and new injustices that are setting fundamentally different challenges to government and civil society.

The political system continues to evolve through a recombinant process of foreign borrowing and home-grown development. This evolutionary process is impossible to squeeze into the dichotomy of dictatorship and democracy, let alone a prediction of democratic transition. In fact, democracy and dictatorship are not, as is commonly assumed, antagonistic political systems. This observation runs deeper than the acknowledgement that democratic 'enclaves' can exist within authoritarian regimes,[12] just as authoritarian enclaves can exist within democratic political systems. Democracy and dictatorship are best used as shorthand references to a range of governmental technologies that can be combined and recombined in real-life political systems regardless of their purported ideological charge. While China continues to change, it is not developing in the direction of a Western multi-party democracy, yet equally it is also no longer a full-blown dictatorship. It is a bit of both and at the same time also something altogether new.

Two terms are often suggested to grasp these developments, namely corporatism and authoritarianism. While each of these terms captures some of what is going on, neither do the developments in China full justice. Corporatism highlights the unity of the social body under the leadership of the state, but underexposes the fragmentary nature and porosity (and global connectedness) of the Chinese system by leaning too much on the twentieth-century assumption that a country does indeed have – or should have – an organic unity of purpose. Authoritarianism more easily fits Chinese reality, but this is because the term itself is largely devoid of content: it does not mean a great deal more than 'non-democratic' and serves as a convenient designation of others who are not like us, replacing the terms dictatorship and totalitarianism of the Cold War era.

This is why the term neo-socialism might be a useful descriptive term that highlights both the recombinant nature of the political system and the party's adherence to its Leninist core. Under current conditions nothing more should be read into neo-socialism. China's evolution is pragmatically determined and not prescribed by an ideology that serves as an anchor or yardstick for policy making. Neo-socialism is therefore a useful shorthand reference to certain aspects of China's system and development, but should not be presented as a new type or model that fits the entirety of China's present and future. The speed and unknown direction of change mean that China is charting the wholly new waters of the twenty-first century in ways that cannot be easily pigeonholed in established ideological categories.

---

[12] On the argument regarding democratic enclaves, see Gilley, Bruce 2010. Democratic Enclaves in Authoritarian Regimes. *Democratization* 17,3:389–415.

With this we are back to the issue of human rights. Chinese citizens do not enjoy the range and depth of human rights as set out by the United Nations declaration of universal human rights. However, it would be foolish to dismiss as phoney or incomplete the freedoms the Chinese have come to enjoy. To do so locks the debate into a discourse that can only conclude that for the Chinese people to be free at last, the current regime will either have to change its ways or, more ominously, will have to be changed to become more like us. Such an approach creates tensions especially in post-colonial settings where the insistence on universal human rights is quickly seen as a foil for continuing Western dominance and the imposition of Western norms of political behaviour. In China, such suspicions run especially deep thanks to a carefully nurtured memory of foreign humiliation, capitalist exploitation and socialist liberation.

The problem with this line of reasoning is that it is based on a Western reading of the nature of the post-Second World War international order. This order was based on two conflicting principles. First, war and decolonization dealt the final blow to empires as legitimate political entities, replacing them with a community of independent, equal and fully sovereign nation-states. Second, the autonomy and sovereignty of these states were constrained by an international order that presumes that it can evaluate individual countries against universal principles of justice, human rights and good governance. In this, a fundamental division and antagonism was seen to run between the 'free world' of democratic countries and an unfree communist bloc.

The Western human rights discourse ignores the fact that this world no longer exists. China has become a political entity that does not fit the old categories of liberal democracy and oppressive dictatorship. Freedom and human rights are shaped and conditioned by the realities of this new political form. Furthermore, China has simply become too strong, too stable and too wealthy to allow the imposition of a discourse on human rights and democracy that takes the West as the norm.

To break free from the fetters of the old human rights discourse and to deal with China as it is rather than what Westerners think it ought to be, I think it is best to start by being honest about why it is that the West is so preoccupied with human rights and democracy to begin with. Are Westerners deep down convinced that Western civilization is superior to any other civilization in the world? If so, they should probably come out of the closet and say as much. Or do they believe that human rights and democracy continue to be a convenient stick to beat their main competitor and potential adversary in the international arena with? If so, they should by now realize that this has been woefully ineffectual, if not outright counter-productive.

We should start with the acknowledgement that any change will only take place within the limits and at the pace that the CCP allows. A genuine concern to improve the freedom, security and quality of life of the Chinese people, especially the most disadvantaged among them, should take the CCP seriously as a viable future for China, instead of treating it as a flawed and therefore ultimately doomed regime. This leaves more room for action than may seem apparent at first sight. As I have shown in this chapter, the CCP is operating in an increasingly complex domestic political field which is only partially of its own making. Only understanding and accepting the constraints and opportunities of China's evolving political field will give us a chance to grasp how injustice, exploitation and dependency are understood and argued against in China itself and to work together with Chinese actors inside and outside the party.

5 | From Empire to Nation, or Why Taiwan, Tibet and Xinjiang Will Not Be Given Independence

To the Communist Party, socialist emancipation and national salvation have always been inseparable. The CCP is heir to a tradition of reform and revolution going back to China's defeat during the First Opium War in 1842. Since then, the concern of countless officials, scholars, students, rebels, activists, writers, scientists and revolutionaries was to 'save the nation' and to overcome the ignominy of 'national humiliation' at the hands of Western and Japanese imperialist aggression. The years immediately after the fall of the Qing dynasty in 1912 in particular were times of rapid radicalization. Appalled by the swift deterioration of the new Republic that succeeded the Empire, patriots trawled Western ideas in search of possible solutions to the country's dire condition, among which Marxism initially was only one. In fact, many of the earliest members of the Communist Party turned to communism only after the success of the Bolshevik Revolution in 1917 showed how powerful a communist nation could suddenly become in a country like Russia which was only a little less poor and backward than their own.

One hundred years on, China as a nation is still very much a work in progress, a project to turn the conquest empire of the Qing dynasty into a modern country and a united nation. In the reform period the relative importance of nation building has increased to the point that nowadays little is heard of a communist utopia. There are three core concepts at the heart of the Communists' national project: the country of the People's Republic of China, the Chinese nation and the Han people. In this chapter I will describe how the CCP brings its neo-socialist arsenal to bear on each of these, enabling it to go far beyond the very real progress made under Mao. China is on its way to becoming a modern and integrated society in which there is paradoxically more and at the same time less space for and tolerance of any form of diversity that challenges the unity of the country, the nation or the people.

5.1 Han and Non-Han

Many nations in the world are imagined as the modern incarnation of
an ancient people, a primordial combination of blood and soil that
present nation building as a natural desire to bring the shape and
boundaries of modern societies in line with cultural and historical realities. More than any other ideology, such nationalism is non-negotiable,
and the fight against its enemies an unquestionable right.

China is one of the best examples of this. In their efforts to find
the Chinese nation, modern nationalists built on a long tradition.
The assumption that the ever-shifting political units in mainland East
Asia are all part of a continuous and united Chinese history is in
itself a product of many centuries of Chinese historiography, of which
modern Chinese nationalism is simply the most recent instalment. To
put it in perspective, this effort should be compared to enlisting, say,
ancient Egypt, the Romans or Charlemagne not just as among the many
sources of Western civilization, but as the ancient equivalents of modern Western political units such as the British Empire or the European
Union. Not entirely a fabrication perhaps, but certainly not self-evident
either.

Until well into the twentieth century, for most people, China as a
culture, society and political unit was rooted in traditional concepts
and practices. Tradition celebrated local identity and culture as much
as a national one, and included ancestor worship, family and marriage,
popular religion, the Chinese script and classical language, trading networks, folklore, calendrical systems, naming practices and more generally a powerful memory of Imperial rule and Confucian civilization.
It would therefore be a mistake to locate the Chinese nation purely in
the modern period. An awareness and identification with China pre-
dated modern nationalism; likewise, the politicization of this awareness happened in different contexts, periods and fashions well before
the nineteenth century. One crucial aspect that was new in modern
nationalism, however, was that 'China' came to be identified with all
of the territories conquered by the non-Chinese dynasty of the Qing, a
reading of the nation that is very much relevant today.

The shifting connections and disjunctions between Chinese political
units, civilization and groups are expressed in the fact that there are
multiple words in both pre-modern and modern Chinese that all translate as 'Chinese' or 'China' in Western languages. *Zhongguo* (China)

and especially *Hua* (Chinese) refer to people who are part of the Chinese civilization and therefore ought to be and wish to be incorporated into a country and be ruled by a state that bears and guards this civilization. In principle, people from any cultural or racial background could become Hua Chinese and be part of Zhongguo China. The word *Han* by contrast denotes the essential difference of native Chinese, both by descent and culture, from non-Chinese living in the same or adjacent territories. This distinction was especially charged during the many conquest dynasties when non-Chinese overlords ruled the whole or part of the territory that is now known as China. In such a context, the Han-non-Han distinction was not just cultural but also political, very similar in fact to ethnic identities in the modern world.

The last Chinese dynasty, the Qing, was a conquest dynasty established by the Manchu people from the area to the Northeast of what was then Ming-dynasty China. Like the Moghul and Russian Empires elsewhere in Asia, it tied together a vast territory and a multitude of societies and cultures. The Manchu rulers of the Qing dynasty imposed a strict segregation between people living under the eight banners (mainly Manchus, but also Mongols and 'martial' Han Chinese) and other subjects. Elite Han Chinese especially felt that they were made to be strangers in their own land occupied by barbarians. The Qing court imposed upon the Han population Manchu-style dress and a plaited Manchu-style queue for men. Being Han meant being different from the Manchus and the other three main categories recognized by the Empire: Tibetans, Mongols and Muslims. As a result, Han became both a stigma and a unifying identity, regardless of the huge difference among the Han across China.

As the Qing got weaker in the course of the nineteenth century and foreign powers got stronger, the stigmatization of Han identity made it easy for patriotism on one hand and loyalty to the dynasty on the other hand to part ways. Calls to strengthen China and save the country increasingly merged with anti-Manchu feelings and Han Chinese chauvinism. A future China would have to be ruled not by barbarians but by Chinese. China would have to become a strong and independent country to survive the Social Darwinian struggle between races and nations and to take its rightful place in the world.

Nationalism was born, but the imagined shape of the new nation retained strong continuities with the Empire that had preceded it.

Some nationalists felt that the new Republic ought to be limited to the central parts of the Empire with a dominant Han Chinese population (similar to the way that elite nationalists a few years later would carve Turkey out of the Ottoman Empire). Quickly, however, the temptations of a traditional approach proved to be too strong. Like all Chinese elites before and after them, nationalists read a unified Chinese culture into Chinese history and Han Chinese identity, unqualified territorial sovereignty into Imperial rule and suzerainty, and contemporary Chinese society into all territories of pre-modern dynasties. Both the Republic and the People's Republic after it were therefore built on a contradiction. Both were simultaneously to be the home of the Han and include all lands that had once been ruled by the Qing, no matter how tenuous this rule had been or how un-Chinese places like Tibet, Xinjiang or Mongolia might be.

The modern Chinese nation thus started as a perfect storm of cultural chauvinism, anachronism and a traditional, dynastic interpretation of history. Early nationalists (Liang Qichao, Kang Youwei) confirmed the diversity of the five main peoples recognized by the Qing (Manchus, Hans, Tibetans, Mongols, Muslims). They expected that eventually all these people would organically melt into a unified Chinese nation. China's 'father of the nation' Sun Yat-sen went further and only paid lip-service to diversity, thinking that non-Han Chinese groups were insignificant compared to the Han. To him, the vast majority of Han Chinese was the backbone of the nation. In his *Three Principles of the People* he famously declared that the Han, 'sharing a common bloodline, language, religion, and customs, are entirely one people.' In the 1930s, nationalist military dictator Chiang Kai-shek went even further: he simply ordained the historic unity of all Chinese without any acknowledgement of the presence of non-Han people.

The Communist Party built on the nationalists' construction of the nation, but developed a more broad-minded interpretation. What remained fundamental was the unity of the Han as the foundation of the nation: regional or ethnic differences among Han Chinese groups were never allowed any form of formal political expression. Likewise, reading the unity of the nation and the sovereignty of the state into the territory of the former Empire remained a sacrosanct principle, including the territory governed by the Nationalist Party after the latter's defeat on the Chinese Mainland and retreat to Taiwan.

The Party's approach to China's non-Han groups, however, would be a different one. In the 1930s, the CCP had already agreed on the principle of 'self-determination' for non-Han groups. Although after 1949 this was watered down to 'autonomy' within the new People's Republic, the Party nevertheless broke with the Nationalist approach to integrate or assimilate non-Han Chinese. The Han-non-Han distinction was thus incorporated into the reading of the Chinese nation. Non-Han groups were termed 'minority nationalities' that together with the majority Han nationality made up the multi-national 'Chinese nation'. This in itself was little more than an amalgam of Qing dynasty governing practices and Nationalist rhetoric. Unlike their predecessors, however, the Communists were determined to weld non-Chinese groups not just into the abstract concept of the nation, but also into the structure of new China's socialist society and political system.

The CCP drew on two sources: Soviet theory of nationhood and Republican ethnological research. Stalin had claimed that nationhood was an objective fact of social reality that could be described, measured and assessed on the basis of language, culture, mode of livelihood and territory. In the early 1950s, the CCP started a systematic enterprise to determine the national composition of Chinese society. As Thomas Mullaney has shown in his work on ethnic classification in the south-western province of Yunnan in 1953–54, the sociologists, anthropologists and folklorists who undertook the job took it far beyond Stalin's original intention. They had to work with an original list of ethnic self-classifications from the PRC's first population census in 1953 that included hundreds of ethnonyms, often of very small and obscure groups. Their work included field visits to the groups in question, but also drew heavily on ethnographic and especially linguistic research from the decades before the establishment of the PRC. The end result of this project was not merely taxonomy of the population. Scientific knowledge and research had been enlisted to produce a blueprint of what the rational and objective ethnic composition of China really was and ought to be, helping people to remove the fog of prejudice, ignorance and obfuscation that had kept them from realizing the actual connections and divisions between the peoples of China.[1]

---

[1] Mullaney, Thomas S. 2011. *Coming to Terms with the Nation: Ethnic Classification in Modern China.* Berkeley: University of California Press.

Science thus created a truth that, once backed up by the state, has become truer with each successive year. The message that minority policies convey is clear: ethnic groups are tolerated as remnants of the past, mere minorities without a future as modern, independent nations equal to the Chinese nation centred on the culturally superior and ethnically undivided Han. To soften the blow, minority status comes with certain political privileges and citizens' rights. Special administrative regions, prefectures and counties provide homes to minority groups. The fifty-six nationalities (the Han plus fifty-five minorities) are routinely trotted out to represent the Chinese nation to domestic and foreign audiences. Despite its ostensible naturalness, this approach to cultural and ethnic diversity has several remarkable features. First, apart from the occasional recognition of a new (usually very small and obscure) minority, the ethnic map of China is permanent and unchanging both in time and space. Although in the fullness of time minorities are expected to assimilate into the Chinese nation, this is postponed to the indefinite future following the natural spread of superior Han culture and socialist modernity. Second, ethnic differences within nationalities are blotted out. This is especially true for the larger nationalities, such as the majority Han and the Yi, Zhuang, Mongols, Uighur, Tibetan and Muslim minorities. Although each of these nationalities are vessels which contain vastly different cultures and groups, the dominance of the state's minority policies has been such that they have come to be considered natural categories and identities, even to the point of being used to mobilize resistance against Chinese domination. Third, minority nationality is a one-size-fits-all concept, applied equally to small fishing tribes like the Nanai or Hezhen along the Amur River that separates the Chinese Northeast from the Russian Far East, a religious minority dispersed across the whole country (the Hui or Chinese Muslims), and large groups occupying a discreet and contiguous territory which had powerful states in the past and continue to have a strong sense of separate nationhood (Tibetans, Uighurs, Mongols).

Minority policies collapse the many degrees and ways of being different into a one-dimensional and Han-centric dichotomy: a group is either Han or it isn't. Groups like the She and Hakka, Muslim Chinese or the Dan boat people have always uncomfortably straddled this divide, arbitrarily ending up at one or the other side or even being split right down the middle. Another example is the Bai minority in Yunnan province. Before being classified as a minority they called themselves not Bai but *Minjia* (civilian households). Although they acknowledged that they had their own language and cultural distinctiveness, the Minjia insisted that they were paragons of Chinese civilization and Confucian orthodoxy. After having become an official minority, a Bai culture and script were created that were ancient and modern all at once, celebrating both their non-Han cultural roots in the ancient Nanzhao and Dali kingdoms and their unique contribution to a socialist and progressive culture. Bai culture quickly became real in all its consequences, especially because the professional elite of Bai cadres, teachers, academics and performers developed a stake in Bai identity. Yet it would be a mistake to see this elite Bai culture only as handmaidens of the state. After the start of the reforms, the Bai region of Dali became a major tourist destination. Bai culture is now a huge asset to local modernization, making the fruits of the state's minority policies first and foremost serve local needs and local people.

The concept of minority nationality works best for groups at various stages of assimilation, integration and absorption at the soft margins of the Han Chinese heartland in the Southeast (Fujian, Taiwan, Jiangxi and Guangdong provinces) and Southwest (Guangxi, Guizhou, Yunnan and the southern part of Sichuan). In these areas Chinese civilization and rule had been gradually extended over many centuries through a combination of migration, intermarriage, acculturation, trade, conquest, occupation and indirect rule. Non-Chinese groups or states, if not already on their way to being Sinicized, usually at least accepted the fact of the superior force of the Chinese state, people and culture. Applied to the peoples at China's traditionally hard borders in the North, West and Northwest (Tibet, Xinjiang, Inner-Mongolia), however, the imposition of minority status was tantamount to demotion following defeat and colonial occupation. In these areas, Chinese civilization and rule had been challenged for millennia by empires, kingdoms and tribal confederacies equal and quite often superior to the might of Chinese empires.

Despite bearing the gifts of development, modernity and socialism, the CCP's efforts to incorporate the northern and western territories into the People's Republic have always run into the resistance of peoples whose claim to separate nationhood often trumped the attraction of inclusion into the Chinese nation. No doubt the best-known in the West is Tibet, where direct and repeated military intervention, the flight of the Dalai Lama to India and heavy-handed direct Chinese rule continue to fuel resistance among large segments of the population. In Xinjiang, the army has been present as much as a military force as a business corporation (the Xinjiang Production and Construction Corps) tasked with semi-colonial rule, resource exploitation, policing, border defence and security work. The administration in Xinjiang was set up to divide-and-rule, with boundaries drawn to divide the majority Uighurs and to pit them against other non-Chinese groups. In Inner-Mongolia, local Mongol Communists with their own strong ties to the Comintern in Moscow initially sought to join the Mongolian People's Republic. Only in the early 1940s were they persuaded to work together with the Chinese Communists to attain Mongolian nationhood as a part of the future People's Republic of China. In 1947, they were indeed awarded with the creation of the Inner Mongolian Autonomous Government. These elites continued to be largely autonomous until they were ousted during the Cultural Revolution, their leader Ulanhu transferred to Beijing and tens of thousands of Mongol Communist cadres killed. After the massacre, nothing stood in the way of Inner-Mongolia rapidly being turned into a Chinese place by large-scale in-migration of Han Chinese and the assimilation of local Mongols, especially those in the cities.

In spite of these chronic problems especially in the North and West of the country, the PRC's minority policies of recognition and limited empowerment were on the whole a marked improvement on ham-fisted Nationalist approaches to non-Han Chinese. After the disruption during the decade of the intolerant Cultural Revolution (1966–76) the minority policies were quickly restored and further elaborated; they remain the cornerstone of the CCP's vision of the nation.

Below this relatively smooth surface, several long-term developments make it unlikely that the current policies can survive for much longer. Fundamentally, minority policies are a specific high-modernist reading of cultural diversity that is predicated on state socialism. Minority nationalities are administrative distinctions defined and imposed by the state in a way similar to other administrative statuses, such as household registration, membership of a work unit or rural collective, being an overseas Chinese or a foreigner, or even gender. Such statuses set the terms under which specific categories of people belong to socialist society and they come with a non-negotiable set of duties, rights, privileges and restrictions regarding residence, employment and so on.

As we saw earlier in chapter 4, recent neo-socialist restructuring of the administration and new patterns of mobility and diversity in China challenge and blur these state-sanctioned cultural categories. The Chinese are becoming individual citizens with rights and responsibilities that they themselves have to defend, use and develop within the parameters set by the law and state policy. Minority statuses that immutably fix one's position, rights and duties and are predicated on a state socialist organization of society are increasingly at odds with these developments. Below, I will discuss these changes under three headings: market-based societal integration and nation building, the production and commodification of diversity, and mobility, globalization and the limits of the nation-state. These three types of changes happen at the same time and they pull individuals, communities and society as a whole in different directions. The outcome is therefore highly uncertain. As I have shown throughout this book, China is a country where many different developments are being telescoped into one brief and intense period of time, and this also has profound implications for the ways in which the unity and diversity of society evolve.

5.2 Unifying Society and the Nation

In 1949, the Chinese nation was still mostly an elite affair. In the 1930s and 1940s the Nationalist government had made an effort to instil a modern sense of belonging into the population and the experiences of the Anti-Japanese War had galvanized large numbers of people to defend China against alien invaders. Nevertheless, the nation remained a thin fabric covering a largely pre-modern society. By 1978, however, a unified modern spoken and written national language was taught in most high schools and universities across the country. National and local media (newspapers, radio and even TV) reached into virtually all areas and households. State socialist construction and Maoist political mobilization had tied people into a united project that was revolutionary and national at the same time, even though relentless class struggle and campaigning simultaneously did much to break down the solidarity that was built up.

Yet it was only the generations after the start of the reforms that fully became nationally Chinese. Neo-socialist governance is directly connected with nation building. Nationalism has become the touchstone of government, while a range of policies directly or indirectly enhance the availability and immediacy of a modern way of life that revolves around citizenship of the People's Republic of China and Han Chinese culture, history, heritage and identity.

A much stronger and better funded central state is the hardware needed to produce unity. The central state has become much more adept at macro-economic control of the economy, strategic planning and vital infrastructural projects. The military, police and intelligence apparatus are much better equipped to deal with disasters, protests and to bring recalcitrant parts of the country to heel. China's increasing military prowess, diplomatic might, technological feats (space exploration!), sports performance and prestigious international events mimic the conspicuous display of might, modernity and wealth by the US, the Soviet Union, Japan and European countries and immeasurably raise the belief and pride in the Chinese nation.

The government is busy constructing a modern infrastructure befitting the twenty-first century, while also undertaking many prestige projects that are chiefly intended as tokens of the government's own strength and effectiveness. The government's enthusiasm is by no means limited to well-known projects in mega-cities, such as the Olympic Games and the central business district in Beijing, or the World Expo and Pudong district in Shanghai. Many smaller city governments also aspire to architectural representations of modernity and power. When doing fieldwork in Honghe near the Vietnamese border in southern Yunnan in 2004, I found that the prefectural government had recently completed its relocation from the picturesque town of Gejiu to the city of Mengzi, where it had built a lavish and hyper-modern government district befitting a small European country.

Less spectacular but arguably more important in the long run is the fact that in the reform era for the first time large numbers of children have grown up speaking the national language standard Chinese (Mandarin) rather than a local language or Chinese dialect as their first language. In part this is because of the introduction of nine years of mandatory and free basic education. The commercialization of the mass media meant that national TV began to cater to popular tastes, creating audiences of hundreds of millions for shows, soaps and movies. More recently, mobile telephony, the internet and social media have united Chinese people across the country into a plethora of virtual communities around any issue, interest or hobby imaginable. The rapid expansion of roads and highways, aviation and high-speed rail has made transportation available to all and affordable to most. Travel, tourism, migration and communications have shrunk China as a social space, lifting people out of their local environment and enabling them to experience and live in China as a whole.

Beyond the government, the growth of a market economy has contributed immeasurably to turning China into an integrated society. National brands for all kinds of products have been created. Although many companies remain firmly rooted in a particular location due to the strong connection between local politics and entrepreneurship, many firms recruit nationally (and even internationally), especially for strategic positions. Conversely, in the absence of lifelong job security, employees are much more willing to relocate to take up a new job. Many young, unattached adults frequently change jobs, housing and place of residence in search of better opportunities or new experiences.

Against this background, it is not so surprising that the 1990s and 2000s have been the age of the growth of popular nationalism, which is sometimes virulently jingoistic or even racist, perhaps more so among youngsters with experience abroad. Some of this is no doubt due to careful nurturing and manipulation by the regime. The Beijing Olympics of 2008 and the Shanghai Expo of 2010 intended to showcase China's successful rise and to instil in the population a sense of national pride and of a destiny about to be fulfilled. Frequent conflicts with Japan about war crimes or territorial issues serve the same function. An equally important explanation is that for many people, it is only in this era that China began to be experienced as a lived-in reality. More diffusely, the government's emphasis on the importance of raising the 'quality' of the people connects individual educational and career ambition to the modernization of society. Government rhetoric often links the two by explicitly urging quality people to contribute to society, most recently in its emphasis on 'core socialist values'. This effort to instil self-discipline and combine individualism with patriotism seems to be starting to bear fruit, as evidenced not only by gratuitous internet nationalism, but also by the spontaneous outpouring of sympathy, donations and voluntary help after the Wenchuan earthquake in 2008.

5.3 New Differences

New connections between places in China and elsewhere have had a profound impact. New differences are emerging and old ones will disappear. The mixing and mingling of people, both Chinese and non-Chinese, make localities no longer just administrative units, ethnic groups no longer confined to their autonomous areas, foreigners no longer a fleeting presence and the category of overseas Chinese no longer restricted to Han Chinese.

Over two hundred million people currently live in another place than their household registration. Much has been written about these migrants, but the secondary literature and Chinese government sources are relatively silent about the fact that this means that it has become commonplace to live in close proximity to people from many different places with different cultures and who speak different languages or dialects. Especially China's larger cities have become pluralistic societies where established residents are sharply distinguished from a broad range of migrant groups. Some of these are transients, moving from job to job and from place to place, but others have become long-term residents. Although some of these groups have turned into residentially concentrated communities with their own leadership and social structure, many others remain socially and administratively visible only as an anonymous part of the undifferentiated 'floating population' or 'rural migrant workers' who are not really a firm and permanent part of urban society. This is a sharp departure from the situation that prevailed in Chinese cities before 1949. People from a particular place tended to specialize in a particular profession or trade and were organized in guilds or associations for a particular area of origin. The city was therefore largely a place where separate communities with different origins co-resided, and much less a space where a local urban community belonged. The city was also administered largely indirectly through and with these organizations and their leaders.

By contrast, nowadays non-recognition of ethnicity beyond the locally resident minority nationalities appears to be a firm principle of governance. This also applies to migrants who are members of a non-Han minority nationality. Non-Han migrants are part of the general migrant population in Chinese cities and are beyond the grip of the administrative structure back home that supports their special minority status. Nevertheless, minority status remains important also for migrants. Like other rural migrants, minority migrants are often embedded in tight networks of workers, recruiters and bosses from their own area. Moreover, news on migrants spreads very rapidly in their home areas and often serves as a barometer for the relationships of a minority with the Han.

The situation and attitude of Han migrants in minority areas is the exact opposite. Han travel to minority areas in increasing numbers. Many come independently as workers, farmers, traders or to start a business, attracted for instance by the opportunities offered by the local minorities tourist industry or the goods and services needed by locally resident Han. Others are recruited by local industry or by the government to dilute the concentration of recalcitrant minorities. The relationship between migrant Han and the local population (often including locally born Han) is fraught with tensions. Migrants see themselves as vectors of superior Han civilization, an attitude that is not lost on the locals. Although Han in-migration might bring employment and opening up of the economy, they are also seen as competitors with an unfair advantage or even agents of the state that wants to turn minority places into Han areas.

In all cases, migration throws together members of minorities and the Han majority, who under state socialism had safely been confined to their own separate worlds. The opportunities and freedom of the market thus make latently conflicting attitudes and interests visible and immediate. The riots in Xinjiang in 2009 are a case in point. Uighur protests started when migrant Uighur women working in Guangdong were molested by Han men, but quickly turned against the Han population in Xinjiang itself. The riots escalated an already tense situation that the existing minority policies are ill-equipped to do anything about. Anti-Han feelings among the Uighurs have risen further, while the government has resorted to an even more heavy-handed approach revolving around the repression of what it considers separatism and terrorism.

During the last ten years migration in China has developed an international dimension. Chinese cities are becoming more cosmopolitan. In addition to foreign ideas, fashions, capital and goods, a rising number of foreign people are flowing into China: tourists, visitors, students, traders, businesspeople, professionals, unskilled workers, and marriage migrants. According to the 2010 census, which for the first time included foreign residents, China currently has a foreign population

of 1 million (including residents from Taiwan, Hong Kong and Macao).
Estimates from different localities add up to double that figure. While
this is still a minute fraction of China's total population of 1.34 billion, the *absolute* number already makes China an immigration country the size of a mid sized European or Asian country. Some of these
are Chinese returnees (overseas Chinese, ethnic minority overseas Chinese, returning students). Others immigrants are from areas adjacent to
China's international borders. Yet others are from Western countries
or countries in Asia, Africa or Latin America. Many foreigners stay
only for a visit or brief sojourn, but a rising number settle for a longer
period, creating communities that are becoming a permanent feature
of the social landscape, especially in China's richer coastal cities. City
governments with large numbers of foreign residents have been prepared to accommodate their needs to a greater extent than for domestic migrants, although with a few exceptions, this still is a far cry from
giving foreign residents any voice in local government.

Immigration to China is fuelled by the opportunities that China's
economic growth is offering to entrepreneurs and traders, the rising
demand for labour and skills, and the safety, political stability and
high standard of living that China has to offer. Local and national governments actively encourage immigrants with skills, capital or expertise, especially Chinese return migrants. Demand for foreign labour,
knowledge and skills is predicated in the short term on the continued
growth of China's export-based economy and, in the medium term, on
a transition to an urban and service-based economy. In the long term,
the impact of population ageing will be much more extreme in China
than in the West or the developed Asian countries, in part because
of the effect of mandatory family planning since 1979. In sum, economic and social development and demographic trends will combine
to create increasing shortages of labour and skills that cannot be met
by the domestic population. In the next thirty years, China is bound
to become a major player and competitor in the global immigration
market.

5.4 New Diversities

A rigid distinction between a uniform Han Chinese majority and the
richly coloured tapestry of recognized minorities continues to be the
centrepiece of the PRC's image of a Chinese nation unified in diversity.

This representation increasingly jars with the changes in Chinese society discussed in the previous two sections. The established minority policies cannot accommodate the new types and expressions of diversity that have been spawned by mobility and liberalization of society. Ethnic minority migrants outside of their autonomous regions or even abroad, Han Chinese migrants in minority areas, and communities of foreign residents create forms of cultural and religious difference that remain invisible through the lens of current policies.

Minority policy is also at odds with individualization and the legitimacy of market competition that have replaced social integration through the state socialist administrative structure. Especially among the upwardly mobile middle classes there is increasing impatience with recognized minorities, who often no longer seem to be suffering from any disadvantages that would justify continued preferential treatment, most jarringly for many being the lower scores required from minorities on the university entrance examination. Education as the sacrosanct channel of legitimate achievement and mobility has proven to be a particularly sensitive trigger for these sentiments. The level playing field that education is supposed to provide is directly violated by these lower score requirements.

In 1989, China's most influential anthropologist and sociologist Fei Xiaotong broke the spell cast by minority policies when he published a book entitled *The Pattern of Unity in Diversity of the Chinese Nation*. Fei called for greater integration of all groups into a united nation centred on its most modern component, Han Chinese culture. More recently, several leading social scientists, most notably anthropologist Ma Rong and economist Hu Angang, have picked up the baton. They argue that the time is over to treat the fifty-five minorities as if they are equal to the Han, while at the same time also asserting that they need special privileges.[2]

These developments and debates have not, as yet, been matched by any formal shift in minority policies; in fact, a new government policy paper in 2009 simply restated the same old principles with only relatively minor modifications. In large part, this may be due to the worsening ethnic conflicts in Tibet and Xinjiang in 2008 and 2009. The

---

[2] Fei's book has never been translated and is only available in Chinese: Fei, Xiaotong. 1989. *Zhonghua minzu duoyuan yiti geju* (The pattern of unity in diversity of the Chinese nation). Beijing: Zhongyang Minzu Xueyuan.

minority policies are based on the formal equality between all fifty-six nationalities, allowing the government to step in when conflicts arise not as the representative of the Han majority, but as impartial arbiter and representative of the whole nation. For now, fifty-six nationalities therefore continue to represent the full official diversity of the Chinese nation. Clearly, the market-driven emerging integration of the nation is still deemed too brittle to allow a fundamental reconsideration of the state's approach to diversity. A validation of domestic or international migrant groups as new ethnic communities is therefore also not (yet) on the books.

Other ways of organizing and presenting difference have developed that have gone some way to get around the limits of official diversity policies. Religion is one of them. Although for many minorities religion and culture are intimately connected, policy strictly separates the two. Religious activities, especially among the troublesome Tibetan Buddhists or Uighur Muslims, are a way of organizing or emphasizing ethnicity that cannot be fully controlled by the state and such slippage between religion and ethnicity is always treated with suspicion. In the context of recent militant mobilization and self-immolations by Buddhist monks in Tibet, even perfectly harmless activities like Buddhist circumambulation in Lhasa are rendered potentially suspect.

Beyond the high-security regions of Tibet and Xinjiang, domestic and foreign migrants across the country often turn to religion for help, support and a way to express their sense of difference from the local population. Thus, Christian churches are focal points for African residents in Guangzhou. Muslim migrants in cities either use local mosques or rent space to set up temporary mosques for themselves. Even in these contexts religion as a source of identity may be potentially difficult to contain. Religion not only links believers to their own community, but also potentially to believers from other backgrounds. Religious communities might even try to recruit and convert, which inevitably arouses deep distrust by the state. In addition, world religions link believers to alternative sources of civilizational and political authority outside China that are beyond the grip the state, and this is bound to set severe limits on the further development of the religious expression of ethnic difference.

Recently, a new and politically less sensitive way of turning difference into identity has spread rapidly, namely the preservation of cultural heritage. Heritage selects from what remains of the past to create meaningful tokens of belonging in the present. Producing heritage turns culture into commodities whose authenticity is validated by a certain authority and which can be consumed as part of tourism, education, training and leisure. Selecting and preserving parts of history, culture and even nature is nothing new in China. As early as 1950, the government ordered the protection of selected sites, objects and animal species. In 1961 the Cultural Relics Bureau was set up, which published a list of 180 national cultural sites. In 1982, the government adopted for the first time the use of the term 'heritage' when it promulgated the heritage protection law and established a national system of bureaus of the State Administration of Cultural Heritage at each level of government. The State Administration of Cultural Heritage manages museums and cultural heritage sites designated by the national or local administration that include pre-modern archaeology and history and the national and revolutionary struggles after 1911.

During the past twenty years, the production, dissemination and consumption of heritage has taken great flight. The PRC has been an enthusiastic supporter of the international movement for the protection of heritage. In 1985 China ratified the World Heritage Convention, joining the international competition to have its heritage sites included on UNESCO's World Heritage List. In 2012 China had forty-seven such sites, second only to Italy with fifty. Sites such as the Great Wall, the Ming Tombs, Dali Old Town in Yunnan or the Potala Palace in Lhasa express both the greatness of Dynastic China and the contributions and historic unity of all nationalities. The international dimension of heritage protection was particularly important in 2006 when the government adopted the inclusion of 'intangible heritage', following the lead of UNESCO three years earlier. Suddenly, not only buildings, sculpture, paintings, instruments or monuments, but also literature, philosophy, dance and even language could be repackaged as heritage. In other words, heritage could now be drawn from all aspects of culture, after having been duly authenticated, sanitized and preserved.

In China, heritage has provided a new language to speak about belonging and diversity that is not constrained by the straightjacket of old socialist minority policies or the single-minded obsession with modernization or economic growth. Both recognized and non-recognized minorities, localities and groups create their own narratives and practices regarding their group's culture, place in Chinese history, and historical and contemporary connections with other groups and

nations. Nominally Han Chinese places like eastern Hui'an County
in Fujian province proudly present their distinctive culture, invariably
including the exotic attire and folkways of their women, as part of a
strategy to develop the tourism industry, a privilege that was reserved
only for recognized minorities in the past. In other places like Ya'an in
Sichuan, temples to local deities were restored, not because these gods
were powerful and widely worshiped, but to attract tourists and other
visitors to the area. Beyond rural folkways and local ethnicity, heritage
has also been used to celebrate the unique contribution to Chinese history and culture of villages, cities or even whole provinces, as with the
many 'red tourism' sites such as Mao's birthplace Shaoshan, restored
Imperial-era streets in Beijing, or even gentrified British-style working
class tenements in Shanghai.

Heritage is thus anything but a 'weapon of the weak'. Authorities have latched onto this internationally recognized concept to gain
greater latitude and creativity in the construction and exploitation of
aspects of local culture beyond the mere preservation of traditional
minority cultures. The development of heritage often involves significant investment for the restoration of buildings, the relocation of people and sometimes even the construction of whole sites from scratch.
Academic specialists often lend their authority and conduct research
into items of heritage and their broader historical context. The production of heritage has liberated the energies of countless ambitious
localities, groups and individuals and has paved the way to imagine
the Chinese nation as made up of endlessly variable components.

This also includes the central government. In the eleventh Five-Year
Plan (2006–10) preservation of 'cultural heritage' was included as
an aspect of the strategy to develop tourism and fight the deleteri-
ous effects of environmental degradation, urbanization and economic
development. The central authorities are also using heritage, history
and archaeology to weave a more finely textured fabric of belonging
to the nation. National museums are being modernized and their col-
lections and displays enriched. To strengthen 'Party spirit', communist
cadre training now routinely includes packaged exposure to some of
the hardships endured by the revolutionaries and touristic fieldtrips to
major sites of the revolutionary struggle. Archaeology, anthropology
and history play a prominent role in the scientific construction of the
Chinese nation, both culturally and genealogically. The *homo erectus*
fossils of Peking Man discovered at Zhoukoudian near Beijing in the

1920s are often presented as proof that modern Chinese (or Asian) man originated in China itself, a unified race untainted by African or European roots. The central authorities have even become adept at manipulating minority heritage. Beijing now insists that the determination of the true incarnation of a Tibetan living Buddha is not up to the Dalai Lama, but must happen by drawing lots from the Golden Urn that was given to Lhasa by the Qing dynasty as a symbol of the Chinese Emperor's suzerainty.

Possibly the best-known aspect of the central government's construction of national heritage is Confucianism. Confucianism has never been included among the officially recognized religions. Politically this has turned out to be a very astute choice. Confucian ethics are about human relations and proper conduct. Unlike world religions such as Buddhism, Christianity, Hinduism or Islam, Confucianism lacks a transcendental component. Like Marxism, Confucianism provides no knowledge about things beyond what can be perceived with our five senses and is not based on dogmatic truth purported to be external to the human condition. Such a system of thought merely requires conviction, unlike belief systems that are based on absolute faith. The lack of a transcendental core opens up the possibility to negotiate or even pick apart the Confucian belief system, selecting the elements that are useful and ignoring others that are not.

Confucianism, in other words, can serve many masters. Specific elements or interpretations of Confucianism blend as much with democratic politics in Taiwan, South Korea and Japan as with the authoritarian system in Singapore and now increasingly the People's Republic of China. During the Maoist period, Confucianism was sharply criticized as the essential core of China's traditional culture that the revolution had overthrown to build a new China. During the earlier phases of the reform period, the government remained mostly silent about Confucianism. It is only since the start of the new millennium that China has experienced a veritable Confucian resurgence, but the language that the government employs is that of culture and heritage, not of religion or ideology. By treating Confucianism as a rich Chinese tradition that can serve the present, the CCP has given itself the space to use elements of Confucianism without violating its commitment to socialism and the principle of Marxist atheism. In 1962, a Confucian temple had featured on the first national list of cultural relics, but now there are at least thirty-nine temples listed as national cultural heritage sites. When attending a conference organized by the International Liaison Department of the CCP's Central Committee in 2014, I discovered that the sage's birthplace Qufu is used by the CCP itself to showcase the splendour of Chinese culture to its foreign guests.

Confucian temples are managed not by religious affairs bureaus, but by the bureaus of State Administration of Cultural Heritage. Confucian ethics with their emphasis on social harmony, education and hard work are enlisted to help raise the quality of citizens. Under Hu Jintao, Confucian concepts like 'harmonious society' and 'putting people first' were included in the CCP's ruling ideology as cues for a more inclusive and sustainable vision of the future. A giant bronze statue of Confucius erected at Tian'anmen Square in 2011 (quickly relocated to a museum) appropriated Confucius as a cultural hero, a symbol of a glorious past and source of pride and self-confidence in the present. The government has set up Confucius institutes across the world to showcase and spread Chinese language, culture and traditions as a world civilization.

At the same time that the CCP and the government discovered Confucianism, a Confucian renaissance also occurred in society. Academic debates on the place of Confucianism include explicit calls to turn Confucianism into a national or civil religion. Confucian semi-religious practices have been invented that include worship at Confucian temples, weddings and mass renewal of wedding vows. Some more zealous Confucians have even set up Confucian associations, in Shenzhen for example, which plan to organize Confucian services and even to build a Confucian academy. More generally, a surge of interest in Confucian ethics has led many parents to use traditional texts for Confucian instruction and study classes.

Confucianism has proven to be very adaptable to neo-socialist society and governance. On one hand, Confucianism has been adopted by individual citizens and autonomous organizations to help shape their own life and China's future. On the other hand, it also easily lends itself to inclusion as part of the increasingly syncretic ruling ideology of the Party whose main components are socialism, nationalism and neoliberalism. Looking somewhat further into the future, the increasing emphasis on Confucianism is part of a shift in the ideological underpinnings of the CCP, discussed earlier in chapter 2. Increasingly, the CCP presents itself less as a guardian of a sacred mission to transform China than as the custodian of peace, prosperity and the people's livelihood, clearing the way for indefinite rule.

5.5 Conclusion: The State of the Nation

The Chinese nation remains a work in progress. Despite appearances to the contrary, its shape and composition have shifted dramatically under neo-socialism and have become much more complex, and even internally contradictory. Viewed from one angle, the nation is a unitary enterprise tying market-driven citizens, organizations, communities and regions together. The central authorities are one of the prime movers here, but the debate on the unity of the nation also reflects rising popular sentiment, especially among the urban middle classes. Looked at from another angle, however, the nation is a kaleidoscopic composite. The pattern of diversity constantly changes under the impact of central policy shifts, local factors and global forces. Although this might be the 'unity in diversity' that central policy proclaims, it is highly variable, constantly shifting and beyond the full control of anybody, including the central authorities.

At the start of the reforms, existing minority policies were elaborated to allow minorities greater room for their own culture, society and avenues to develop their economies. More recently, the concept of heritage has extended these opportunities to a much greater range of groups, communities and localities. Celebrating, producing, packaging and consuming diversity from below increasingly complements the rigid structures imposed from above, turning China into a much more lived-in and dynamic nation than it was even twenty years ago. Many different ways of becoming modern are now being tolerated without the expectation that this should produce a homogenous culture and society. This also extends to transnational connections. The freedom and opening up to the outside world during the reform period has given many minorities new ways to establish links with groups, religions or even nations whose cultures they share. In many cases, these are extensions of existing cross-border connections fuelled by new migratory flows to and from China. Examples are Dai religious and ethnic relations with other Tai groups in Laos, Thailand and Burma, the Miao (Hmong) diaspora in Southeast Asia and North America and Chinese Korean labour and marriage migrants in South Korea. Chinese Muslims even travel to Mecca on the *hajj* pilgrimage; others live and study in Middle Eastern countries. The government has gone as far as coining the oxymoronic neologism of 'minority nationality overseas Chinese' in an attempt to tie these migrants back into the Chinese

nation through the connections with their minority nationality home-
land, just like it has already done for many decades with Han overseas
Chinese.

To a greater extent than is often realized, ethnic minorities have
become free to forge links abroad and to partake in modern civilizations that are alternatives to China's own modernity and civilizational
expansion across the world. In this sense, minorities are not treated any
differently from other Chinese citizens with the right to foreign travel,
study and settlement. However, this freedom ends when these civilizational alternatives are taken back to China to counter the nation-
building project. Tibetan connections with the Dalai Lama's government in India or Uighur separatists in Central Asia or the Middle
East are treated with the full repressive force of the state. The issue
of minorities thus shows the extent of the freedoms gained under neo-
socialist governance, but also its other face, that of the security state
which is fighting back with all its modern might against its enemies,
both foreign and domestic.

There is little if any possibility of a more lenient treatment that
would allow minority areas such as Tibet and Xinjiang greater autonomy or even independence. The inclusion of these territories is part and
parcel of the nation-building project that took shape at the end of the
nineteenth century. This project is defined by the territory controlled
by the Qing dynasty and by the desire to right the wrongs inflicted
by Western Imperialist powers, Japan and the CCP's archenemy, the
Guomindang in Taiwan. As many foreign governments and their diplo-
mats who got entangled into these issues have learnt, little gain can be
expected from questioning China's unified nationhood. However, at a
more practical level there might be more leeway. To the CCP, the nation
is also an extremely flexible concept that can include almost any type
of autonomy, freedom, rights or claims as long as ultimate and largely
token sovereignty is respected. Hong Kong and Macao immediately
come to mind, and there is no reason why similar solutions could not
be found for Taiwan, and possibly even Tibet, Xinjiang or any other
territory claimed by the PRC.

Market reform, modernization and state building have generated the
resources and capabilities to strengthen the fabric of the nation and
to assert its cohesion, identity and security. Although still a work in
progress, the Chinese nation is much stronger, more self-confident and

more secure than at the start of the reform period. Furthermore, neo-socialism has also given citizens, governments, enterprises and other institutions much greater scope to pursue their own agendas. On the whole, this has strengthened rather than diminished the integration of society and the awareness of nationhood. China is no longer a collection of self-contained units only held together by the Party and the plan, but has become a society of mutually dependent yet autonomous individuals.

This is, however, only one side of the equation. The greater integration of the nation and the modernization of the state have also led to an increasing intolerance of and the capacity to crack down on expressions of diversity that do not fit into the mould of a unified country pursuing middle-class prosperity and happiness within the boundaries set by the Party. The state is still at a loss to cope with demands – often peaceful, sometimes violent – for greater ethnic, religious or political freedom, feeling compelled to hang on to policies and principles that date from the state socialist past. Self-confident and increasingly empowered middle-class citizens subscribe to nationalism and universalist principles of fairness and often have little patience for the outdated privileges of recognized minorities or the demands for greater autonomy (let alone independence) in Tibet, Xinjiang and Taiwan. China has become a society with a much greater scope for differences between people, religions and life styles without, as yet, a policy framework in place that would enable a better accommodation and higher tolerance of diversity.

6 | *Not Just a Chinese Century*

When the People's Republic embarked upon its reforms in the late 1970s, it did not simply 'open up' to take advantage of the opportunities that the world had to offer. China's opening up coincided with, and was part of, a fundamental restructuring of the capitalist world order that was taking place at the time and that continues until this day. These changes are often captured under the headings of the end of the Cold War, or the rise of neoliberalism and globalization, and have opened up spaces around the world that China can and sometimes must fill. It does so together with a growing list of other rising countries, such as Brazil, India, Indonesia, Turkey or, in the slightly longer run, Iran or South Africa. China's rise is thus a vital part of rather than the only source and cause of a fundamental restructuring of the global order. Although China has the very considerable advantages of size and being a first mover, there is nothing uniquely Chinese or historically inevitable about its rise. History has no memory and China isn't special. Despite its current growth, wealth and power, it is not China's destiny to 'rule the world', although it is very likely to become (and in fact already is) a very significant power.[1]

To say that the world will be much more than a Chinese place does not mean that this book's China-centric view is inappropriate. Quite the contrary, looking at the world from Chinese perspectives will facilitate the realization that the emerging world order is fraught with uncertainty rather than the straightforward passing of the baton into Chinese hands. Even though the world is becoming more Chinese with every passing year, it is also becoming more Indian, Latin American, Islamic, and even more European and American. The future is very

---

[1] This phrase has been taken from the title of Jacques, Martin. 2012. *When China Rules the World: The End of the Western World and the Birth of a New Global Order*. London: Penguin. Jacques has been one of most widely read proponents of the inevitability of China's rise.

unlikely to be one of China superseding the West or more specifically the US. Neither is it likely that a separate Chinese world will develop in parallel with a Western world. Globalizing Chinese capital, people, goods and culture merge with those from other parts of the world. Globalization does not equal Americanization, Japanization, Sinification, Islamization or Westernization, terms that describe the struggle between separate and unequal worlds. Globalization entails the creation of hybrid forms, forces and flows that connect differently at various parts of the globe beyond the control of any of the centres that have spawned them. The question that I will tackle in this chapter is therefore not when or how China will rule the world or what China as a hegemonic power will be like, but rather what the global shifts in economic, political and cultural power look like from Chinese points of view and what the Chinese contribution to these shifts might be, a perspective that I have termed Chinese globalization.[2]

The argument that I will present here is not simply that the future will be all about global forces, processes and actors. As even some of the most ardent believers in globalization admit, the nation-state is and will remain the most important domain where globalization is inflected; likewise, the connections between national and international factors shape and constrain the ways that Chinese globalization plays out.[3] The crucial question to ask is If and To what extent the government will attempt and be able to harness the forces of Chinese globalization to serve the power of the country, the nation and the state. The capacity of the neo-socialist state to operate outside China is rapidly changing. Its potential and limits remain largely unknown. This chapter will therefore start with a discussion of how the country of China is rising as a player and a presence in the international domain, followed by a discussion of processes of globalization and the global impact of the neo-socialist state that make Chinese people, organizations, goods and culture an increasingly normal component of the world we all live in. I will then return to the issue of the global reach of the neo-socialist state.

---

[2] Pieke, Frank N., Nyíri, Pál, Thunø, Mette, Ceccagno, Antonella. 2004. *Transnational Chinese: Fujianese Migrants in Europe.* Stanford, CA: Stanford University Press, chapter 1.

[3] See Sassen, Saskia. 2006. *Territory, Authority, Rights: From Medieval to Global Assemblages.* Princeton, NJ: Princeton University Press.

6.1 Rising China

With surprisingly little discussion or debate a consensus has emerged over the past ten years (not least in China itself) that China's economic success makes it inevitable that it will become an international superpower. China's rise is routinely compared with the period of a century ago when the US took over the reins of world domination from Great Britain. Much less is said about the fact that the rise of the US then coincided with the transition from a world dominated by empires to a world system of nominally equal and sovereign nation-states divided into two opposing blocs, one capitalist, the other communist, just like nowadays the shift to Chinese world power coincides with the end of that Cold War era, globalization, and the emergence of a multipolar world. In both cases, I would argue that the fundamental shift in the world order is more important than which specific country dominates it.

Leaving this broader context to one side for the time being, China's rise as a global power is usually seen as taking place in three different domains, namely the international economy, military and strategic relations, and global governance. A fourth domain, soft power, touches upon the broader questions of globalization, so I will return to later on in this chapter. Although China presents a different face in each of these domains, the questions that should be asked are relatively straightforward, although not necessarily easy to answer. How far off from superpower status is China? When will China eclipse the US? How keen is China to translate its economic weight into military might and diplomatic prowess, and how long will that take? Will the transition from US to Chinese hegemony be gradual and smooth or punctuated by sudden confrontations or conflicts?

The moment when China will become the world's largest economy is a matter of a few years, or a decade at most. In 2013, the US economy was almost double the size of the Chinese in terms of its nominal GDP (US$17 trillion for the US compared to US$9.3 trillion for China), but this severely underestimates the real size of the Chinese economy, especially given the undervaluation of the Chinese yuan. In terms of purchasing power parity gross national income (PPP GNI) the Chinese economy in 2013 was already almost as large as the US's (US$16 trillion for China and US$17 trillion for the US), although this should not be given overly much weight as China also has to buy things on the world market at international prices. Granted, China's economy is no longer growing as fast as it used to and the US economy has recently picked up speed, but there is still so much more room for the Chinese economy to grow (if only because of the sheer size of its population that will not start to shrink for another fifteen years or so) that China's economy becoming larger than the US's is virtually certain.[4]

Size matters, but economic dominance is about more than just dollars and cents. The Chinese economy still largely leans on manufacture for export that takes advantage of cheap labour rather than high added value. The real money from production in China is often earned by companies based in Japan, South Korea, Taiwan, the US and Europe that control the brands, designs, patents, distribution and market access. The domestic economy is hamstrung by an exceptionally high savings rate that stuns the growth in domestic demand that could reduce the dependence on export. Large parts of China are still dirt-poor and face an uphill battle to join the prosperous parts of the country. Although Chinese companies now feature prominently among the world's largest, with a very few exceptions they remain rooted in the Chinese economy and are yet to become genuinely global players.

Although these issues are real, it would be disingenuous to conclude that China doesn't have what it takes to become an economic superpower. There is nothing insurmountable about any of these problems, and neither does China's socialist political system preclude finding solutions for them. There are surely many challenges ahead and overcoming them won't be easy, but half the battle is to be aware of the problems and to have the desire, capacity and staying power to solve them. Whatever else one might think about the political system, these qualities certainly do not seem to be lacking in the CCP leadership.

Unless a radical change happens in China or the world, in ten years from now the impact of the Chinese economy around the world will match that of the US or the EU. No longer will many things simply be made in China. They will be created, made and sold across the world by global Chinese companies, who no longer invest abroad to serve their domestic agenda but as part of a global corporate strategy. The domestic economy will have become an engine of growth for the world

---

[4] 2013 GDP and PPP NGI data are from the World Bank, http://datacatalog .worldbank.org/, checked 24 March 2015.

economy for foreign and Chinese companies alike. The flip side of the coin is that the world economy will also become more vulnerable to adverse events in China or structural weaknesses of the Chinese economy, of which ageing and the shrinking of the workforce and the population as a whole are potentially the most serious.

Becoming the largest economy in itself does not make for superpower status, as the rise of Japan in the 1970s and 1980s clearly illustrated: economically a powerhouse, politically a dwarf. Strategically and militarily, the People's Republic of China is still a considerable way off superpower ambitions, let alone superpower status. The military has been modernized and particularly building up the navy has been prioritized. Military expenditure is now the second-largest in the world at roughly one-sixth of US spending (US$114 billion for China and US$614 billion for the US in 2013). This looks relatively small, but several factors have to be taken into account. First, China's military spending in nominal US dollars is indeed much less than that of the US, but it is much more in purchasing power parity terms, perhaps even as much as US$500 billion. Second, China does not need to wait for full parity with the US to become a major military power. Third, China's military spending has been rising faster than economic growth, growing by 10 per cent in 2015 in an economy that had grown by just 7.5 per cent in 2014. Fourth, Chinese military spending as a percentage of total GDP is only about half that of the US (2.0 per cent for China and 3.8 per cent for the US). In this regard, China is in line with military powers that are close allies of the US, such as France (2.2 per cent), the UK (2.3 per cent) or South Korea (2.8 per cent), while the percentage of the US military spending is comparable to that of its main military rival, Russia (4.1 per cent). As a military spender, therefore, China seems to be playing a long game. The government does not seem to be interested in putting undue strain on the government's budget and the economy in the short term, but behaves like a country that wishes to maintain a credible military force without the ambition to confront the hegemony of the US, at least for the time being. In the longer term, however, if the increases in the military budget continue at levels significantly above economic growth, spending will eventually rival that of the US, clearing the way for a potentially credible claim to hegemonic power status by mid century.[5]

---

[5] Figures on military spending for 2013 are from the Stockholm International Peace Research Institute, see Perlo-Freeman, Sam, Solmirano, Carina. 2013.

In the long term China might thus become a globally hegemonic military power. At present, however, its strategic ambitions are largely defined by narrow territorial, regional and security issues. Taiwan, the Senkaku Islands, the South China Sea and areas along the Sino-Indian border continue to be territories where China's claims of sovereignty are vigorously contested by other countries or governments. The Taiwan issue, in particular, will remain a massive preoccupation as long as the US continues militarily to back up the island's de facto independent statehood. The ramifications of these claims are much more than just strategic. Territorial issues are a constant reminder that the Chinese revolution is not yet complete and that the enemy is still on the doorstep. This is useful domestically to generate patriotic dedication to the Party, but it constrains the options that the government can entertain in its relationships with neighbouring countries. As a still wounded nation, China simply lacks the credibility to lead Asia. China might be feared, admired or needed, but as long as it insists in claiming territories all around it, it will never be trusted. Asian nations will continue to look at the US (and to Russia or the EU to a more limited extent) for protection against Chinese hegemonic incursions, all essentially at no political cost to the US itself. As long as this continues to be the case, China will only be considered a safe ally in places far away from it. Against this background it is no surprise that China has been most successful as a genuine global power among African and to a lesser extent Latin American countries.

As Chinese enterprises and individuals fan out across the world and the economy becomes more dependent on supplies and markets far away from home, the government is increasingly concerned that it is unable to defend the country's direct interests as these are becoming more global. The crisis in Libya in 2011 was a particularly important wake-up call; the government found itself without the military capacity to protect the interests of the unexpectedly large number of its citizens and companies that became caught up in the civil war that broke out there. Projection of power along strategic shipping lanes and even

Trends in World Military Expenditure, 2013, online at http://books.sipri.org/product_info?c_product_id=476, checked 25 March 2015; on projections for 2045, see *Global Strategic Trends – Out to 2045*, Ministry of Defence UK (2014), pp. 93–94, online at www.gov.uk/government/uploads/system/uploads/attachment_data/file/348164/20140821_DCDC_GST_5_Web_Secured.pdf, checked 25 March 2015; on China's 2015 military budget hike, see GlobalSecurity.org. 2015. China's Defense Budget, online at www.globalsecurity.org/military/world/china/budget.htm, checked 25 March 2015.

space exploration feature increasingly prominently in Chinese policy documents, most recently in the 2015 Military Strategy White Paper. It should be emphasized, however, that China's strategy of what it calls 'active defence', at this point in time at least, sees as the main strategic issues China's territorial integrity, terrorism and local conflicts across the world, rather than hegemonic competition with other major powers.[6]

In terms of global governance China's evolution roughly keeps pace with, or might be just slightly ahead of its military and strategic profile. The opening up to the outside world started not with the reforms in 1978, but much earlier with the Chinese-US rapprochement pioneered by Zhou Enlai, Henry Kissinger, Mao Zedong and Richard Nixon in 1970–72 and the PRC's admission to the United Nations in 1971. From the word go, opening up and participation in the institutions of global governance have gone together. Until the early to mid 2000s China was largely content with the recognition and prestige that came with participation in international organizations and NGOs, signing treaties and learning how to extract maximum benefit (funding, expertise, best practice) for itself, while minimizing any undesirable impact and interference in its own domestic affairs. Only recently has China become uneasy and less patient with the Western imprint of many of these institutions, profiling itself increasingly as the champion of the non-Western world in which many UN organizations – particularly the International Monetary Fund and the World Bank – are perceived as oppressive instruments of Western hegemony.

Many Western observers continue to hope that China will eventually assimilate the liberal norms and values associated with the institutions of international governance. Alternatively, China might want to use its increasing economic and diplomatic weight to try to change the established international institutions from within. At present, there is little sign of either scenario happening, although China's clout within international organizations is certainly increasing. A more important development is the establishment of new institutions that shadow or even challenge established US and EU-dominated ones and more directly serve China's agenda. The best-known examples are the Shanghai Cooperation Organization (mainly security-oriented) and the Asia

---

[6] The full text of the 2015 Military Strategy White Paper is available at http://eng.mod.gov.cn/Database/WhitePapers/, checked 6 June 2015.

Infrastructure Investment Bank (AIIB, to rival the World Bank and the Asia Development Bank). The accession of the UK on 12 March 2015 as a founder member of the AIIB in defiance of US pressure, closely followed by Germany, France and Italy took even Beijing by surprise. The mid 2010s are becoming a watershed in international governance, and much sooner than expected. Only time will tell if the established institutions will be able to cope with or even absorb the new ones created under Chinese leadership, or whether global governance will become an arena for international cooperation and for global competition.

China is currently moving fast in the international arena, spearheading a world order where political power shifts away from the US, the EU and Japan. Yet a lot of water will have to flow under the bridge before this becomes a reality. Some American scholars have gone even further, questioning the very capacity of China's political system or regime to pull off a transition to superpower status. While not denying the underlying trend of rising economic, military and political power, they consider China a 'fragile' or 'partial' power, or at the 'tipping point' of regime transition.[7] They offer two arguments. The first is what they believe to be the inherent vulnerability of the political system. This argument is valid but its conclusion is not. China's political system has indeed many weaknesses and this book has documented many, but to read into them evidence of the inevitable breakdown of the system and the fall of the CCP is another thing altogether. This argument amounts to a simple regurgitation of the old anti-communist faith in the inherent superiority of (Western, American) democracy.[8] China indeed faces a crisis of political legitimacy, mounting corruption, deep factional divides within the leadership, an economic growth model that is running out of steam and so on, but the same things can be said in slightly amended form for most countries in the world, not least the US with a dysfunctional political system that makes a mockery of democracy including the office of the Presidency itself, a

---

[7] Nathan, Andrew J. 2013. China at the Tipping Point? Foreseeing the Unforeseeable. *Journal of Democracy* 24,1:20–25, Shambaugh, David. 2012. *China Goes Global: The Partial Power.* New York: Oxford University Press, Shirk, Susan L. 2007. *China: Fragile Superpower.* Oxford: Oxford University Press.

[8] Shambaugh, David. 2015. The Coming Chinese Crackup. *Wall Street Journal,* 6 March, online at www.wsj.com/articles/the-coming-chinese-crack-up-1425659198, checked 27 March 2015.

society deeply divided along racial, class and regional lines, a debilitating national debt, overfunded and overstretched armed forces, and so on. But should the conclusion from this evidence be that the US will collapse?

The second argument against China's impending rule in my view cuts closer to the truth. In the words of American political scientist David Shambaugh, China 'is *not influential* in many parts of the world or on major international issues. China is not shaping events and actively contributing to solving problems. Rather, it is quite risk-averse and narrowly self-interested ... Beijing is not doing enough to shoulder its appropriate share of international responsibility and to be a world leader.'[9] This observation that China is still some way off from being willing and able to exercise a global leadership role is true but also somewhat beside the point as it is rapidly becoming less true with each year that passes. China's rise really just started to take shape fifteen years ago. For it to have grown into a world leadership position already would have been impossible, especially because US power is as yet anything but declining. However, more is involved than just time. The world has changed and continues to change and to expect that China will simply become a US 2.0 as a world leader is reading the past into the future. With the rise of so many new powers global hegemony will increasingly become impossible, as the US is already beginning to find out.

Global dominance based on the belief in the superiority of one's own society, culture and political system no longer makes sense. Unlike Maoist times, there are no signs that China is even remotely interested in exporting its model of governance. Competition over global governance in future is more likely to pit the interests of rising powers, most of which are in fact democratic countries (India, Indonesia, Brazil, Turkey and South Africa), against those of the established powers (US, EU, Japan). Twenty-first-century international competition and conflict will be very different from twentieth-century ones. Ideological divides or differences in political systems are less important. Instead, the new conflicts between the established and the outsiders will be deeply emancipatory in nature, informed by the memories of two centuries of colonial and neo-colonial conquest and oppression and the mounting evidence that rapid economic development, prosperity

---

[9] Shambaugh, David. 2012. *China Goes Global: The Partial Power.* New York: Oxford University Press, p. 309, emphasis in original.

and global power have nothing to do with the intrinsic superiority of Western civilization.

6.2 Labour

So how Chinese is the world becoming? In this section and the next I will focus on the two aspects of Chinese globalization that are the most talked about, namely the migration of people and the investment of capital. In the nineteenth and early twentieth centuries, Western and Japanese businesses and residents had turned China's treaty ports into hubs of global connections. Foreign goods, ideas, ideologies, religions, trends, fashions and lifestyles found their way to China to such an extent that one could say that Shanghai was one the most cosmopolitan cities in the world, on a par with New York, London, Berlin or Paris.

As foreign influence spread in China, Chinese influence on the world mainly took the form of migration. After the defeat in the First Opium War in 1842 the Chinese government could no longer curtail mass emigration. Millions of people signed up as indentured labourers to work in support of European expansion in Southeast Asia, Latin America and the Caribbean, North America and Siberia. They opened up land, logged trees, built railways and roads, worked on plantations and (during the First World War) even dug trenches for the allied forces in Europe. Millions more followed of their own volition seeking employment or business opportunities, or looking to make a quick fortune in the newly discovered gold fields in the Americas, Australia or Africa. By the first part of the twentieth century, Chinese communities were found in almost all countries in the world. Chinese emigration tapered off in the twentieth century, coming to an almost complete standstill after the victory of the CCP in 1949, with the important exception of illegal emigration across the border into Hong Kong.[10]

This situation contrasts sharply with Chinese migration today. China is still one of the most important countries of origin, but has also increasingly become a destination for international migrants. The most important characteristic of international migration from China is the

---

[10] The next few pages on Chinese international migration draw on Pieke, Frank N., Speelman, Tabitha. 2016. Chinese Investment Strategies and Migration: Does Diaspora Matter? In *Chinese Migration and Economic Relations with Europe: The Silk Road Revisited*, ed. Marco Sanfilippo, Agnieszka Weinar, pp. 12–32. Abingdon, UK: Routledge.

incredible diversity of migratory flows. Unlike thirty years ago, Chinese emigrants now come from all kinds of social and cultural backgrounds, hail from all over China, and include business and government expatriates, investors and entrepreneurs, students, professionals, contract workers, seafarers, unskilled job seekers, and family and marriage migrants.

The main driver, at least initially, of the new migration from the PRC was a gradual but fundamental relaxation of the country's emigration policy from the early 1970s onward. The PRC now allows foreign travel and emigration to virtually all Chinese citizens who can produce evidence of the right of legitimate entry to a foreign country. As a consequence, the types, origins and destinations of Chinese migration have changed and proliferated. Emigration is no longer limited to a few pockets of Chinese society and even includes members of China's power elite, who enjoy residences across the world and send their children abroad to prestigious schools and universities. Their travel and residence abroad are not only part of a cosmopolitan lifestyle and business interests. They also serve as a hedge against future changes in the political wind, similar in many respects to the Hong Kong's capitalist elite 'astronaut' families with residences in one or more Western countries.[11]

An important component is migration for educational or professional reasons. Self-funded study abroad was permitted in the early 1990s; by 2010, 93 per cent of Chinese students abroad were self-financed.[12] As a result, Chinese educational migration has proliferated, both in terms of sheer numbers and in the range of student backgrounds, destinations, and degrees pursued. As China got richer, foreign study came within reach of the offspring of China's burgeoning entrepreneurial elite and even the salaried middle classes. According to a report of the European Commission and the Chinese Ministry of

---

[11] Details on Chinese leaders' asset holdings abroad were exposed by a team of journalists in January 2014, see Walker Guevara, Marina, Ryle, Gerard, Olesen, Alexa, Cabra, Mar, Hudson, Michael, Giesen, Christoph. 2014. Leaked Records Reveal Offshore Holdings of China's Elite. *International Consortium of Investigative Journalists*, 21 January, online at www.icij.org/offshore/ leaked-records-reveal-offshore-holdings-chinas-elite, checked 9 June 2015.

[12] Ye Zi, Zhongguo zaiwai liuxuesheng 127 wan ren – cheng shijie zuida shengyuanguo (China's students abroad reach 1,270,000, becoming the world's largest source country), http://news.xinhuanet.com/overseas/2011-04/18/c_ 121317007.htm.

Education, the total number of Chinese students in the EU in 2010 was between 118 700 and 120 000, or about six times more than in 2000. This number is comparable to the US, which had 127 600 Chinese students in 2010. Of the total number of Chinese students in the EU, 40 per cent was in the UK, 23 per cent in France, and 20 per cent in Germany.[13] In the UK, China is the number one foreign country of origin for higher education students.[14]

Only a minority of these students ever return to China, but find employment, obtain permanent residency and ultimately acquire citizenship abroad. This pattern is particularly pronounced in the US, but is also significant in Western Europe, Australia and Japan. Direct emigration of professionals from the PRC is also significant and on the rise, not only to regions and countries that one might expect (North America, Western Europe, Australia and New Zealand, Singapore and Hong Kong), but also to African countries which to a Western observer might seem less obvious. Until the early 2000s, the lack of student return and professional emigration was a matter that raised remarkably few questions in China itself. In fact, the opportunity to study abroad has been for many aspiring Chinese individuals and families, one of the great gifts of the reform era. However, as the economy has grown, students and professionals abroad are increasingly seen to constitute a brain drain. At the end of 2011 the accumulated number of Chinese students abroad was 2 244 100, of whom 818 400 or 36 per cent have returned to China. This is considered very low by policy makers and advisors, especially in view of the fact that the higher the educational qualifications attained, the lower the chance that a student returns.[15]

Policy has increasingly emphasized return, as part of the 'inviting in' of foreign businesses and individuals since the late 1990s. Despite the relatively low return percentage, Chinese returnees are very prominent

[13] Commission, European, China, Ministry of Education in. 2011. *EU-China Student and Academic Staff Mobility: Present Situation and Future Developments*, online at http://ec.europa.eu/education/international-cooperation/documents/china/mobility_en.pdf, accessed 4 August 2015.

[14] Higher Education Statistics Agency, press release 172 – Non-UK domicile students, 23 February 2012, online at www.hesa.ac.uk/index.php?option=com_content&task=view&id=2371&Itemid=161, accessed 7 June 2015.

[15] Wang, Huiyao. 2012. *China's Competition for Global Talents: Strategy, Policy and Recommendations*. Vancouver, BC: Asia Pacific Foundation of Canada, online at www.asiapacific.ca/sites/default/files/filefield/researchreportv7.pdf.

among academics and senior administrators in higher education and research institutions, especially the more prestigious and better funded ones. Others are high-tech entrepreneurs or independent professionals; yet others work for large multinationals or government. Governments actively court overseas graduates and scholars and encourage them to set up businesses or contribute their knowledge, skills and patents to partnerships with Chinese businesses. Educated Chinese abroad are increasingly talked about in terms of *brain gain*, a talent pool abroad waiting for China to tap into when needed.

Another policy response to the perceived brain drain has been the encouragement of direct labour export, especially after 2003. According to the Ministry of Commerce, in 2010, 346 888 workers were dispatched abroad, more than 80 per cent within Asia. Labour export on fixed-term contracts through recognized agencies was vigorously promoted in the 2000s as an alternative to unregulated migration. Contract labour fits much better than individual migration with the government's aspirations to manage the freedom of the population. In Asian countries such as South Korea, Japan and Singapore that have the will and the means to control who comes and who stays, Chinese contract labour with mandatory return has grown enormously. However, elsewhere in Asia and Africa contract labour is simply a separate flow associated with Chinese investments and projects in addition to unregulated migration.

Emigration and, more broadly travel abroad, have become a lucrative business: 98 million outbound Chinese tourists spent 129 billion US dollars in 2013, taking first place in the ranking of international tourism expenditure.[16] Inside China, countless agencies and individuals assist aspiring migrants as intermediaries or in securing or manufacturing the necessary documentation. Current estimates place the number of ethnic Chinese residents worldwide between 35 and 50 million, with the vast majority still in Southeast Asia, especially Indonesia, Thailand and Malaysia. Growth is most conspicuous in those parts of the world that had only small numbers of Chinese before the 1980s. Europe, for instance, currently has about 2 million ethnic Chinese,

---

[16] On tourist numbers, see www.travelchinaguide.com/tourism/2014statistics/ outbound.htm, checked 9 June 2015; on tourist money spent, see World Tourism Organization (UNWTO). 2014. *Tourism Highlights – 2014 Edition.* Madrid: UNWTO, online at www2.unwto.org/sites/all/files/pdf/unwto_ highlights14_en.pdf, checked 9 June 2015.

Africa has at least five hundred thousand.[17] However, in terms of absolute numbers more traditional destinations are equally if not more important. In the 2010 US population census, the number of Chinese residents stood at 3.3 million, up from 2.7 million in 2000.[18] Singapore has been admitting very large numbers of migrants in a deliberate drive to increase its population and wants to admit millions more. Some are admitted only as temporary workers; others are permanent immigrants. In either case, the majority are from China: between 1990 and 2008 close to one million PRC nationals migrated to the city-state.[19]

Simply by force of numbers, the Chinese presence in the world is large and rapidly growing, making the world a more Chinese place with businesses, culture, media, clubs, temples, churches and organizations proliferating in even the most remote corners of the earth. Central and local governments in China itself have also elected to engage Chinese abroad more actively through overseas Chinese organizations, delegations, conferences and even job or investment fairs. Traditional overseas Chinese and their native places have ceased to be a government priority, increasingly connected as they are to illegality, asylum seeking and human smuggling. National policy focusses mainly on students, entrepreneurs and professionals and increasingly emphasizes

[17] The figure for Africa is from Li, Pengtao. 2010. Zhong-Fei guanxi de fazhan yu Feizhou Zhongguo xin yimin (The development of Chinese–African relations and new Chinese migrants in Africa). *Huaqiao Huaren lishi yanjiu* 2010,4:24–31; Ma, Emmanuel Mung. 2008. Chinese and China's Foreign Policy in Africa. *Journal of Chinese Overseas* 4,1:91–109, provides an estimate of the number of Chinese in Africa of 270 000–520 000; the figure for Europe is my own extrapolation based on 2008 Eurostat data on the number of Chinese citizens in Europe and proportions in the UK 2011 census and the 2011 population records of the Dutch National Bureau of Statistics of the number of Chinese citizens, second-generation Chinese and self-identified Chinese; for the UK census, see www.ons.gov.uk/ons/publications/re-reference-tables.html?edition=tcm%3A77-286262, accessed 8 June 2015; for the Dutch data, see Gijsberts, Mérove, Huijnk, Willem, Vogels, Ria. 2011. *Chinese Nederlanders: van horeca naar hogeschool* (Chinese Dutch: from catering trade to university). The Hague: Sociaal en Cultureel Planbureau, pp. 29 and 41.

[18] For the 2010 census figure, see www.census.gov/prod/cen2010/briefs/c2010br-11.pdf; for the 2000 census figure, see www.census.gov/newsroom/releases/archives/census_2000/cb02-cn59.html, both accessed 8 June 2015.

[19] On Chinese immigration to Singapore, see Yeoh, Brenda S. A., Liu, Weiqiang. 2013. Chinese Migration to Singapore: Discourses and Discontents in a Globalizing Nation-State. *Asian and Pacific Migration Journal* 22,1:31–54.

return as part of the 'inviting in' of foreign businesses and individuals. Despite a relatively low actual return percentage, returnees are very prominent among academics and senior administrators in higher education and research institutions, especially the more prestigious and better funded ones. Others are high-tech entrepreneurs or independent professionals; yet others work for large multinationals or government. Educated Chinese abroad are increasingly talked about in terms of *brain gain*, a vast talent pool abroad waiting for China to tap into.

6.3 Capital

In many Western countries Chinese migration is viewed with suspicion. Illegal Chinese immigration in the US or Europe became a staple of media reporting in the 1990s and early 2000s. More recently, changes in Chinese migration, stricter and more sophisticated border controls and especially the mounting refugee crisis from Africa and the Middle East have diverted public attention away from illegal migration. Instead, investment became the focus of Western misgivings about China's rise.

Few contest the wisdom and success of the unprecedented capital flows into China. Foreign investment has transformed the economy, society and to a certain extent politics without anyone batting an eye. The more recent flows of capital out of China, however, are routinely met with suspicion, particularly in the West. China is said to be 'buying the world', undermining the control of countries over their economy and stripping them of their natural resources and technologies. As with so many other issues regarding China, this rhetoric pits 'China' against 'the West' using a powerful combination of fact, fiction and fear.

A high-profile example of this is provided by the problems that Huawei, one of China's largest private companies, has run into trying to get into the US market. The information and communications technology company's efforts to invest and market in the US have continued to be frustrated by Congressional and government obstruction on the grounds that Huawei has close links with the Chinese government and particularly the military. US intelligence researcher Eric Anderson has documented the Huawei case in great detail. He concludes that these fears cannot be substantiated and must be traced not to fact but a deep-seated American 'Sinophobia'. Anderson's verdict might seem extreme, but the impression remains that Chinese companies that venture abroad are often treated as guilty until proven innocent.[20]

China is not buying up the world, but neither is Chinese foreign investment a mere drop in the ocean devoid of any strategic implications. According to figures from the United Nations Conference on Trade and Development, foreign direct investment flowing out of China has increased from just a few billion dollars annually in the 1990s and early 2000s to US$101 billion in 2013. Moreover, inward foreign direct investment in China at US$124 billion (flow) and US$957 billion (stock) in 2013 has remained stagnant in recent years; in 2014 the flow of outbound investment overtook inward investment for the first time. The accumulated total amount (stock) of Chinese outward foreign direct investment for that year was US$614 billion. Nevertheless, Chinese levels of overseas direct investment still pale in comparison with those of the US, whose investment flow in 2013 was US$338 billion with a total stock of US$6350 billion, but are beginning to rival Japan at US$136 billion (flow) and US$993 billion (stock).[21]

The question is, where does all this money go? Data from the Heritage Foundation in the US on Chinese overseas investment are disaggregated by country and sector, allowing a first view of what it is that Chinese outbound investments are seeking. The Foundation reports a slightly higher worldwide total of US$870 billion in 2014. Of this total, energy was by far the most important sector (396 billion), followed at some considerable distance by transportation (135 billion) and metals (125 billion). Turning to individual countries, the biggest recipients are the US (80 billion) and Australia (61 billion), but for very different reasons. In Australia, Chinese investment overwhelmingly targets metals and energy, i.e. resource extraction; in the US, the picture is one of a Chinese presence across all major sectors of the economy. Finance, energy and real estate are the biggest, but a significant share of investment is put in technology and agriculture as well. Elsewhere a similar contrast obtains between countries targeted for resource extraction

---

[20] Anderson, Eric C. 2012. *Sinophobia: The Huawei Story*. n.p.: Eric C. Anderson.
[21] Figures for 2013 are from the annex tables of UNCTAD, *World Investment Report 2014*, online at http://unctad.org/en/Pages/DIAE/World%20Investment %20Report/Annex-Tables.aspx, checked 11 June 2015. On outbound investment overtaking inbound investment in 2014, see *China Daily*. 2014. China Cuts US Treasuries Holdings to Diversify Forexreserves, 18 April, online at www.chinadaily.com.cn/business/2015-04/18/content_20468133.htm, checked 13 June 2015.

(Canada, Nigeria, the Middle East, Brazil, Central Asia) and countries whose general economic structure has opportunities to offer to Chinese investors (many European countries especially the UK, and surprisingly Russia). Finally, investment in other East Asia countries is only modest and mainly in real estate.[22]

Some Chinese investment, particularly in resource-rich parts of the world, serves strategic objectives of the central government. China's economy needs reliable sources of resources, ranging from oil to ores and from lumber to agricultural products (soya beans and palm oil for instance). Other strategic investments or foreign aid are intended to facilitate Chinese commercial expansion or to buy the cooperation and goodwill of particular governments. This is particularly true of the much-publicized Chinese expansion into Africa, Southeast Asia and Latin America, but has recently also been extended to Europe, albeit on a more reciprocal basis in return for European investment in Central Asia. The central government combines state-backed loans, foreign aid, gifts and private investment to further commercial objectives, gain access to resources and secure political support. Investment often includes turnkey projects, large-scale deployment of Chinese staff and workers, acquisition of land and construction of infrastructure, the latter also including hospitals, schools or other not-for-profit projects, most famously the US$200 million African Union Conference Centre in Addis Ababa. Most investment, however, is commercial: Chinese firms, like businesses the world over, expand abroad seeking profits, inputs, markets, brands, technology, diversification or vertical integration.

There is therefore a plan, but the plan only very partially explains what happens. The Chinese economy is too large, too diverse, too decentralized and too capitalist to fit into the straightjacket of a 'China Inc.' controlled from Beijing. Local governments pursue their own agenda for economic growth, including trade and investment abroad. Moreover, national strategizing often makes for bad business decisions. The Chinese oil industry may serve as perhaps a somewhat extreme example, but an important one given the large share of the energy sector in China's foreign investment. Chinese state-owned oil companies (Sinopec, China National Petroleum and China National Offshore Oil

[22] See www.heritage.org/research/projects/china-global-investment-tracker-interactive-map, checked 11 June 2015.

Corporation) were involved in US$130 billion in overseas acquisitions during the period 2008–13. They have become very large, internationally operating corporations listed at place 3, 4 and 79 respectively on the Global Fortune-500 list in 2014. Yet their global strategy appears hamstrung by political goals that emphasize national control over oil and gas supplies through global acquisition of reserves, low prices in China, and the build-up of and control over a national infrastructure of tankers, pipelines and refineries across the world. Expansion and putting matters in Chinese hands rather than shareholder value are the overriding concerns imposed on these oil companies, depressing their profit margins and increasing their dependence on state financing and loans. The lure of global profit opportunities nevertheless proves difficult to resist: most of the oil obtained by these companies outside the Middle East was sold on the international market rather than shipped to China.

Another and much more visible component of a national plan for foreign investment is the so-called 'trade and economic cooperation zones' in developing countries. Currently nineteen such zones exist in Asia, Africa and Latin America. Trade and cooperation zones are modelled on China's own investment zones (including but not limited to the four initial special economic zones in the 1980s), and provide the infrastructure that Chinese companies need but is not immediately available in developing countries. The Chinese Ministry of Commerce initiates and coordinates the negotiations with local governments, tendering for the construction and financing of the zones. Investments are intended to be export-oriented, to develop horizontal linkages with the local economy, and to employ a decent share of local workers. The majority of zones are still under construction and only a few Chinese firms have actually made an investment and started production. Although a cautious optimism regarding the developmental gains from these zones seems justified, it is unlikely that they will generate the kind of development that investment zones in China such as Shenzhen, Binhai or Pudong have generated.

A particularly interesting aspect that reveals the limits of viewing Chinese overseas investment through the prism of a purported national strategy is the acquisition of agricultural land abroad. 'Land grabbing' was an allegation swiftly made when news of Chinese agribusinesses in Africa first appeared in the media, conjuring up a Malthusian image of an overpopulated China desperately exporting its excess labour and seeking sources of food for its starving millions. Reality turns out to be considerably less apocalyptic. China continues to be a net exporter of food, although this is likely to change in the future as more agricultural land is lost to development and Chinese diets shift to the consumption of more meat. The Chinese have indeed started commercial farms in Africa, Siberia, Central Asia and, more recently, in Latin America. However, the evidence from Africa, where this issue has been most researched, reveals that the majority of these farms are commercial investments often made together with local entrepreneurs, employing local labour and serving the local market. Chinese farms add to the availability and variety of foodstuffs and contribute to food self-sufficiency in a continent that has long relied on the importation of food; only a minority of farms produce agricultural commodities for export, both food (sugar, palm oil) and non-food (biofuel, sisal). Chinese agribusiness abroad pales in comparison with those serving European markets. Chinese 'agro-imperialism' as a concerted strategy to export China's excess population and to feed a country with too many people and too little land simply does not exist.

Despite the visible and invisible hand of the Chinese government, most Chinese investment abroad is best understood when seen as the outcome of decisions made by individual enterprises. This does not mean that there is never a strategic aspect to specific outbound investments, but rather that this strategy would be impossible to implement without commercial considerations as a foundation. So what is it that makes Chinese enterprises look abroad for investment opportunities if economic growth in China itself is still much more vigorous than anywhere else in the world?

At present, China has only a few companies that are or are likely to become truly global. A global company's activities overseas are part of an integrated strategy of worldwide expansion, access to resources, market opportunities and product development. Most Chinese firms do not yet fit this description. They seek to expand abroad as an extension of their domestic activities and strategy, and their global activities are limited to one or just a few aspects of their operations. Chinese companies are young and have, on the whole, only limited experience operating abroad: the vast majority are ill prepared to compete at an international level. Yet many companies feel compelled to expand beyond China. Not infrequently, an ill-informed bandwagon effect or prestige considerations play an important role when a company ventures abroad because their peers or competitors do so as well. More strategically, companies expand abroad because of extreme competition, overcapacity or an already large market share in their sector domestically. For many companies, expansion abroad is not a luxury but a must, the best way to leverage their business assets. Expansion abroad usually takes place through mergers or acquisitions of existing businesses rather than so-called 'greenfield' projects, giving the Chinese partner or owner access to advanced technology, global brands or international best practices that help boost their domestic market share at the same time as they acquire access to foreign markets. The foreign partner profits from a fresh injection of cash, economies of scale and better access to the Chinese market. In fact, many foreign companies acquired by Chinese companies would not have survived on their own, creating a win-win for all concerned.

We are at the early stages of Chinese outward investment. Only a few companies are gradually becoming known to the Western public while several more have become reputable global players in particular market segments. The best-known examples are Alibaba (e-commerce), Huawei (information and communication technology), Lenovo (personal computers) and Haier (domestic appliances). All are rapidly growing, but in global terms they are still medium-sized companies owned privately or by local governments in China. Most genuinely large Chinese companies remain unfamiliar outside China, often because they are state-owned and thus more bound to domestically centred strategies, despite having substantial holdings abroad.

The conclusion that follows from all this is ironic: China's industrial policy is caught between contradictory objectives. The central government wants Chinese companies to become global players. For this reason, it created a team of national champions at the end of the 1990s that were given a whole range of privileges, yet were also allowed to become market-oriented autonomous firms. Despite spectacular successes in the last fifteen years, domestic privilege has turned into a gilded cage. Many national champions have grown dependent on their monopolistic or oligopolistic positions and continued financial support from the state and state-owned banks. Their operations are insufficiently competitive to take on global companies in their sector outside China itself. If the government truly wishes state-owned companies to become global players, the time has come to abandon protectionism and let them face the rigours of free market competition, first domestically and then internationally. This will also allay the fears and suspicions, particularly in the US, that Chinese foreign investment is part of a national strategy with not just economic but also political or security goals. This will also mean that these companies can no longer be beholden to national priorities and national goals. In time, they must be allowed to evolve into multinationals that are fully part of the capitalist global order, beyond the control of the Party and be Chinese largely in name.

6.4 A Chinese World?

China's position in the world is at a crucial juncture. Since about 2005 and with a clear acceleration after Xi Jinping came to power in 2012, the country is transitioning to a dominant position in the world. Some aspects of this transition are happening earlier and faster than others. Production and trade of goods for the world market and the emigration of people already took off in the 1980s and 1990s and have progressed furthest. More recently, capital and companies have rapidly expanded their global presence. The government has begun to shape rather than merely use the system of global governance and is rapidly building up its strategic and military presence. In the West, some of this is welcomed as a new source of wealth and economic growth, but suspicion and fear are equally much in evidence: will China's rise herald in a new world no longer dominated by Western civilization?

The Chinese government itself increasingly buys into the narrative of global dominance, turning China into a country that is becoming not only more self-confident and assertive, but also more corporatist and hegemonic virtually with each month that passes. The global strategy of the Chinese government follows logically from certain aspects of neo-socialist governance. The government believes in the dynamism of the market and the autonomy of economic actors, but also invests heavily in its capacity to harness that very same dynamism and autonomy in the service of collective goals set by the Communist Party.

This is illustrated by the recent furore over China's 'One Belt, One Road' plan. Announced first in late 2013, this plan proposes to invest hundreds of billions of dollars in infrastructure development across mainland Asia and the sea routes in Southeast and South Asia. The plan involves many partners and serves many masters, both in China and abroad. It aims to turn the Chinese economy away from the Pacific towards growth in Central Asia, South Asia, the Middle East and Europe. The plan should also ensure strategic control over supply routes of oil, gas and other natural resources from Central Asia, the Middle East and beyond that Africa. Infrastructure projects provide new contracts for China's huge construction sector and will be a welcome outlet for China's foreign currency reserves. Despite professions to the contrary, by linking the world's largest population centres (China, South Asia, Europe) the plan will reduce US dominance in world affairs, which is why specifically European co-funding and participation is so hugely important. To the government, 'One Belt, One Road' is the centrepiece of China's 'second opening up' after the first opening up in 1978 and the most telling expression of China's self-declared peaceful rise that will bring harmony and prosperity to the world instead of dominance and conflict characteristic of US hegemony.

Initiatives like the 'One Belt, One Road' illustrate the recent evolution of China's neo-socialist state on the global stage. The central government sets highly ambitious long-term targets with the goal of positioning China for a leading role in the world. In doing so, it reveals its Leninist roots within a corporatist mind-set that enlists all forces and resources for a common and unquestionable goal. However, just below the surface neo-socialist global strategy reveals many of the same domestic characteristics arising, as documented throughout this book, from the simultaneous symbiosis and contradictions between high-modern socialist state building and the development of a capitalist market economy. Sub-national governments, individual government departments, state-owned enterprises and banks, and private enterprises are principally moved by the opportunities that the global economy has to offer, which shape their strategies of global expansion and associated vested interests. The central government has considerable power and financial clout to incentivize, cajole or sometimes even force China's global actors to contribute to its strategic vision, but is certainly not all-powerful. Beyond Leninist party control and discipline, China's global actors have no innate structural incentives to submit to China's national interests, whatever these might be; if necessary, they will resort to time-tested domestic tactics to stall, dodge or even subvert the government's grand vision. Despite the increasingly corporatist face that China is now showing internationally, there are therefore limits to the power of the neo-socialist state in shaping and controlling Chinese globalization.

Detecting and understanding the contours of these limits is the key challenge for anybody who wishes to analyse China's global role in the years to come. The potential as well as the limits of neo-socialist global ambitions are even more evident regarding an aspect of Chinese globalization about which I have so far remained silent namely culture. While Chinese people, goods and capital leave an ever-larger imprint on the world, Chinese culture lags far behind. Chinese life styles, products, politics and society singularly fail to appeal to people outside China. This issue runs deeper than the absence of Chinese 'soft power', a problem identified by the Chinese government some ten years ago. Clumsy neo-socialist remedies, such as the much-maligned Confucius institutes, have not been terribly successful in addressing this problem. In cooperation with local universities, the Chinese government has established Confucius institutes across the globe to teach and promote Chinese language and culture. However, among Western audiences these institutes have only served to prove that the Chinese government is indeed a communist dictatorship determined to undermine the freedoms that are the foundation of Western democracy. The man who coined the term soft power, Joseph Nye, himself has stated that the Chinese government has failed to understand that a country's soft power comes from civil society, not the government, concluding that '[a]s long as China fans the flames of nationalism and holds tight the reins of Party control, its soft power will always remain limited.'[23]

The exception to the lack of appeal of things Chinese are certain aspects of traditional or high-modern culture. Traditional Chinese painting, ceramics, music and material culture have a (very profitable) elite niche market; modern literature, film and avant-garde art likewise have a strong elite appeal: arguably the best-known Chinese artist worldwide is Ai Weiwei. However, in all these cases it is the *Chineseness* that sells either because of its exotic quality or because of its association with resistance or dissidence. Conspicuous difference makes Chinese culture both highly visible in a global context and sets it apart. Nobel prizes for Literature for Gao Xingjian in 2000 and Mo Yan

---

[23] Joseph Nye. 2015. The Limits of Chinese Soft Power. *Project Syndicate*, 10 July, online at www.project-syndicate.org/commentary/china-civil-society-nationalism-soft-power-by-joseph-s-nye-2015-07, accessed 25 August 2015.

in 2012 and numerous international awards for China's most famous film director Zhang Yimou notwithstanding, China has not achieved what Koichi Iwabuchi has felicitously termed an 'odourless' global cultural presence. Countless products, brands, games, TV programmes, cartoons, movies, music and fashions are invented, produced and marketed in countries like Japan, Hong Kong and Korea in very much the same way as in Western countries. Japanese manga or Korean TV soaps, for instance, are attractive to audiences abroad (and not least in China itself) because they are part of an unmarked global modernity that is recognizably different from the perceived provincialism of local cultural products. This modernity is no longer primarily associated with the culture of its origin. Pokémon, Super Mario or karaoke are hardly the shock troops of a global Japanese cultural hegemony, just as Hollywood movies, Coca Cola or MacDonald's are no longer 'American', but are appropriated locally the world over in ways of life that are modern, fashionable or cool.[24]

China remains short on this odourless global presence. To a certain extent this is caused by a lack of time. In most parts of the world the impact of Chinese investment, people and power has only begun to be felt a little over ten years ago and as such, the recent international success of fashion designer Guo Pei may be a first sign of what is to come. Yet the neo-socialist project itself also stands in the way. The government actively intervenes in the evolution of Chinese society by shaping and directing the autonomy of individuals, institutions and firms. Such social engineering reduces the independent production and spread of life styles, ideas, products and culture, principally within China but increasingly also abroad. Much creative energy is spent testing the 'high voltage wire' of official displeasure and much less on thinking about global consumers. Neo-socialism has bred a vibrant but largely inward looking cultural production. As in other authoritarian countries, technologies that enable globalization, especially the internet, are also used to erect walls, both within China and between China and the world. The result is the exact opposite of what the government says it wants. While China globalizes it also remains isolated, depriving the world of many of the contributions that it could make to global cultural modernity.

[24] Iwabuchi, Koichi. 2002. *Recentering Globalization: Popular Culture and Japanese Transnationalism.* Durham, NC: Duke University Press.

6.5 Conclusion: Prospects of Chinese Globalization

Just as China is becoming more global, so is the world becoming more Chinese. Starting in the late 1970s, reform, liberalization and modernization in China itself coincided with globalization and the rise of neoliberalism in the world around it. This combination has resulted in a deep penetration of global forces in China itself shaped by a unique configuration of neoliberalism and socialist governance. Regarding China's relations with the world, proactive neo-socialist governance is increasingly in evidence as well. China's role in the existing system of international relations and global governance is evolving. From a largely passive participant stirred into action chiefly when its own immediate interests are at stake, it is becoming an active player that makes its influence felt across the globe and is beginning to shape the institutions of global governance.

Beyond the sphere of international relations, the impact of neo-socialist governance is also in evidence in the way that Chinese people and capital move between China and foreign countries. Migrants are increasingly 'invited in' to serve the government's strategic objectives: leveraging the economy beyond the middle income trap and becoming a source of innovation and development independently from the world's advanced economies. Returnees are a key component of developing the skills and knowledge needed for Chinese enterprises to become globally competitive, a part of the 'going out' policy that the government embarked on in the late 1990s in the run-up to WTO accession in 2001 and that created the framework for the surge in outward foreign investment.

The government's going out strategy serves several objectives. The country's huge foreign exchange reserves (3.73 trillion US dollars in 2015[25]) have to be invested somewhere and preferably not all of it in US government bonds. Second, investment abroad is needed to ensure a continued supply of natural resources, especially oil, gas, metals and timber. Third, Chinese companies venturing abroad is a key prop of the strategy of structural change to the economy away from labour-intensive export processing to knowledge-intensive industry and services. Fourth, national pride is at stake. China can only call itself a respectable player in world affairs if Chinese companies become

---

[25] http://blogs.wsj.com/moneybeat/2015/04/16/keeping-yuan-stable-hits-chinas-currency-reserves/, checked 13 June 2015.

world-beating competitors on a par with the largest multi-national corporations.

In this chapter I have documented two very different faces of the interaction between China and the world. In the arena of international relations, China and the US are bracing themselves for global rivalry. A combination of diplomacy, international governance, military build-up, outward investment, trade, foreign aid and soft power is rapidly turning China into a global force. Xi Jinping and others of his generation do not waver in their implementation of a master plan to realize their dream of superpower status in twenty to thirty years from now. The US government, too, displays an increasingly confrontational attitude, apparently eager to take on a new adversary after the fall of the Soviet Union and the largely successful containment of Islamic terrorism. Both countries are beginning to frame their relationship not just in terms of competition for hegemony in world affairs, but as a showdown between civilizations that are as irreconcilably as they are convinced of their own superiority.

However, below the surface things are less straightforward. Strategic rivalry is complicated by the complementarity between the American and Chinese economies and the far-reaching integration of China in the global system. China and the US are competitors and rivals that cannot do without each other, making any attempt at 'containment' of China, if the US government would ever want to, utterly impossible. This is just one aspect of the complexity of Chinese interests and relationships abroad. Another aspect is the conflicting interests between various actors within China itself. Central government agencies often have conflicting interests or fail to coordinate their efforts. Provincial or other local governments have their own strategic and economic interests abroad that may not coincide with those of the Centre. Government strategy is often at odds with the commercial interests of Chinese firms. Chinese people continue to move abroad for all kinds of reasons that can only be imperfectly aligned with the interests of the government. Chinese firms that locate operations abroad or are managed according to international standards also grow more independent from the government departments that may still formally control them.

The world of the twenty-first century is very different from that of the twentieth century. Globalization uproots capital, people, goods, culture and information instead of creating parallel worlds each separately focussed on and controlled by their own centre. Chinese globalization, too, does not create a separate Chinese world. General globalization processes that create a high degree of mutual dependence put a very high price tag on isolation and confrontation. Against this background, the main issue is not how China and the US will shape their rivalry for superpower status or how other major power centres, such as the EU, Russia or Japan, will align themselves. The main question that will determine the shape tomorrow's world is whether the CCP will be willing and able to extend its project beyond China in an effort to contain and direct Chinese globalization processes.

If the Party indeed manages to enlist more and more of China global actors for its own strategic purposes, it will eventually not only constrain the further development of Chinese society, economy and culture, but will also turn China's emerging rivalry with the US into a confrontation between different worlds. So far, the evidence presented in this chapter tilts in favour of the independence of Chinese global actors whose profits, freedom and opportunities usually induce them to make their own decisions. This ought to be encouraged, facilitated and even insisted upon, not because the West doesn't want China to 'win' but to avoid the emergence of a zero-sum game over world dominance. Twentieth-century history provides ample evidence that the long-term stability and prosperity of our future world depends on restraining the desire to play the 'great game'.

7 | Conclusion: The Communist Party and China's Future

For China to meet both reform and post-reform challenges, the continued rule of the Communist Party is not the main obstacle, but instead, the most important condition. This involves much more than merely the routine, and in itself correct, observation that CCP rule keeps China united and ensures stability and peace. Designing and implementing the necessary policies demands the kind of skill, organization, staying power and legitimacy that only the Communist Party possesses. Although this assessment runs counter to the view that the problems and issues that China faces are inherent to fundamental flaws of the system that must eventually bring communism to its knees, it is intended neither as a whitewash for these problems, nor as a denial that the Party can, and indeed must do a lot better than at present.

The CCP's development can be divided in three distinct phases, each with its own characteristics, strengths and weaknesses. Twice has the Party needed to reinvent itself fundamentally to survive. Twice has it done so successfully, the first time between 1935 and 1942 and the second time between 1989 and 1992. Between its foundation in Shanghai in 1921 and the rectification in Yan'an in 1942, the CCP was a revolutionary party that was fragmented, ideologically divided and at the mercy of forces more powerful than itself: Stalin and the Comintern, warlords, the Nationalist Party and the Japanese army. After his arrival in Yan'an at the end of the Long March in 1935, Mao Zedong turned the Party into a personal dictatorship, a military machine and a totalitarian organization that defeated its enemies and transformed China into a communist state. Maoist dictatorship subsequently also destroyed many of the gains of the revolution, ultimately leaving China poor, weak and divided. Many aspects of communist dictatorship were changed during the first decade of reform in the 1980s, but a new phase in CCP politics and organization only really got underway after the crackdown on the Tian'anmen Movement in 1989 and Deng Xiaoping's Southern Tour in 1992. A unique blend of socialist authoritarianism and liberalization has grown out of this, changing China into an economic powerhouse and emerging global power.

This book has documented and discussed many aspects of this transformation. China has now moved beyond the project of the reform of state socialism to what I have termed neo-socialism. The gains of marketization, liberalization and global capitalism have been parlayed into strengthened state capacity, a stronger, larger and more Leninist party, a vibrant society and autonomous civil society, a growing economy and rising standards of living, a nation that has been forged into a more integrated community, and a powerful and respected country across the world.

Despite the many successes and the appearance of confidence, several of the problems that the CCP currently faces are an indication that certain aspects of the neo-socialist approach need to be reconsidered. If the Party wishes to continue its leading role in politics and society, a more fundamental rethink of its mission is required than the current leadership is prepared to undertake, perhaps not as radical as during the two earlier occasions that the Party reinvented itself in 1942 and 1992, but certainly involving much more than a few adjustments.

China's neo-socialist achievements such as economic performance, the reduction of poverty, the creation of a social security and health insurance system and the high-speed rail network are proudly presented as evidence of the superiority of Party leadership and the blessings of consultative instead of multi-party democracy, particularly when contrasted with Europe's lacklustre economies and the US's dysfunctional political system. There is more than simple gloating over success at stake here. The Party now claims the indefinite right to rule no longer only as the engineer of a sacred transformative mission (previously 'revolution', now 'reform'), but also as the best and most trusted custodian of the collective interests of the Chinese people. Party rule is not simply a perpetual dictatorship but is presented as being conditional on its continued success in creating prosperity, national strength and social harmony. Without the support and approval of the people, the Party leadership insists, Party rule would quickly come to an end. Gradually but deliberately, socialist or nationalist transformation is morphing into something remarkably akin to the dynastic Mandate of Heaven proven by social harmony and the prosperity and satisfaction of the people.

Despite the language of harmony, collective interests and wellbeing, there is also a hard and even dictatorial aspect to the CCP's new-found assertiveness, a trend that started around the Seventeenth Party congress in 2007 and has become noticeably more pronounced after Xi Jinping became Party general secretary in 2012. An increasing emphasis on unity, social stability and social governance also signalled a return to an approach to governance in which the Party and the state have become more prominent again. A corollary of this new authoritarian expression is that the Party has rolled back the autonomy of social organizations, activists and political entrepreneurs and more recently also the media and the academic world. More worrying and partially driving this development have been the divisions within the Party leadership. The fall of Bo Xilai in 2011 triggered a full-fledged purge of the Party which at the time of writing (August 2015) shows no signs of abating. Internationally, a similar trend is in evidence. China increasingly presents a corporate face to the outside world and an ambition to become a global power prepared to compete with and possibly confront its rivals or adversaries. Strategies are increasingly formulated based on the assumption that China is an entity with shared corporate interests that have to be pursued against those of other countries: a sharply realist view of international relations projected onto the global economy.

Both domestically and internationally these trends threaten to undo some of the most important achievements of neo-socialism of the past 25 years, and in fact appear counter-productively and needlessly regressive. China no longer needs to behave like a wounded nation facing far superior adversaries. The Chinese economy has become so complex that its countless producers, consumers and regulators cannot and should not be squeezed into a China Inc. directed from above. Political entrepreneurs, social organizations, the media and academics do not need more social governance, but less. Competitiveness and revanchist sentiments entice the national government to make decisions that belong on an Olympic track, not in the economy or international relations. Policy making should, in the final analysis, have nothing to do with becoming number 1 or beating one's opponents, but with the prosperity and wealth of the country and its people.

It is easy simply to conclude from this that the communist leopard has not changed its spots after all. In fact, the desire to be number 1 runs much deeper in ways that have nothing to do with communism at all. Since the Opium Wars, opening up to the world beyond China has always been fraught with contradictions: the Chinese nation had to be saved from extinction, yet this could only be done by jettisoning

Chinese and adopting foreign ways. Since the 1990s, this long-standing conundrum has given rise to what Xiang Biao has called the 'Pacific paradox'. As Chinese students, intellectuals and political leaders became more familiar with the West – and more particularly with the US – in the 1980s and 1990s, they also became more aware of the shortcomings of Western culture. They became more particular in choosing what China should borrow and what it should reject, and more culturally chauvinistic. Yet at the same time, Western ways continue to be relevant to China's future, because these ways best serve the purposes of global capitalism and geopolitics, which China must participate in because it is the only game in town: 'China has to compete with the US to survive, and to do that, China *has to* become like the US, for instance by developing capitalism and building up military might.'[1]

The Pacific paradox has become increasingly conspicuous in the choices that the Communist Party leadership is making. The CCP is emphasizing global competition and therefore the need to participate in the global game, but is also saying that this must be done to preserve China's civilization and on China's terms. China's rise thus serves two masters: joining the global order and becoming just like the US, and carving out a unique space to defend China, defeat its enemies and preserve what is unique and special about China. The rising combativeness of the Xi-Li regime in the international arena is therefore not unqualified. It is coupled with a continued desire to be a fully functional part of the world order and at the same time to become like its main competitors. This ambiguity presents a historic chance to change the nature of the international game. The question is whether leaders across the world will take this opportunity instead of opting to play by starkly realist rules. The establishment of the Asian International Investment Bank in 2015 is an example of what can go wrong. For several years, European partners were actively courted by China to join the new bank. This would have given Europe the opportunity to shape the governance of the bank to suit European interests. Instead, Europe ignored the Chinese overtures until 2015, when the shape, size and mission of the bank had largely been set. As a result, European and

[1] Xiang, Biao. 2014. The Pacific Paradox: The Chinese State in Transpacific Interactions. In *Transpacific Studies: Framing an Emerging Field*, ed. Janet Hoskins, Viet Thanh Nguyen, pp. 85–105. Honolulu: University of Hawai'i Press.

other Western countries are now participating in a brand-new international organization largely on Chinese terms.

A similar split attitude undergirds the regime's stance on the transformation of Chinese society since 1989. Many of the freedoms that the Chinese had become accustomed to have recently been curtailed to preserve the unity of the Party and with it, the uniquely communist and Chinese nature of the political system. Yet no attempt is made to undo the fundamental evolution of society caused by marketization and individualization. The leadership remains convinced that mimicking the success of the West will continue to make China richer and more powerful in its engagement of the West.

Borrowing an anthropological term, this latest instalment of a long-standing 'internal cultural debate' in China is made especially virulent because it has become mixed up with internal power politics in the CCP.[2] After the fall of Bo Xilai China has witnessed a return to pre-1989 factional policies that are likely to lead to some equivalent of the 'release and restrain' policy cycle caused by confrontations between competing leaders and their factions. To defeat their enemies within the Party, the Xi-Li leadership has tightened the noose on the expression of political disagreement that might feed on and amplify any divisions at the heart of the Party. The question is not so much if, but rather when the current restraining phase of the cycle will end and a more permissive political environment will return. Yet despite the harsh political climate since 2013, China's autonomous and diverse society and wider political field have not disappeared and will continue to develop as soon as the policy cycle loosens up again.

This raises the question of whether the disjunction between a fundamentally changed society and basically unchanged party politics is sustainable in the longer term. The leadership obviously thinks there is no such contradiction and maintains that it should be judged by its results, backed up by ideological innovation, Party unity and social governance. Moreover, the economic deterioration in 2015 (stock exchange crash, sliding economic growth, devaluation of the Chinese yuan) will further strengthen the leadership's conviction that at this point in time any further liberalization may quickly turn dissatisfaction with the performance of the economy into political instability. Nevertheless, in the

---

[2] Moeran, Brian. 1984. Individual, Group and Seishin: Japan's Internal Cultural Debate. *Man, New Series* 19,2:252–66.

slightly longer term the development of the society and the economy will continue to widen the range and force of a multitude of opinions and interests. Consultative democracy, lobbying, social organizations, petitioning and the legal system will have to be complemented by a more direct way of informing policy making and implementation from beyond the sacred void. Furthermore, structural solutions need to be found to break through the many vested interests among the power elite that continue to remain unchecked. This is not to insist that a multi-party democracy be installed. What is needed, however, is a further opening up of the political system by moving beyond the neo-socialist strategy and reinventing core aspects of the Party and other parts of the political system. The Party leadership should be bold and work to develop a political system that is more in tune with a society that is modern, vigorous, diverse and independent, giving the Party strong institutional tools to continue its rule in the decades to come. If the Party decides to steer such a course towards a more open political process, the following issues will have to be addressed.

First, a more radical separation between Party and society is needed. Currently, all rights and freedoms of individuals, corporations, associations and organizations under the rule of law or social governance are ultimately conditional on Party scrutiny. This works as long as Chinese citizens allow themselves to be thought of as minors in need of adult supervision. The rise in political activity across China is a sign that this is no longer the case. Instead, the Party ought to wean itself from its preoccupation with social stability and trust the society that it has created. Ideological and religious differences or conflict and competition are not necessarily bad or a threat to stability. Quite the contrary, they are signs of a vigorous, stable and mature society.

Second, transparency and accountability are essential. The Party should change the nature of the political game. Much clearer procedures and rules should be put in place for political competition, lobbying and debate and decision making inside and outside the Party. To fight systemic corruption, Party leaders ought to make their own financial and business interests public. Rules and procedures should be put in place to prevent leaders from being involved in decisions from which they themselves could gain.

In such a future, the Communist Party will still have a vital role to play as the ultimate arbiter which formulates, bears and guarantees a mission and consensus that transcends crude interests and ordinary politics. However, to ensure broad support, the debates and formulation of the principles and ultimate objectives of politics within the Party should be open to public scrutiny, a twenty-first-century version of Leninist democratic centralism or Confucian consensus building that opens up the sacred void at the centre of the Party. This would change the Communist Party from a secretive organization to a 'superego' of China's future that is open-ended. Could it be time to loosen, not shorten the reins of power?

Further Reading

Chapter 1: Introduction

The Tian'anmen Movement in Beijing in the spring of 1989: Frank N. Pieke, Frank N. Pieke. 1996. The Ordinary and the Extraordinary: An Anthropological Study of Chinese Reform and the 1989 People's Movement in Beijing. London: Kegan Paul International; Craig Calhoun. 1994. Neither Gods nor Emperors: Students and the Struggle for Democracy in China. Berkeley: University of California Press; Tong Shen. 1990. Almost a Revolution: The Story of a Chinese Student's Journey from Boyhood to Leadership in Tiananmen Square. Boston: Houghton Mifflin. On the details of the military suppression, see Timothy Brook. 1999. Quelling the People: The Military Suppression of the Beijing Democracy Movement Stanford: Stanford University Press. A very recent addition of memories of the suffering during the movement in the city of Chengdu is Louisa Lim. 2014. The People's Republic of Amnesia: Tiananmen Revisited. Oxford: Oxford University Press.

Chapter 2: Why the CCP will not Fall from Power

Communism before 1949: On the origins of communist and socialist thought in the decade after the fall of the Qing dynasty in 1911, see Arif Dirlik. 1989. The Origins of Chinese Communism. New York: Oxford University Press. On the early history of the CCP, see S.A. Smith. 2000. A Road Is Made: Communism in Shanghai 1920–1927. Richmond, Surrey: Curzon; Hans Van de Ven. 1991. From Friend to Comrade: The Founding of the Chinese Communist Party, 1920–1927. Berkeley: University of California Press. On the CCP struggles after the breakdown of the First United Front with the Guomindang in 1927, see Gregor Benton. 1992. Mountain Fires: The Red Army's Three-Year War in South China, 1934–1938. Berkeley: University of California Press. On the CCP during the Second World War, see Gregor Benton. 1999. New Fourth Army: Communist Resistance along the Yangtze and the Huai, 1938–1941. Richmond, Surrey: Curzon; Rana Mitter. 2014. China's War with Japan, 1937–1945: The Struggle for Survival. London: Penguin.

The CCP turning conquest into revolution: David Crook & Isabel Crook. 2010[1959]. Revolution in a Chinese Village: Ten Mile Inn. Abingdon: Routledge; Kenneth Lieberthal. 1980. Revolution and Tradition in Tientsin, 1949–1952. Stanford: Stanford University Press. On the development of work units and collectives, see David Bray. 2005. Social Space and Governance in China: The *Danwei* System from Origins to Reform. Stanford: Stanford University Press; Sulamith Heins Potter & Jack M. Potter. 1990. China's Peasants: The Anthropology of a Revolution. Cambridge: Cambridge University Press.

Pre-reform CCP rule: Eddy U. 2007. Disorganizing China: Counter-Bureaucracy and the Decline of Socialism. Stanford: Stanford University Press; Andrew G. Walder. 1986. Communist Neo-Traditionalism: Work and Authority in Chinese Industry. Berkeley: University of California Press; for a broader sweep of the politics and society of the Maoist period, see Andrew G. Walder. 2015. China Under Mao: A Revolution Derailed. Cambridge, Mass.: Harvard University Press. On the organizational politics of the party and the state, see Franz Schurmann. 1968. Ideology and Organization in Communist China. Second edition. Berkeley: University of California Press; Kenneth Lieberthal & Michel Oksenberg. 1988. Policy Making in China: Leaders, Structures, and Processes. Princeton, N.J.: Princeton University Press; Vivienne Shue. 1988. The Reach of the State: Sketches of the Chinese Body Politic. Stanford: Stanford University Press. On Campaign-style politics under Mao, see David E. Apter & Tony Saich. 1994. Revolutionary Discourse in Mao's Republic. Cambridge, Massachusetts: Harvard University Press; Dali Yang. 1996. Calamity and Reform in China: State, Rural Society, and Institutional Change Since the Great Leap Famine. Stanford: Stanford University Press; Frank Dikötter. 2010. Mao's Great Famine: The History of China's Most Devastating Catastrophe, 1958–1962. London: Bloomsbury; 2013. The Tragedy of Liberation: A History of the Chinese Revolution, 1945–1957. London: Bloomsbury; Roderick MacFarquhar & Michael Schoenhals. 2006. Mao's Last Revolution. Cambridge, Mass.: Belknap Press of Harvard University Press; Andrew G. Walder. 2009. Fractured Rebellion: The Beijing Red Guard Movement. Cambridge, Mass.: Harvard University Press. On CCP political language, see Michael Schoenhals. 1992. Doing Things with Words in Chinese Politics: Five Studies. Berkeley: Institute of East Asian Studies.

CCP line struggles and factionalism: The classic works on factionalism under Mao are Andrew Nathan. 1973. A Factionalism Model for CCP Politics. In *China Quarterly*, pp. 34–66; Frederick C. Teiwes. 1993. Politics and Purges in China: Rectification and the Decline of Party Norms, 1950–1965 Armonk, N.Y.: M.E. Sharpe; Tang Tsou. 1976. Prolegomenon to the Study of Informal Groups in CCP Politics. In *China Quarterly*, pp. 98–114. While Nathan assumes a rule-bound form of factional competition, Tsou and Teiwes highlight the confrontations over policies and principles and the winner-take-all nature of inner-party politics. For applications of the factionalism model to the post-reform era, see Ben Hillman. 2010. Factions and Spoils: Examining Political Behavior within the Local State in China. In *China Journal*, pp. 1–18; Victor C. Shih. 2007. Factions and Finance in China: Elite Conflict and Inflation. Cambridge: Cambridge University Press.

Party and state building after the start of the reforms: Frank N. Pieke. 2009. The Good Communist: Elite Training and State Building in Today's China. Cambridge: Cambridge University Press; Dali L. Yang. 2004. Remaking the Chinese Leviathan: Market Transition and the Politics of Governance in China. Stanford: Stanford University Press; Kjeld Erik Brødsgaard. 2002. Institutional Reform and the *Bianzhi* System in China. In *The China Quarterly*, pp. 361–86; Patricia M. Thornton. 2013. The Advance of the Party: Transformation or Takeover of Urban Grassroots Society. In *China Quarterly*, pp. 1–18; Pierre Landry. 2008. Decentralized Authoritarianism in China: The Communist Party's Control of Local Elites in the Post-Mao Era. Cambridge: Cambridge University Press; Maria Edin. 2003. State Capacity and Local Agent Control in China: CCP Cadre Management from a Township Perspective. In *The China Quarterly*, pp. 35–52; David Shambaugh. 2008. China's Communist Party: Atrophy and Adaptation. Washington, D.C. and Berkeley: Woodrow Wilson Center Press and University of California Press.

The local state: Marc Blecher & Vivienne Shue. 1996. Tethered Deer: Government and Economy in a Chinese County. Stanford: Stanford University Press; Thomas P. Bernstein & Xiaobo Lü. 2003. Taxation without Representation in Contemporary Rural China. Cambridge: Cambridge University Press; Linda Chelan Li. 2012. Rural Tax Reform in China: Policy Processes and Institutional Change. Abingdon: Routledge; You-tien Hsing. 2010. The Great Urban Transformation: Politics of Land and Property in China. Oxford: Oxford University Press; Jean C. Oi et al. 2012. Shifting Fiscal Control to Limit Cadre Power in China's Townships and Villages. In *China Quarterly*, pp. 649–75; Graeme Smith. 2010. The Hollow State: Rural Governance in China. In *China Quarterly*, pp. 601–18. On collusion between local officials and business, see David L. Wank. 1999. Commodifying Communism: Business, Trust, and Politics in a Chinese City. Cambridge: Cambridge University Press, John Osburg. 2013. Anxious Wealth:

Money and Morality among China's New Rich. Stanford: Stanford University Press; Graeme Smith. 2009. Political Machinations in a Rural County. In *China Journal*, pp. 29–59.

The legal system and the rule of law: The most thorough work on building up the legal system remains Randall Peerenboom. 2002. China's Long March toward Rule of Law. Cambridge: Cambridge University Press. For a more recent overview, see Pitman Potter. 2013. China's Legal System. Cambridge: Polity Press; On the use of the law against the state, see Hualing Fu & Richard Cullen. 2008. Weiquan (Rights Protection) Lawyering in an Authoritarian State: Building a Culture of Public-Interest Lawyering. In *China Journal*, pp. 111–27: The University of Chicago Press on behalf of the College of Asia and the Pacific, The Australian National University; Susanne Brandtstädter. 2011. The Law Cuts Both Ways: Rural Legal Activism and Citizenship Struggles in Neosocialist China. In *Economy and Society*, pp. 266–88.

Marketization of welfare and public services: Studies on the creation of specific markets include Jane Duckett. 2011. The Chinese State's Retreat from Health: Policy and the Politics of Retrenchment. Abingdon: Routledge; Mark W. Frazier. 2010. Socialist Insecurity: Pensions and the Politics of Uneven Development in China. Ithaca, NY: Cornell University Press; Andrew B. Kipnis. 2011. Governing Educational Desire: Culture, Politics, and Schooling in China. Chicago: University of Chicago Press; Daniela Stockmann. 2013. Media Commercialization and Authoritarian Rule in China. Cambridge: Cambridge University Press.

Non-state political action: On petitioning, see Yongshun Cai. 2010. Collective Resistance in China: Why Popular Protests Succeed or Fail. Stanford: Stanford University Press; Xi Chen. 2012. Social Protest and Contentious Authoritarianism in China. Cambridge: Cambridge University Press; Lianjiang Li et al. 2012. Petitioning Beijing: The High Tide of 2003–2006. In *China Quarterly*, pp. 313–34; Kevin J. O'Brien & Lianjiang Li. 2006. Rightful Resistance in Rural China. Cambridge: Cambridge University Press. On elections, see Joseph Fewsmith. 2013. The Logic and Limits of Poltical Reform in China. Cambridge: Cambridge University Press; Baogang He. 2007. Rural Democracy in China: The Role of Village Elections. Houndsmills: Palgrave Macmillan; Gunter Schubert & Anna L. Ahlers. 2012. Participation and Empowerment at the Grassroots: Chinese Village Elections in Perspective. Lanham: Lexington; Stig Thøgersen et al. 2008. Consultative Elections of Chinese Township Leaders. In *China Information*, pp. 67–89. On social management and social governance, see Frank N. Pieke. 2012. The Communist Party and Social Management in China. In *China*

Information, pp. 149–65; Ching Kwan Lee & Yonghong Zhang. 2013. The Power of Instability: Unraveling the Microfoundations of Bargained Authoritarianism in China. In *American Journal of Sociology*, pp. 1475–508.

Chapter 3: China's Economy will Continue to Grow, but not Forever

Market transition: The most consistent advocate of market transition in China has been Victor Nee, see Victor Nee. 1989. A Theory of Market Transition: From Redistribution to Markets in State Socialism. In *American Sociological Review*, pp. 663–81; Victor Nee & Sonja Opper. 2012. Capitalism from Below: Markets and Institutional Change in China. Cambridge, MA: Harvard University Press; others include Ronald Coase & Ning Wang. 2012. How China Became Capitalist. Houndsmills: Macmillan and Nicholas R. Lardy. 2014. Markets over Mao: The Rise of Private Business in China. Washington, D.C.: Peterson Institute for International Economics. Market transition believers include several eminent Chinese economists, see for instance Barry Naughton. 2013. Wu Jinglian: Voice of Reform in China. Cambridge, MA: The MIT Press.

Reforming the state sector and industrial policy: Margaret M. Pearson. 2005. The Business of Governing Business in China: Institutions and Norms of the Emerging Regulatory State. In *World Politics*, pp. 296–322; Jean C. Oi & Chaohua Han. 2011. China's Corporate Restructuring: A Multi-step Process. In *Going Private in China: The Politics of Corporate Restructuring and System Reform*, ed. Jean C. Oi, pp. 18–37. Stanford: Walter H. Shorenstein Asia-Pacific Research Center; Peter Nolan. 2001. China in the Global Economy: National Champions, Industrial Policy and the Big Business Revolution. Houndmills, Basingstoke: Palgrave; Roselyn Hsueh. 2011. China's Regulatory State: A New Strategy for Globalization. Ithaca: Cornell University Press; Sarah Eaton. 2015. The Advance of the State in Contemporary China: State-Market Relations in the Reform Era. Cambridge: Cambridge University Press.

Special Economic Zones and foreign investment: Lanqing Li. 2009. Breaking Through: The Birth of China's Opening-up Policy. Hong Kong: Oxford University Press; You-tien Hsing. 1998. Making Capitalism in China: The Taiwan Connection. Oxford: Oxford University Press; Yasheng Huang. 2003. Selling China: Foreign Direct Investment during the Reform Era. Cambridge: Cambridge University Press and Mary Elizabeth Gallagher. 2005. Contagious Capitalism: Globalization and the Politics of Labor in China. Princeton: Princeton University Press; Eric Thun. 2006. Changing Lanes in China: Foreign Direct Investment, Local Governments, and Auto Sector

Development. Cambridge: Cambridge University Press. On the changes in a village that happens to be located in China's largest special economic zone Shenzhen, see Anita Chan et al. 2009. Chen Village: Revolution to Globalization. Berkeley: University of California Press.

Demographic development and family planning: James Z. Lee & Feng Wang. 1999. One Quarter of Humanity, Malthusian Mythology and Chinese Realities 1700–2000. Cambridge, MA: Harvard University Press; Susan Greenhalgh. 2008. Just One Child: Science and Policy in Deng's China. Berkeley: University of California Press; Susan Greenhalgh & Edwin A. Winckler. 2005. Governing China's Population: From Leninist to Neoliberal Biopolitics. Stanford: Stanford University Press; Xizhe Peng. 2011. China's Demographic History and Future Challenges. In *Science*, pp. 581–7; Karen Eggleston et al. 2013. Will Demographic Change Slow China's Rise? In *The Journal of Asian Studies*, pp. 505–18. On population "quality", see Ann Anagnost. 2004. The Corporeal Politics of Quality (*Suzhi*). In *Public Culture*, pp. 189–208; Andrew Kipnis. 2007. Neoliberalism Reified: *Suzhi* Discourse and Tropes of Neoliberalism in the People's Republic of China. In *Journal of the Royal Anthropological Institute (N.S.)*, pp. 383–400. On labour and labour markets, see Albert Park et al. 2010. Can China Meet Her Employment Challenges? In *Growing Pains: Tensions and Opportunities in China's Transformation*, ed. Jean Oi, Scott Rozelle, Xueguang Zhou, pp. 27–55. Stanford: Stanford Asia-Pacific Research Center; Sarosh Kuruvilla et al. 2011. From Iron Rice Bowl to Informalization: Markets, Workers, and the State in a Changing China. Ithaca: ILR Press.

Innovation and higher-education: On universities, see Ruth Hayhoe et al. 2011. Portraits of 21st Century Chinese Universities: In the Move to Mass Higher Education. Dordrecht: Springer; Robert A. Rhoads et al. 2014. China's Rising Research Universities: A New Era of Global Ambition. Baltimore: Johns Hopkins University Press. On talent programmes, see Denis Fred Simon & Cong Cao. 2009. China's Emerging Technological Edge: Assessing the Role of High-End Talent. Cambridge: Cambridge University Press; David Zweig & Huiyao Wang. 2013. Can China Bring Back the Best? The Communist Party Organizes China's Search for Talent. In *The China Quarterly*, pp. 590–615. More generally, on human capital and student migration, see Biao Xiang & Wei Shen. 2009. International Student Migration and Social Stratification in China. In *International Journal of Educational Development*, pp. 513–22; Bernard P. Wong. 2006. The Chinese in Silicon Valley: Globalization, Social Networks, and Ethnic Identity. Lanham, Md.: Rowman & Littlefield; Gracia Liu-Farrer. 2011. Labour Migration from China to Japan: International Students, Transnational Migrants.

London: Routledge; Vanessa L. Fong. 2011. Paradise Redefined: Transnational Chinese Students and the Quest for Flexible Citizenship in the Developed World Stanford: Stanford University Press. On creative clusters and art districts, see Michael Keane. 2011. China's New Creative Clusters: Governance, Human Capital and Investment. London: Routledge; Yue Zhang. 2014. Governing Art Districts: State Control and Cultural Production in Contemporary China. In *China Quarterly*, pp. 827–48.

Environment: the best-know dystopic overviews of environmental degradation are Elizabeth Economy. 2004. The River Runs Black: The Environmental Challenge to China's Future. Ithaca: Cornell University Press; Vaclav Smil. 1984. The Bad Earth: Environmental Degradation in China. Armonk, N.Y.: M.E. Sharpe. On environmentalism, see Michael Hathaway. 2013. Environmental Winds: Making the Global in Southwest China. Berkeley: University of California Press; Guobin Yang & Craig Calhoun. 2007. Media, Civil Society, and the Rise of a Green Public Sphere in China. In *China Information*, pp. 211–36; Bryan Tilt. 2015. Dams and Development in China: The Moral Economy of Water and Power. New York: Columbia University Press. On the impact of pollution and the role of local cadres, see Anna Lora-Wainwright et al. 2012. Learning to Live with Pollution: The Making of Environmental Subjects in a Chinese Industrialised Village. In *China Journal*, pp. 106–24; Bryan Tilt. 2010. Struggling for Sustainability in Rural China: Environmental Values and Civil Society. New York: Columbia University Press. Anna Lora-Wainwright. 2013. Fighting for Breath: Living Morally and Dying of Cancer in a Chinese Village. Honolulu: University of Hawai'i Press; Sarah Eaton & Genia Kostka. 2014. Authoritarian Environmentalism Undermined? Local Leaders' Time Horizons and Environmental Policy Implementation in China. In *China Quarterly*; Thomas Heberer & Anja Senz. 2011. Streamlining Local Behaviour through Communication, Incentives and Control: A Case Study of Local Environmental Policies in China. In *Journal of Current Chinese Affairs*, pp. 77–112.

Chapter 4: Freedom without Universal Human Rights

Human rights in China: Rosemary Foot. 2001. Rights beyond Borders: The Global Community and the Struggle over Human Rights in China. Oxford: Oxford University Press; Anne Kent. 1999. China, the United Nations, and Human Rights – The Limits of Compliance. Philadelphia; Sonya Sceats & Shaun Breslin. 2012. China and the International Human Rights System. London: Chatham House; Marina Svensson. 2002. Debating Human Rights in China: A Conceptual and Political History. Lanham: Rowman & Littlefield; Gudrun Wacker. 2013. Norms without Borders? Human Rights in China. In *China across the Divide: The Domestic and Global in Politics and Society*, ed. Rosemary Foot, pp. 175–99. Oxford: Oxford University Press, Pitman Potter. 2013. China's Legal System. Cambridge: Polity Press, pp. 186–193.

The individual and society: On individualization, see Yunxiang Yan. 2010. The Chinese Path to Individualization. In *The British Journal of Sociology*, pp. 489–512: Blackwell Publishing Ltd; Li Zhang & Aihwa Ong. 2008. Privatizing China: Socialism from Afar. Ithaca: Cornell University Press; Yunxiang Yan. 2009. The Good Samaritan's New Trouble: A Study of the Changing Moral Landscape in Contemporary China. In *Social Anthropology*, pp. 9–24; Vanessa L. Fong. 2004. Only Hope: Coming of Age under China's One-Child Policy. Stanford: Stanford University Press; Lisa Rofel. 2007. Desiring China: Experiments in Neoliberalism, Sexuality, and Public Culture. Durham: Duke University Press. On charity and volunteer work: André Laliberté et al. 2011. Religious Philanthropy and Chinese Civil Society. In *Chinese Religions: Communities, Practices and Contemporary Issues*, ed. David A. Palmer, Glenn Shive, Philip Wickeri, pp. 139–51. New York: Oxford University Press; Vivienne Shue. 2006. The Quality of Mercy: Confucian Charity and the Mixed Metaphors of Modernity in Tianjin. In *Modern China*, pp. 411–52; Ning Zhang. 2012. The Wenchuan Earthquake, Social Organizations, and the Chinese State. In *Urban Anthropology*, pp. 211–46. On connections and the art of using them: Frank N. Pieke. 1995. Bureaucracy, Friends, and Money: The Growth of Capital Socialism in China. In *Comparative Studies in Society and History*, pp. 494–518; Yunxiang Yan. 1996. The Flow of Gifts: Reciprocity and Social Networks in a Chinese Village. Stanford: Stanford University Press; Mayfair Mei-hui Yang. 1994. Gifts, Favors & Banquets: The Art of Social Relationships in China. Ithaca: Cornell University Press; Thomas Gold et al. 2002. Social Connections in China: Institutions, Culture, and the Changing Nature of Guanxi. Cambridge: Cambridge University Press.

Rural-urban migration: Rachel Murphy. 2002. How Migrant Labor is Changing Rural China. In *Cambridge modern China series*. Cambridge: Cambridge University Press; Biao Xiang. 2005. Transcending Boundaries. Zhejiangcun: The Story of a Migrant Village in Beijing. Leiden: Brill Hairong Yan. 2008. New Masters, New Servants: Migration, Development, and Women Workers in China. Durham: Duke University Press; Tiantian Zheng. 2009. Red Lights: The Lives of Sex Workers in Postsocialist China. Minneapolis: University of Minnesota Press. On forced migration, see Jun Jing. 2003. Dams and Dreams: A Return-to-Homeland Movement in Northwest China. In *Living with Separation in China: Anthropological Accounts*, ed. Charles Stafford, pp. 113–29. London: Routledge; for recent adjustments to the methods of resettlement, see Sabrina Habich. 2015. Strategies of Soft Coercion in Chinese Dam Resettlement. In *Issies & Studies*, pp. 165–99. On cross-border marriages, see Caroline Grillot. 2012. Cross-Border Marriages between Vietnamese Women and Chinese Men: Their Integration of Otherness and the Impact of Popular Representations. In *Wind over Water: Migration in an East Asian Context*, ed. David Haines, Keiko Yamanaka, Shinji Yamashita, pp. 125–37. New York: Berghahn; Hsiu-Hua Shen. 2005. 'The first Taiwanese Wives' and 'the Chinese Mistresses': The International Division of Labour in Familial and Intimate Relations across the Taiwan Strait. In *Global Networks*, pp. 419–37; Wen-Shan Yang & Melody Chia-Wen Lu. 2010. Asian Cross-border Marriage Migration: Demographic Patterns and Social Issues. Amsterdam: Amsterdam University Press.

New and second-generation rural-urban migrants: Jenny Chan & Mark Selden. 2014. China's Rural Migrant Workers, the State, and Labor Politics. In *Critical Asian Studies*, pp. 599–620; Ye Liu et al. 2012. The Social Networks of New-generation Migrants in China's Urbanized Villages: A Case Study of Guangzhou. In *Habitat International*, pp. 192–200; Xingzhou Wang. 2008. An Investigation into Intergeneration Differences between Two Generations of Migrant Workers. In *Social Sciences in China*, pp. 136–56; T. E. Woronov. 2011. Learning to Serve: Urban Youth, Vocational Schools and New Class Formations in China. In *The China Journal*, pp. 77–99. On the "urban villages" where many transient youth find temporary accommodation, see Helen F. Siu. 2007. Grounding Displacement: Uncivil Urban Spaces in Postreform South China. In *American Ethnologist*, pp. 329–50.

Social stratification and social mobility: Yanjie Bian. 2002. Chinese Social Stratification and Social Mobility. In *Annual Review of Sociology*, pp. 91–116 and more recently John Knight. 2014. Inequality in China: An Overview. In *The World Bank Research Observer*, pp. 1–19; Li Shi et al. 2013. Rising Inequality in China: Challenges to a Harmonious Society. Cambridge: Cambridge University Press; Martin King Whyte. 2010. Myth of the Social Volcano: Perceptions of Inequality and Distributive Injustice in Contemporary China. Stanford: Stanford University Press; Li Zhang. 2010. In Search of Paradise: Middle Class Living in a Chinese Metropolis. Ithaca: Cornell University Press; Yingjie Guo. 2008. Class, Stratum and Group: The Politics of Description and Prescription. In *The New Rich in China: Future Rulers, Present Lives*, ed. David S.G. Goodman, pp. 38–52. Abingdon: Routledge; Ching Kwan Lee & Yuan Shen. 2009. China: The Paradox and Possibility of a Public Sociology of Labor. In *Work and Occupations*, pp. 110–25. On the new rich, see David S.G. Goodman.

2008. The New Rich in China: Future Rulers, Present Lives. London: Routledge; Andrew G. Walder et al. 2013. Social Stratification in Transitional Economies: Property Rights and the Structure of Markets. In *Theory & Society*, pp. 561–88; John Osburg. 2013. Anxious Wealth: Money and Morality among China's New Rich. Stanford: Stanford University Press; Lisa Hoffman. 2010. Patriotic Professionalism in Urban China: Fostering Talent. Philadelphia: Temple University Press; Thomas Heberer. 2007. Doing Business in Rural China: Liangshan's New Ethnic Entrepreneurs. Seattle: University of Washington Press. On the old and the new proletariat, see Mun Young Cho. 2013. The Specter of "the People": Urban Poverty in Northeast China. Ithaca: Cornell University Press; William Hurst. 2009. The Chinese worker after Socialism. Cambridge: Cambridge University Press; Jaesok Kim. 2013. Chinese Labor in a Korean Factory: Class, Ethnicity, and Productivity on the Shop Floor in Globalizing China. Stanford: Stanford University Press; Ching Kwan Lee. 2007. Against the Law: Labor Protest in China's Rustbelt and Sunbelt. Berkeley: University of California Press.

Consumerism and life styles: Amy Hanser. 2008. Service Encounters: Class, Gender, and the Market for Social Distinction in Urban China. Stanford: Stanford University Press; Karl Gerth. 2010. As China Goes, So Goes the World: How Chinese Consumers Are Transforming Everything. New York: Hill & Wang; Kevin Latham et al. 2006. Consuming China: Approaches to Cultural Change in Contemporary China London: Routledge; Shaoguang Wang. 1995. The Politics of Private Time: Changing Leisure Patterns in Urban China. In *Urban Spaces in Contemporary China: the Potential for Autonomy and Community in Post-Mao China*, ed. Deborah Davis, Richard Kraus, Barry Naughton, Elizabeth J. Perry, pp. 149–72. Washington, D.C.: Woodrow Wilson Center Press and Cambridge University Press. On sex cultures and sexualities, see James Farrer. 2002. Opening Up: Youth Sex Culture and Market Reform in Shanghai. Chicago: University of Chicago Press; Elaine Jeffreys. 2004. China, Sex and Prostitution. London: RoutledgeCurzon; 2006. Sex and Sexuality in China. Abingdon: Routledge; Lucette Yip Lo Kam. 2013. Shanghai Lalas: Female Tongzhi Communities and Politics in Urban China. Hong Kong: Hong Kong University Press; Lisa Rofel. 2007. Desiring China: Experiments in Neoliberalism, Sexuality, and Public Culture. Durham: Duke University Press. On consumption, life style and health, see Nancy Chen. 2003. Breathing Spaces: Qigong, Psychiatry, and Healing in China. New York: Columbia University Press; Judith Farquhar & Qicheng Zhang. 2012. Ten Thousand Things: Nurturing Life in Contemporary Beijing. New York: Zone books; David A. Palmer. 2007. Qigong Fever: Body, Science and Utopia in China. London: Hurst & Co.; Chee-Beng Tan & Yuling Ding. 2010. The Promotion of Tea in South China: Re-Inventing

Tradition in an Old industry. In *Food & Foodways*, pp. 121–44; Mei Zhan. 2009. Other-Worldly: Making Chinese Medicine through Transnational Frames. Durham: Duke University Press.

Religion: on religious policy, see Vincent Goossaert & David A. Palmer. 2011. The Religious Question in Modern China. Chicago: University of Chicago Press, chapter 12; an excellent case study of the way that CCP's religious affairs work in practice, see Yoshiko Ashiwa & David L. Wank. 2006. The Politics of a Reviving Buddhist Temple: State, Association, and Religion in Southeast China. In *Journal of Asian Studies*, pp. 337–59. On religion between communities and the state: on the scope and impact of the localization of governance through religious, kinship and other communal institutions, see Lily L. Tsai. 2007. Accountability without Democracy: Solidary Groups and Public Goods Provision in Rural China. Cambridge: Cambridge University Press; for more detailed case studies, see Adam Yuet Chau. 2006. Miraculous Response: Doing Popular Religion in Contemporary China. Stanford: Stanford University Press; Frank N. Pieke. 2003. The Genealogical Mentality in Modern China. In *Journal of Asian Studies*, pp. 101–28; Stig Thøgersen. 2002. A County of Culture: Twentieth-Century China Seen from Village Schools of Zouping, Shandong. Ann Arbor: University of Michigan Press; John M. Flower. 2004. A Road Is Made: Roads, Temples, and Historical Memory in Ya'an County, Sichuan. In *The Journal of Asian Studies*, pp. 649–85: Association for Asian Studies. On organized religion: David Ownby. 2009. Falun Gong and the Future of China. Oxford: Oxford University Press; David A. Palmer. 2007. Qigong Fever: Body, Science and Utopia in China. London: Hurst & Co.; Thomas David DuBois. 2005. The Sacred Village: Social Change and Religious Life in Rural North China. Honolulu: University of Hawaii Press; Henrietta Harrison. 2013. The Missionary's Curse and Other Tales from a Chinese Catholic Village. Berkeley: University of California Press; Richard Madsen. 1998. China's Catholics: Tragedy and Hope in an Emerging Civil Society. Berkeley: University of California Press; David Moser. 2013. An Invisible Path: 'Urban Buddhists' in Beijing and Their Search for Meaning. In *Restless China*, ed. Perry Link, Richard P. Madsen, Paul Pickowicz, pp. 167–90. Lanham: Rowman & Littlefield; Nanlai Cao. 2011. Constructing China's Jerusalem: Christians, Power, and Place in Contemporary Wenzhou. Stanford: Stanford University Press.

Non-state social organizations: on origins in the 1980s and 1990s, see Margaret M. Pearson. 1994. The Janus Face of Business Associations in China: Socialist Corporatism in Foreign Enterprises. In *The Australian Journal of Chinese Affairs*, pp. 25–46; Gordon White et al. 1996. In Search of

Civil Society: Market Reform and Social Change in Contemporary China. Oxford: Clarendon Press. On contemporary civil society: Timothy Hildebrandt. 2013. Social Organizations and the Authoritarian State in China. Cambridge: Cambridge University Press; Jessica C. Teets. 2013. Let Many Civil Societies Bloom: The Rise of Consultative Authoritarianism in China. In *Chna Quarterly*, pp. 19–38; Michael Hathaway. 2013. Environmental Winds: Making the Global in Southwest China. Berkeley: University of California Press; Chris King-Chi Chan & Pun Ngai. 2009. The Making of a New Working Class? A Study of Collective Actions of Migrant Workers in South China. In *The China Quarterly*, pp. 287–303; Jenny Chan & Mark Selden. 2014. China's Rural Migrant Workers, the State, and Labor Politics. In *Critical Asian Studies*, pp. 599–620; Ching Kwan Lee & Yuan Shen. 2011. The Anti-solidarity Machine? Labor Non-governmental Organizations in China. In *From Iron Rice Bowl to Informalization: Markets, Workers, and the State in a Changing China*, ed. Sarosh Kuruvilla, Ching Kwan Lee, Mary E. Gallagher, pp. 173–87. Ithaca: ILR Press; Mingwei Liu. 2011. "Where There Are Workers, There Should Be Trade Unions": Union Organizing in the Era of Growing Informal Employment. In *From Iron Rice Bowl to Informalization: Markets, Workers, and the State in a Changing China*, ed. Sarosh Kuruvilla, Ching Kwan Lee, Mary E. Gallagher, pp. 157–72. Ithanca: ILR Press.

Intellectuals, dissidents and political reform: on the 1980s, see Merle Goldman. 1994. Sowing the Seeds of Democracy in China: Political Reform in the Deng Xiaoping Era. Cambridge, Massachusetts: Harvard University Press. On the 1990s, see Teresa Wright. 2004. Intellectuals and the Politics of Protest: The Case of the China Democracy Party. In *Chinese Intellectuals between state and Market*, ed. Edward Gu, Merle Goldman, pp. 158–80. London: Routledge. On recent developments, see Liu Xiaobo, see Jean-Phillipe Béja et al. 2012. Liu Xiaobo, Charter 08 and the Challenges of Political Reform in China. Hong Kong: Hong Kong University Press; William A. Callahan. 2013. China Dreams: 20 Visions of the Future. Oxford: Oxford University Press; Émilie Frenkiel. 2015. Conditional Democracy: The Contemporary Debate on Political Reform in Chinese Universities. Colchester: ECPR Press; Mark Leonard. 2008. What Does China Think? London: Fourth Estate; 2012. China 3.0. London: European Council on Foreign Relations.

Non-state political entrepreneurs: A general statement of the growth of non-state politics is Andrew Mertha. 2009. "Fragmented Authoritarianism 2.0": Political Pluralization of the Chinese Policy Process. In *China Quarterly*, pp. 995–1012. Studies of specific aspects of political entrepreneurship include Susanne Brandtstädter. 2011. The Law Cuts

Both Ways: Rural Legal Activism and Citizenship Struggles in Neosocialist China. In *Economy and Society*, pp. 266–88; Fu Hualing & Richard Cullen. 2011. Climbing the Weiquan Ladder: A Radicalizing Process for Rights-Protection Lawyers. In *The China Quarterly*, pp. 40–59; Timothy Hildebrandt. 2013. Social Organizations and the Authoritarian State in China. Cambridge: Cambridge University Press, chapter 7; Zhengxu Wang et al. 2013. Leadership in China's Urban Middle Class Protest: The Movement to Protect Homeowners' Rights in Beijing. In *China Quarterly*, pp. 411–31; Yue Zhang. 2014. Governing Art Districts: State Control and Cultural Production in Contemporary China. In *China Quarterly*, pp. 827–48, p. 843; Scott Kennedy. 2005. The Business of Lobbying in China. Cambridge, Massachusetts: Harvard University Press.

Chapter 5: From Empire to Nation, or Why Taiwan, Tibet and Xinjiang will not be Given Independence

Pre-modern sources of Chineseness: Myron L. Cohen. 2005. Being Chinese: The Peripheralization of Traditional Identity. In *Kinship, Contract, Community, and State: Anthropological Perspectives on China*, pp. 39–58. Stanford: Stanford University Press; Joseph R. Levinson. 1958, 1964, 1965. Confucian China and Its Modern Fate: A Trilogy. Berkeley: University of California Press; Prasenjit Duara. 1995. Rescuing History from the Nation: Questioning Narratives of Modern China. Chicago: University of Chicago Press.

Barbarians and Chinese: on barbarians as rulers, see Mark Elliott. 2012. *Hushuo*: The Northern Other and the Naming of the Han Chinese. In *Critical Han Studies: The History, Representation, and Identity of China's Majority*, ed. Thomas S. Mullaney, James Leibold, Stéphane Gros, Eric Vanden Bussche, pp. 173–90. Berkeley: University of California Press; Mark C. Elliott. 2001. The Manchu Way: The Eight Banners and Ethnic Identity in Late Imperial China. Stanford: Stanford University Press; Edward J.M. Rhoads. 2000. Manchu & Han: Ethnic Relations and Political Power in Late Qing and Early Republican China, 1861–1928. Seattle: University of Washington Press. The classic study on China's frontiers is Owen Lattimore. 1962[1940]. Inner Asian Frontiers of China. Boston: Beacon Press; for a more recent study, see Thomas J. Barfield. 1989. The Perilous Frontier: Nomadic Empires and China, 221 B.C. to A.D. 1757. Oxford: Blackwell. On Chinese expansion towards the South and the incorporation of non-Han groups, see Melissa J. Brown. 2004. Is Taiwan Chinese? The Impact of Culture, Power, and Migration on Changing Identities. Berkeley: University of California Press; C. Patterson Giersch. 2006. Asian Borderlands: The Transformation of Qing China's Yunnan Frontier. Cambridge, Mass.:

Harvard University Press; John R. Shepherd. 1993. Statecraft and Political Economy on the Taiwan Frontier, 1600–1800. Stanford: Stanford University Press.

Early twentieth-century nationalism and ethnic chauvinism: Pamela Kyle Crossley. 2005. Nationality and Difference in China: The Post-imperial Dilemma. In *The Teleology of the Modern Nation-State: Japan and China*, ed. Joshua Fogel, pp. 138–55. Philadelphia: University of Pennsylvania Press; Frank Dikötter. 1992. The Discourse of Race in Modern China. London: Hurst; James Leibold. 2012. Searching for Han: Early Twentieth-Century Narratives of Chinese Origins and Development. In *Critical Han Studies: The History, Representation, and Identity of China's Majority*, ed. Thomas S. Mullaney, James Leibold, Stéphane Gros, Eric Vanden Bussche, pp. 210–33. Berkeley: University of California Press; Edward J.M. Rhoads. 2000. Manchu & Han: Ethnic Relations and Political Power in Late Qing and Early Republican China, 1861–1928. Seattle: University of Washington Press.

CCP minority policies: on their origin and growth in the 1950s, see Thomas S. Mullaney. 2011. Coming to Terms with the Nation: Ethnic Classification in Modern China. Berkeley: University of California Press. The best recent studies on China's minorities policies are Elena Barabantseva. 2011. Overseas Chinese, Ethnic Minorities, and Nationalism: De-Centering China London: Routledge; James Leibold. 2013. Ethnic Policy in China: Is Reform Inevitable? Honolulu: East-West Center. On Tibetans: Melvyn C. Goldstein. 2013. A History of Modern Tibet, Volume 3: The Storm Clouds Descend, 1955–1957. Berkeley: University of California Press; Hui Wang. 2011. The 'Tibet Issue' between East and West. In *Chinese Sociology and Anthropology*, pp. 7–30. On Uighurs: Ildikó Bellér-Hann. 2014. The Bulldozer State: Chinese Socialist Development in Xinjiang. In *Ethnographies of the State in Central Asia*, ed. Madeleine Reeves, Johan Rasanayagam, Judith Beyer, pp. 173–97. Bloomington, Indiana: Indiana University Press; Gardner Bovingdon. 2010. The Uyghurs: Strangers in Their Own Land. New York: Columbia University Press; Joanne Smith Finlay. 2013. The Art of Symbolic Resistance: Uyghur Identities and Uyghur-Han Relations in Contemporary Xinjiang. Leiden: Brill. On Mongols: Uradyn Erden Bulag. 2010. Collaborative Nationalism: The Politics of Friendship on China's Mongolian Frontier. Lanham: Rowman Littlefield; David Sneath. 2000. Changing Inner Mongolia : Pastoral Mongolian Society and the Chinese State. Oxford: Oxford University Press.

Constructing and living in the nation: Andrew Kipnis. 2012. Constructing Commonality: Standardization and Modernization in Chinese

Nation-Building. In *Journal of Asian Studies*, pp. 731–55; Rachel Murphy & Vanessa L. Fong. 2009. Media, Identity, and Struggle in Twenty-First-Century China London: Routledge; Pál Nyíri. 2006. Scenic Spots: Chinese Tourism, the State, and Cultural Authority. Seattle: University of Washington Press; Guobin Yang. 2009. The Power of the Internet in China: Citizen Activism Online. New York: Columbia University Press; William A. Callahan. 2010. China: The Pessoptimist Nation. Oxford: Oxford University Press; Vanessa Fong. 2004. Filial Nationalism among Teenagers with Global Identities. In *American Ethnologist*, pp. 631–48; Pál Nyíri et al. 2010. China's Cosmopolitan Nationalists: 'Heroes' and 'Traitors' of the 2008 Olympics. In *The China Journal*; Lisa Hoffman. 2010. Patriotic Professionalism in Urban China: Fostering Talent. Philadelphia: Temple University Press.

Migration and diversity: On the accommodation of diversity in late Imperial cities, see William T. Rowe. 1989. Hankow: Conflict and Community in a Chinese City, 1976-1895. Stanford: Stanford University Press. On migrant communities in post-reform cities, see Biao Xiang. 2005. Transcending Boundaries. Zhejiangcun: The Story of a Migrant Village in Beijing. Leiden: Brill. On Han Chinese migrants in minority areas, see Mette Halskov Hansen. 2005. Frontier People: Han Settlers in Minority Areas of China. London: Hurst. On the rising prominence of foreign residents, see Frank N. Pieke. 2012. Immigrant China. In *Modern China*, pp. 40–77.

Heritage, history and identity: for an overview, see Tami Blumenfeld & Helaine Silverman. 2013. Cultural Heritage Politics in China. New York: Springer; Robert J. Shepherd & Larry Yu. 2013. Heritage Management, Tourism, and Governance in China: Managing the Past to Serve the Present. New York: Springer. On case studies on the use of history and heritage to assert local or non-Han belonging, see Stevan Harrell & Yongxiang Li. 2003. The History of the History of the Yi: Anthropological Narratives of Recovery and Progress in China. In *Modern China*, pp. 362–96: Sage Publications, Inc.; Ralph A. Litzinger. 2000. Other Chinas: The Yao and the Politics of National Belonging. Durham: Duke University Press; Sara L. Friedman. 2006. Intimate Politics: Marriage, the Market, and State Power in Southeastern China. Cambridge: Harvard University East Asian Center, chapter 6; John M. Flower. 2004. A Road Is Made: Roads, Temples, and Historical Memory in Ya'an County, Sichuan. In *The Journal of Asian Studies*, pp. 649–85: Association for Asian Studies; Emily Chao. 2012. Lijiang Stories: Shamans, Taxi Drivers, and Runaway Brides in Reform-era China. Seattle: University of Washington Press; Tim Oakes. 2013. Heritage as Improvement: Cultural Display and Contested Governance in Rural China.

In *Modern China*, pp. 380–407; Sigrid Schmalzer. 2008. The People's Peking Man: Popular Science and Human Identity in Twentieth-Century China. Chicago: University of Chicago Press; Martin Saxer. 2014. Re-Fusing Ethnicity and Religion: An Experiment on Tibetan Grounds. In *Journal of Current Chinese Affairs*, pp. 181–204.

Red tourism: Yiping Li et al. 2010. Red Tourism: Sustaining Communist Identity in a Rapidly Changing China. In *Journal of Tourism and Cultural Change*, pp. 101–19; Yoko Takayama. 2012. Red Tourism in China. In *India, Russia, China: Comparative Studies on Eurasian Culture and Society*, ed. Tetsuo Mochizuki, Shiho Maeda. Sapporo: Slavic Research Center, Hokkaido University113-130.

Confucianism: Anna Sun. 2013. Confucianism as a World Religion: Contested Histories and Contemporary Realities. Princeton: Princeton University Press; for a partisan essay on the Confucian renaissance, see Daniel A. Bell. 2008. China's New Confucianism:Politics and Everyday Life in a Changing Society. Princeton: Princeton University Press.

Minority transnational connections: on minority nationality overseas Chinese, see Elena Barabantseva. 2012. Who Are 'Overseas Chinese Ethnic Minorities'? China's Search for Transnational Ethnic Unity. In *Modern China*, pp. 78–109; Chris Vasantkumar. 2012. What Is This "Chinese" in Overseas Chinese? Sojourn Work and the Place of China's Minority Nationalities in Extraterritorial Chinese-ness. In *The Journal of Asian Studies*, pp. 423–46. On Chinese Korean transnational and translocal links, see Outi Luova. 2006. Mobilizing Transnational Ethnic Linkages for Economic Development: The Case of Yanbian Korean Autonomous Prefecture. In *China Information*, pp. 33–68 and Wooyeal Paik & Myungsik Ham. 2012. From Autonomous Areas to Non-Autonomous Areas: The Politics of Korean Minority Migration in Contemporary China. In *Modern China*, pp. 110–33. On the hajj and Muslim transnationalism, see Jackie Armijo. 2008. Chinese *Madrasas* and linkages to Islamic Schools Abroad. In *The Madrasa in Asia: Political Activism and Transnational Linkages*, ed. Farish A. Noor, Yoginder Sikand, Martin Van Bruinessen, pp. 169–87. Amsterdam: Amsterdam University Press; Maris Boyd Gilette. 2003. The 'Glorious Returns' of Chinese Pilgrims to Mecca In *Living with Separation in China: Anthropological Accounts*, ed. Charles Stafford, pp. 130–57. London: Routledge. On the Miao diaspora, see Nicholas Tapp. 2010. The Impossibility of Self: An Essay on the Hmong Diaspora. Berlin: LIT; On Hui modernity and cosmopolitanism, see Maris Boyd Gilette. 2000. Between Mecca and Beijing: Modernization and Consumption Among Urban Chinese Muslims.

Stanford: Stanford University Press. On Dai transnational connections, see Susan K. McCarthy. 2009. Communist Multiculturalism: Ethnic Revival in Southwest China. Seattle: University of Washington Press, chapter 3.

Chapter 6: Not Just a Chinese Century

Military modernization: Ji You. 2016. China's Military Transformation. Cambridge: Polity; David Lampton. 2008. The Three Faces of Chinese Power: Might, Money, and Minds. Berkeley: University of California Press, chapter 2; Sarah Kirchberger. 2015. Assessing China's Naval Power: Technological Innovation, Economic Constraints, and Strategic Implications. Berlin: Springer; David Shambaugh. 2012. China Goes Global: The Partial Power. New York: Oxford University Press, chapter 7.

China's role in global governance: Peter Ferdinand & Jue Wang. 2013. China and the IMF: From Mimicry towards Pragmatic International Institutional Pluralism. In *International Affairs*, pp. 895–910: Blackwell Publishing Ltd; Iain Alistair Johnston. 2008. Social States: China and International Institutions, 1980–2000. Princeton: Princeton University Press; Ann Kent. 2010. Beyond Compliance: China, International Organizations, and Global Security. Stanford: Stanford University Press; David Shambaugh. 2012. China Goes Global: The Partial Power. New York: Oxford University Press, chapter 4; On environmental diplomacy and climate change, see Joanna Lewis. 2013. China's Environmental Diplomacy: Climate Change, Domestic Politics, and International Engagement. In *China across the Divide: The Domestic and Global in Politics and Society*, ed. Rosemary Foot, pp. 200–25. Oxford: Oxford University Press.

Cosmopolitan pre-1949 Shanghai: Robert A. Bickers. 2011. The Scramble for China: Foreign Devils in the Qing Empire: 1832–1914. London: Allen Lane; Karl Gerth. 2003. China Made: Consumer Culture and the Creation of the Chinese Nation. Cambridge, Massachusetts: Harvard University Asia Center; Wen-hsin Yeh. 2008. Shanghai Splendor: A Cultural History, 1843–1949. Berkeley: University of California Press.

History of the overseas Chinese: The doyen of the field of overseas Chinese studies is Wang Gungwu, see Gregor Benton & Hong Liu. 2004. Diasporic Chinese Ventures: The Life and Work of Wang Gungwu. London: RoutledgeCurzon; an authoritative, albeit somewhat outdated source of information is Lynn Pan. 1998. The Encyclopedia of the Chinese Overseas. Singapore: Archipelago Press and Landmark Books.Joanna Lewis. 2013. China's Environmental Diplomacy: Climate Change, Domestic Politics, and International

Engagement. In *China across the Divide: The Domestic and Global in Politics and Society*, ed. Rosemary Foot, pp. 200–25. Oxford: Oxford University Press.

Investment in Africa: Deborah Brautigam. 2009. The Dragon's Gift: The Real Story of China in Africa. Oxford; Shaun Breslin. 2013. China and the South: Objectives, Actors and Interactions. In *Development and Change*, pp. 1273–94; Deborah Bräutigam & Xiaoyang Tang. 2014. 'Going Global in Groups': Structural Transformation and China's Special Economic Zones Overseas. In *World Development*, pp. 78–91; Deborah Bräutigam. 2015. Will Africa Feed China? New York: Oxford University Press; Hairong Yan & Barry Sautman. 2010. Chinese Farms in Zambia: From Socialist to Agro-Imperialist Engagement? In *African and Asian Studies*, pp. 307–33.

Globalization of Chinese firms: Joel Backaler. 2014. China Goes West: Everything You Need to Know about Chinese Companies Going Global. Houndmills: Palgrave Macmillian; Arthur Yeung et al. 2011. The Globalization of Chinese Companies: Strategies for Conquering International Markets. Singapore: John Wiley & Sons (Asia).

Confucius Institutes: Marshall Sahlins. 2015. Confucius Institutes: Academic Malware. Chicago: Prickly Paradigm Press; for a more detached assessment, see Christopher R. Hughes. 2014. Confucius Institutes and the University: Distinguishing the Political Mission from the Cultural. In *Issues & Studies*, pp. 45–83.

References

Anagnost, Ann. 2004. The Corporeal Politics of Quality (*Suzhi*). *Public Culture* 16,12:189–208.

Anderson, Benedict. 1991. *Imagined Communities: Reflections on the Origins and Spread of Nationalism*. London: Verso.

Anderson, Eric C. 2012. *Sinophobia: The Huawei Story*. n.p.: Eric C. Anderson.

Ang, Yuen Yuen. 2012. Counting Cadres: A Comparative View of the Size of China's Public Employment. *China Quarterly* 211:676–96.

Apter, David E., Saich, Tony. 1994. *Revolutionary Discourse in Mao's Republic*. Cambridge, MA: Harvard University Press.

Arendt, Hannah. 1951. *The Origins of Totalitarianism*. New York: World.

Armijo, Jackie. 2008. Chinese Madrasas and Linkages to Islamic Schools Abroad. In *The Madrasa in Asia: Political Activism and Transnational Linkages*, ed. Farish A. Noor, Yoginder Sikand, Martin Van Bruinessen, pp. 169–87. Amsterdam: Amsterdam University Press.

Ashiwa, Yoshiko, Wank, David L. 2006. The Politics of a Reviving Buddhist Temple: State, Association, and Religion in Southeast China. *Journal of Asian Studies* 65,2:337–59.

Backaler, Joel. 2014. *China Goes West: Everything You Need to Know about Chinese Companies Going Global*. Houndsmills, UK: Palgrave Macmillan.

Barabantseva, Elena. 2011. *Overseas Chinese, Ethnic Minorities, and Nationalism: De-Centering China*. London: Routledge.

2012. Who Are 'Overseas Chinese Ethnic Minorities'? China's Search for Transnational Ethnic Unity. *Modern China* 38,1:78–109.

Barfield, Thomas J. 1989. *The Perilous Frontier: Nomadic Empires and China, 221 B.C. to A.D. 1757*. Oxford: Blackwell.

Barmé, Geremie R. 1999. *In the Red: On Contemporary Chinese Culture*. New York: Columbia University Press.

Béja, Jean-Phillipe, Fu, Hualing, Pils, Eva, eds. 2012. *Liu Xiaobo, Charter 08 and the Challenges of Political Reform in China*. Hong Kong: Hong Kong University Press.

Bell, Daniel A. 2008. *China's New Confucianism: Politics and Everyday Life in a Changing Society*. Princeton, NJ: Princeton University Press.

Bellér-Hann, Ildikó. 2014. The Bulldozer State: Chinese Socialist Development in Xinjiang. In *Ethnographies of the State in Central Asia*, ed. Madeleine Reeves, Johan Rasanayagam, Judith Beyer, pp. 173–97. Bloomington: Indiana University Press.

Benton, Gregor. 1992. *Mountain Fires: The Red Army's Three-Year War in South China, 1934–1938*. Berkeley: University of California Press.

1999. *New Fourth Army: Communist Resistance along the Yangtze and the Huai, 1938–1941*. Richmond, UK: Curzon.

Benton, Gregor, Liu, Hong, eds. 2004. *Diasporic Chinese Ventures: The Life and Work of Wang Gungwu*. London: RoutledgeCurzon.

Bernstein, Thomas P., Lü, Xiaobo. 2003. *Taxation without Representation in Contemporary Rural China*. Cambridge: Cambridge University Press.

Bian, Yanjie. 2002. Chinese Social Stratification and Social Mobility. *Annual Review of Sociology* 28:91–116.

Bickers, Robert A. 2011. *The Scramble for China: Foreign Devils in the Qing Empire: 1832–1914*. London: Allen Lane.

Blumenfeld, Tami, Silverman, Helaine, eds. 2013. *Cultural Heritage Politics in China*. New York: Springer.

Bovingdon, Gardner. 2010. *The Uyghurs: Strangers in Their Own Land*. New York: Columbia University Press.

Brady, Anne-Marie. 2008. *Marketing Dictatorship: Propaganda and Thought Work in Contemporary China*. Lanham, MD: Rowman and Littlefield.

Brandtstädter, Susanne. 2011. The Law Cuts Both Ways: Rural Legal Activism and Citizenship Struggles in Neosocialist China. *Economy and Society* 40,2:266–88.

Bräutigam, Deborah. 2009. *The Dragon's Gift: The Real Story of China in Africa*: Oxford: Oxford University Press.

2015. *Will Africa Feed China?* New York: Oxford University Press.

Bräutigam, Deborah, Tang, Xiaoyang. 2014. 'Going Global in Groups': Structural Transformation and China's Special Economic Zones Overseas. *World Development* 63,0:78–91.

Bray, David. 2005. *Social Space and Governance in China: The Danwei System from Origins to Reform*. Stanford, CA: Stanford University Press.

Breslin, Shaun. 2013. China and the South: Objectives, Actors and Interactions. *Development and Change* 44,6:1273–94.

Brødsgaard, Kjeld Erik. 2012. Politics and Business Groups Formation in China: The Party in Control? *China Quarterly* 211:625–48.

Brook, Timothy. 1999. *Quelling the People: The Military Suppression of the Beijing Democracy Movement*. Stanford, CA: Stanford University Press.

2009. The Politics of Religion: Late-Imperial Origins of the Regulatory State. In *Making Religion, Making the State: The Politics of Religion in Modern China*, ed. Yoshiko Ashiwa, David L. Wank, pp. 22–42. Stanford, CA: Stanford University Press.

Brown, Melissa J. 2004. *Is Taiwan Chinese? The Impact of Culture, Power, and Migration on Changing Identities*. Berkeley: University of California Press.

Bulag, Uradyn Erden. 2010. *Collaborative Nationalism: The Politics of Friendship on China's Mongolian Frontier*. Lanham, MD: Rowman and Littlefield.

Cai, Yongshun. 2010. *Collective Resistance in China: Why Popular Protests Succeed or Fail*. Stanford, CA: Stanford University Press.

Callahan, William A. 2010. *China: The Pessoptimist Nation*. Oxford: Oxford University Press.

2013. *China Dreams: 20 Visions of the Future*. Oxford: Oxford University Press.

2014. Citizen Ai: Warrior, Jester and Middleman. Working Paper Series 212. Asian Research Institute, online at www.ari.nus.edu.sg/docs/wps/wps14_212.pdf.

Cao, Nanlai. 2011. *Constructing China's Jerusalem: Christians, Power, and Place in Contemporary Wenzhou*. Stanford, CA: Stanford University Press.

Chan, Chris King-Chi, Ngai, Pun. 2009. The Making of a New Working Class? A Study of Collective Actions of Migrant Workers in South China. *China Quarterly* 198:287–303.

Chan, Jenny, Selden, Mark. 2014. China's Rural Migrant Workers, the State, and Labor Politics. *Critical Asian Studies* 46,4:599–620.

Chang, Ha-Joon. 2007. *Bad Samaritans: The Guilty Secrets of Rich Nations and the Threat to Global Prosperity*. London: Random House.

Chao, Emily. 2012. *Lijiang Stories: Shamans, Taxi Drivers, and Runaway Brides in Reform-era China*. Seattle: University of Washington Press.

Chau, Adam Yuet. 2006. *Miraculous Response: Doing Popular Religion in Contemporary China*. Stanford, CA: Stanford University Press.

Chen, Nancy. 2003. *Breathing Spaces: Qigong, Psychiatry, and Healing in China*. New York: Columbia University Press.

Chen, Xi. 2012. *Social Protest and Contentious Authoritarianism in China*. Cambridge: Cambridge University Press.

Cho, Mun Young. 2013. *The Specter of 'the People': Urban Poverty in Northeast China*. Ithaca, NY: Cornell University Press.

Coase, Ronald, Wang, Ning. 2012. *How China Became Capitalist*. Houndsmills, UK: Macmillan.

Cohen, Myron L. 2005. Being Chinese: The Peripheralization of Traditional Identity. In *Kinship, Contract, Community, and State: Anthropological Perspectives on China*, pp. 39–58. Stanford, CA: Stanford University Press.

Crook, David, Crook, Isabel. 2010[1959]. *Revolution in a Chinese Village: Ten Mile Inn*. Abingdon, UK: Routledge.

Crossley, Pamela Kyle. 2005. Nationality and Difference in China: The Post-imperial Dilemma. In *The Teleology of the Modern Nation-State: Japan and China*, ed. Joshua Fogel, pp. 138–55. Philadelphia: University of Pennsylvania Press.

Cui, Zhiyuan. 2011. Partial Intimations of the Coming Whole: The Chongqing Experiment in Light of the Theories of Henry George, James Meade, and Antonio Gramsci. *Modern China* 36,6:646–60.

De Kloet, Jeroen. 2010. *China with a Cut: Globalisation, Urban Youth and Popular Music*. Amsterdam: Amsterdam University Press.

Dikötter, Frank. 1992. *The Discourse of Race in Modern China*. London: Hurst.

2010. *Mao's Great Famine: The History of China's Most Devastating Catastrophe, 1958–1962*. London: Bloomsbury.

2013. *The Tragedy of Liberation: A History of the Chinese Revolution, 1945–1957*. London: Bloomsbury.

Dirlik, Arif. 1989. *The Origins of Chinese Communism*. New York: Oxford University Press.

Duara, Prasenjit. 1988. *Culture, Power, and the State: Rural North China, 1900–1942*. Stanford, CA: Stanford University Press.

1995. *Rescuing History from the Nation: Questioning Narratives of Modern China*. Chicago: University of Chicago Press.

DuBois, Thomas David. 2005. *The Sacred Village: Social Change and Religious Life in Rural North China*. Honolulu: University of Hawai'i Press.

Duckett, Jane. 2011. *The Chinese State's Retreat from Health: Policy and the Politics of Retrenchment*. Abingdon, UK: Routledge.

Durkheim, Emile. 1965. *The Elementary Forms of the Religious Life*. New York: Free Press.

Eaton, Sarah. 2013. Political Economy of the Advancing State: The Case of China's Airlines Reform. *China Journal* 69:64–86.

Eaton, Sarah, Kostka, Genia. 2014. Authoritarian Environmentalism Undermined? Local Leaders' Time Horizons and Environmental Policy Implementation in China. *China Quarterly* 218:359–80.

Economy, Elizabeth. 2004. *The River Runs Black: The Environmental Challenge to China's Future*. Ithaca, NY: Cornell University Press.

Eggleston, Karen, Oi, Jean C., Rozelle, Scott, Sun, Ang, Walder, Andrew, Zhou, Xueguang. 2013. Will Demographic Change Slow China's Rise? *Journal of Asian Studies* 72,3:505–18.

Elliott, Mark C. 2001. *The Manchu Way: The Eight Banners and Ethnic Identity in Late Imperial China*. Stanford, CA: Stanford University Press.

    2012. Hushuo: The Northern Other and the Naming of the Han Chinese. In *Critical Han Studies: The History, Representation, and Identity of China's Majority*, ed. Thomas S. Mullaney, James Leibold, Stéphane Gros, Eric Vanden Bussche, pp. 173–90. Berkeley: University of California Press.

European Commission, Ministry of Education in China. 2011. *EU-China Student and Academic Staff Mobility: Present Situation and Future Developments*.

Farquhar, Judith, Zhang, Qicheng. 2012. *Ten Thousand Things: Nurturing Life in Contemporary Beijing*. New York: Zone Books.

Farrer, James. 2002. *Opening Up: Youth Sex Culture and Market Reform in Shanghai*. Chicago: University of Chicago Press.

Fei, Xiaotong. 1989. *Zhonghua minzu duoyuan yiti geju* (The pattern of unity in diversity of the Chinese nation). Beijing: Zhongyang Minzu Xueyuan.

Ferdinand, Peter, Wang, Jue. 2013. China and the IMF: From Mimicry towards Pragmatic International Institutional Pluralism. *International Affairs* 89,4:895–910.

Fewsmith, Joseph. 2013. *The Logic and Limits of Political Reform in China*. Cambridge: Cambridge University Press.

Flower, John M. 2004. A Road Is Made: Roads, Temples, and Historical Memory in Ya'an County, Sichuan. *Journal of Asian Studies* 63,3:649–85.

Fong, Vanessa. 2004. Filial Nationalism among Teenagers with Global Identities. *American Ethnologist* 31,4:631–48.

    2004. *Only Hope: Coming of Age under China's One-Child Policy*. Stanford, CA: Stanford University Press.

    2011. *Paradise Redefined: Transnational Chinese Students and the Quest for Flexible Citizenship in the Developed World*. Stanford, CA: Stanford University Press.

Frazier, Mark W. 2010. *Socialist Insecurity: Pensions and the Politics of Uneven Development in China*. Ithaca, NY: Cornell University Press.

Frenkiel, Émilie. 2015. *Conditional Democracy: The Contemporary Debate on Political Reform in Chinese Universities*. Colchester, UK: ECPR Press.

Friedman, Sara L. 2006. *Intimate Politics: Marriage, the Market, and State Power in Southeastern China.* Cambridge, MA: Harvard University East Asian Center.

Fu, Hualing, Cullen, Richard. 2008. Weiquan (Rights Protection) Lawyering in an Authoritarian State: Building a Culture of Public-Interest Lawyering. *China Journal* 59:111–27.

Fukuyama, Francis. 1992. *The End of History and the Last Man.* New York: Free Press.

Gallagher, Mary Elizabeth. 2005. *Contagious Capitalism: Globalization and the Politics of Labor in China.* Princeton, NJ: Princeton University Press.

Gellner, Ernest. 1983. *Nations and Nationalism.* Ithaca, NY: Cornell University Press.

Gerth, Karl. 2003. *China Made: Consumer Culture and the Creation of the Chinese Nation.* Cambridge, MA: Harvard University Asia Center.

2010. *As China Goes, So Goes the World: How Chinese Consumers Are Transforming Everything.* New York: Hill and Wang.

Giersch, C. Patterson. 2006. *Asian Borderlands: The Transformation of Qing China's Yunnan Frontier.* Cambridge, MA: Harvard University Press.

Gijsberts, Mérove, Huijnk, Willem, Vogels, Ria. 2011. *Chinese Nederlanders: van horeca naar hogeschool* (Chinese Dutch: from catering trade to university). The Hague: Sociaal en Cultureel Planbureau.

Gilette, Maris Boyd. 2000. *Between Mecca and Beijing: Modernization and Consumption among Urban Chinese Muslims.* Stanford, CA: Stanford University Press.

2003. The 'Glorious Returns' of Chinese Pilgrims to Mecca. In *Living with Separation in China: Anthropological Accounts*, ed. Charles Stafford, pp. 130–57. London: Routledge.

Gilley, Bruce. 2010. Democratic Enclaves in Authoritarian Regimes. *Democratization* 17,3:389–415.

Gold, Thomas, Guthrie, Doug, Wank, David L., eds. 2002. *Social Connections in China: Institutions, Culture, and the Changing Nature of Guanxi.* Cambridge: Cambridge University Press.

Goldman, Merle. 1994. *Sowing the Seeds of Democracy in China: Political Reform in the Deng Xiaoping Era.* Cambridge, MA: Harvard University Press.

Goldstein, Melvyn C. 2013. *A History of Modern Tibet, Volume 3: The Storm Clouds Descend, 1955–1957.* Berkeley: University of California Press.

Goodman, David S. G., ed. 2008. *The New Rich in China: Future Rulers, Present Lives.* London: Routledge.

Goossaert, Vincent, Palmer, David A. 2011. *The Religious Question in Modern China*. Chicago: University of Chicago Press.

Greenhalgh, Susan. 2008. *Just One Child: Science and Policy in Deng's China*. Berkeley: University of California Press.

Greenhalgh, Susan, Winckler, Edwin A. 2005. *Governing China's Population: From Leninist to Neoliberal Biopolitics*. Stanford, CA: Stanford University Press.

Grillot, Caroline. 2012. Cross-Border Marriages between Vietnamese Women and Chinese Men: Their Integration of Otherness and the Impact of Popular Representations. In *Wind over Water: Migration in an East Asian Context*, ed. David Haines, Keiko Yamanaka, Shinji Yamashita, pp. 125–37. New York: Berghahn.

Guo, Yingjie. 2008. Class, Stratum and Group: The Politics of Description and Prescription. In *The New Rich in China: Future Rulers, Present Lives*, ed. David S. G. Goodman, pp. 38–52. Abingdon, UK: Routledge.

Halskov Hansen, Mette. 2005. *Frontier People: Han Settlers in Minority Areas of China*. London: Hurst.

Hanser, Amy. 2008. *Service Encounters: Class, Gender, and the Market for Social Distinction in Urban China*. Stanford, CA: Stanford University Press.

Harrell, Stevan, Li, Yongxiang. 2003. The History of the History of the Yi: Anthropological Narratives of Recovery and Progress in China. *Modern China* 29,3:362–96.

Harrison, Henrietta. 2001. *China*. London: Bloomsbury.

2013. *The Missionary's Curse and Other Tales from a Chinese Catholic Village*. Berkeley: University of California Press.

Hathaway, Michael. 2013. *Environmental Winds: Making the Global in Southwest China*. Berkeley: University of California Press.

Hayhoe, Ruth, Li, Jun, Lin, Jing, Zha, Qiang, eds. 2011. *Portraits of 21st Century Chinese Universities: In the Move to Mass Higher Education*. Dordrecht, Netherlands: Springer.

He, Baogang. 2007. *Rural Democracy in China: The Role of Village Elections*. Houndsmills, UK: Palgrave Macmillan.

Heberer, Thomas. 2007. *Doing Business in Rural China: Liangshan's New Ethnic Entrepreneurs*. Seattle: University of Washington Press.

Heberer, Thomas, Senz, Anja. 2011. Streamlining Local Behaviour through Communication, Incentives and Control: A Case Study of Local Environmental Policies in China. *Journal of Current Chinese Affairs* 40,3:77–112.

Heilmann, Sebastian, Perry, Elizabeth. 2011. Embracing Uncertainty: Guerrilla Policy Style and Adaptive Governance in China. In *Mao's Invisible*

Hand: The Political Foundations of Adaptive Governance in China, ed. Sebastian Heilmann, Elizabeth Perry, pp. 1–29. Cambridge, MA: Harvard University Asia Center.

Heins Potter, Sulamith, Potter, Jack M. 1990. *China's Peasants: The Anthropology of a Revolution*. Cambridge: Cambridge University Press.

Hildebrandt, Timothy. 2013. *Social Organizations and the Authoritarian State in China*. Cambridge: Cambridge University Press.

Hillman, Ben. 2010. Factions and Spoils: Examining Political Behavior within the Local State in China. *China Journal* 64:1–18.

Hoffman, Lisa. 2010. *Patriotic Professionalism in Urban China: Fostering Talent*. Philadelphia: Temple University Press.

Hofman, Irna. 2015. Opening up markets or fostering a new satellite state? Detangling the impetuses of Chinese land investments in Tajikistan. Unpublished paper.

Holz, Carsten A. 2007. Have China Scholars All Been Bought? *Far Eastern Economic Review* 170,3:36–40.

Howell, Jude. 2014. NGOs and Service Sub-contracting: New Form of Social Welfare or Social Appeasement? Paper presented at the conference Governance, Adaptability and System Stability under Contemporary One-Party Rule: Comparative Perspectives, Nanchang, 27–29 March.

Hsing, You-tien. 2010. *The Great Urban Transformation: Politics of Land and Property in China*. Oxford: Oxford University Press.

Hsu, Francis L. K. 1967[1948]. *Under the Ancestors' Shadow: Kinship, Personality and Social Mobility in China*. Stanford, CA: Stanford University Press.

Hsueh, Roselyn. 2011. *China's Regulatory State: A New Strategy for Globalization*. Ithaca, NY: Cornell University Press.

Hualing, Fu, Cullen, Richard. 2011. Climbing the Weiquan Ladder: A Radicalizing Process for Rights-Protection Lawyers. *China Quarterly* 205:40–59.

Huang, Yasheng. 2003. *Selling China: Foreign Direct Investment during the Reform Era*. Cambridge: Cambridge University Press.

2008. *Capitalism with Chinese Characteristics: Entrepreneurship and the State*. Cambridge: Cambridge University Press.

Hughes, Christopher R. 2014. Confucius Institutes and the University: Distinguishing the Political Mission from the Cultural. *Issues and Studies* 50,4:45–83.

Iwabuchi, Koichi. 2002. *Recentering Globalization: Popular Culture and Japanese Transnationalism*. Durham, NC: Duke University Press.

Jacques, Martin. 2012. *When China Rules the World: The End of the Western World and the Birth of a New Global Order*. London: Penguin.

Jeffreys, Elaine. 2004. *China, Sex and Prostitution*. London: Routledge-Curzon.

ed. 2006. *Sex and Sexuality in China*. Abingdon, UK: Routledge.

Jing, Jun. 2003. Dams and Dreams: A Return-to-Homeland Movement in Northwest China. In *Living with Separation in China: Anthropological Accounts*, ed. Charles Stafford, pp. 113–29. London: Routledge.

Johnston, Iain Alistair. 2008. *Social States: China and International Institutions, 1980–2000*. Princeton, NJ: Princeton University Press.

Jowitt, Ken. 1992. The Leninist Phenomenon. In *New World Disorder: The Leninist Extinction*, pp. 1–49. Berkeley: University of California Press.

Kam, Lucette Yip Lo. 2013. *Shanghai Lalas: Female Tongzhi Communities and Politics in Urban China*. Hong Kong: Hong Kong University Press.

Keane, Michael. 2011. *China's New Creative Clusters: Governance, Human Capital and Investment*. London: Routledge.

Kennedy, Scott. 2005. *The Business of Lobbying in China*. Cambridge, MA: Harvard University Press.

Kent, Anne. 1999. *China, the United Nations, and Human Rights – The Limits of Compliance*: Philadelphia: University of Pennsylvania Press.

Kim, Jaesok. 2013. *Chinese Labor in a Korean Factory: Class, Ethnicity, and Productivity on the Shop Floor in Globalizing China*. Stanford, CA: Stanford University Press.

Kipnis, Andrew. 2007. Neoliberalism Reified: *Suzhi* Discourse and Tropes of Neoliberalism in the People's Republic of China. *Journal of the Royal Anthropological Institute (N.S.)* 13:383–400.

2011. *Governing Educational Desire: Culture, Politics, and Schooling in China*. Chicago: University of Chicago Press.

2012. Constructing Commonality: Standardization and Modernization in Chinese Nation-Building. *Journal of Asian Studies* 71,3:731–55.

Kirchberger, Sarah. 2012. Evaluating Maritime Power: The Example of China. In *Power in the 21st century: International Security and International Political Economy in a Changing World*, ed. Enrico Fels, Jan-Frederik Kremer, Katharina Kronenberg, pp. 151–75. Berlin: Springer.

Knight, John. 2014. Inequality in China: An Overview. *The World Bank Research Observer* 29,1:1–19.

Kuruvilla, Sarosh, Lee, Ching Kwan, Gallagher, Mary E., eds. 2011. *From Iron Rice Bowl to Informalization: Markets, Workers, and the State in a Changing China*. Ithaca, NY: ILR Press.

Laliberté, André, Palmer, David, Wu, Keping. 2011. Religious Philanthropy and Chinese Civil Society. In *Chinese Religions: Communities,*

Practices and Contemporary Issues, ed. David A. Palmer, Glenn Shive, Philip Wickeri, pp. 139–51. New York: Oxford University Press.

Landry, Pierre. 2008. *Decentralized Authoritarianism in China: The Communist Party's Control of Local Elites in the Post-Mao Era*. Cambridge: Cambridge University Press.

Lardy, Nicholas R. 2014. *Markets over Mao: The Rise of Private Business in China*. Washington, DC: Peterson Institute for International Economics.

Laruelle, Marlène, Peyrouse, Sébastien. 2012. *The Chinese Question in Central Asia: Domestic Order, Social Change, and the Chinese Factor*. London: Hurst.

Latham, Kevin, Thompson, Stuart, Klein, Jacob, eds. 2006. *Consuming China: Approaches to Cultural Change in Contemporary China* London: Routledge.

Lattimore, Owen. 1962[1940]. *Inner Asian Frontiers of China*. Boston: Beacon Press.

Lee, Ching Kwan. 2007. *Against the Law: Labor Protest in China's Rustbelt and Sunbelt*. Berkeley: University of California Press.

Lee, Ching Kwan, Shen, Yuan. 2009. China: The Paradox and Possibility of a Public Sociology of Labor. *Work and Occupations* 36,2:110–25.

2011. The Anti-solidarity Machine? Labor Non-governmental Organizations in China. In *From Iron Rice Bowl to Informalization: Markets, Workers, and the State in a Changing China*, ed. Sarosh Kuruvilla, Ching Kwan Lee, Mary E. Gallagher, pp. 173–87. Ithaca, NY: ILR Press.

Lee, Ching Kwan, Zhang, Yonghong. 2013. The Power of Instability: Unraveling the Microfoundations of Bargained Authoritarianism in China. *American Journal of Sociology* 118,6:1475–508.

Lee, James Z., Wang, Feng. 1999. *One Quarter of Humanity, Malthusian Mythology and Chinese Realities 1700–2000*. Cambridge, MA: Harvard University Press.

Leibold, James. 2012. Searching for Han: Early Twentieth-Century Narratives of Chinese Origins and Development. In *Critical Han Studies: The History, Representation, and Identity of China's Majority*, ed. Thomas S. Mullaney, James Leibold, Stéphane Gros, Eric Vanden Bussche, pp. 210–33. Berkeley: University of California Press.

2013. *Ethnic Policy in China: Is Reform Inevitable?* Honolulu: East-West Center.

Leonard, Mark. 2008. *What Does China Think?* London: Fourth Estate.

ed. 2012. *China 3.0*. London: European Council on Foreign Relations.

Levinson, Joseph R. 1958, 1964, 1965. *Confucian China and Its Modern Fate: A Trilogy*. Berkeley: University of California Press.

Li, Lanqing. 2009. *Breaking Through: The Birth of China's Opening-Up Policy.* Hong Kong: Oxford University Press.

Li, Lianjiang, Liu, Mingxing, O'Brien, Kevin J. 2012. Petitioning Beijing: The High Tide of 2003–2006. *China Quarterly* 210:313–34.

Li, Linda Chelan. 2012. *Rural Tax Reform in China: Policy Processes and Institutional Change.* Abingdon, UK: Routledge.

Li, Pengtao. 2010. Zhong-Fei guanxi de fazhan yu Feizhou Zhongguo xin yimin (The development of Chinese-African relations and new Chinese migrants in Africa). *Huaqiao Huaren lishi yanjiu* 2010,4:24–30.

Li, Yiping, Hu, Zhi Yi, Zhang, Chao Zhi. 2010. Red Tourism: Sustaining Communist Identity in a Rapidly Changing China. *Journal of Tourism and Cultural Change* 8,1–2:101–19.

Lieberthal, Kenneth. 1980. *Revolution and Tradition in Tientsin, 1949–1952.* Stanford, CA: Stanford University Press.

Lieberthal, Kenneth, Oksenberg, Michel. 1988. *Policy Making in China: Leaders, Structures, and Processes.* Princeton, NJ: Princeton University Press.

Litzinger, Ralph A. 2000. *Other Chinas: The Yao and the Politics of National Belonging.* Durham, NC: Duke University Press.

Liu, Mingwei. 2011. 'Where There Are Workers, There Should Be Trade Unions': Union Organizing in the Era of Growing Informal Employment. In *From Iron Rice Bowl to Informalization: Markets, Workers, and the State in a Changing China*, ed. Sarosh Kuruvilla, Ching Kwan Lee,Mary E. Gallagher, pp. 157–72. Ithaca, NY: ILR Press.

Liu, Ye, Li, Zhigang, Breitung, Werner. 2012. The Social Networks of New-Generation Migrants in China's Urbanized Villages: A Case Study of Guangzhou. *Habitat International* 36:192–200.

Liu-Farrer, Gracia. 2011. *Labour Migration from China to Japan: International Students, Transnational Migrants.* London: Routledge.

Lora-Wainwright, Anna. 2013. *Fighting for Breath: Living Morally and Dying of Cancer in a Chinese Village.* Honolulu: University of Hawai'i Press.

Lora-Wainwright, Anna, Zhang, Yiyun, Wu, Yunmei, Van Rooij, Benjamin. 2012. Learning to Live with Pollution: The Making of Environmental Subjects in a Chinese Industrialised Village. *China Journal* 68: 106–24.

Luova, O. 2006. Mobilizing Transnational Ethnic Linkages for Economic Development: The Case of Yanbian Korean Autonomous Prefecture. *China Information* 20:33–68.

Ma, Emmanuel Mung. 2008. Chinese and China's Foreign Policy in Africa. *Journal of Chinese Overseas* 4,1:91–109.

MacFarquhar, Roderick, Schoenhals, Michael. 2006. *Mao's Last Revolution.* Cambridge, MA: Belknap Press of Harvard University Press.

Madsen, Richard. 1998. *China's Catholics: Tragedy and Hope in an Emerging Civil Society.* Berkeley: University of California Press.

Manion, Melanie. 2004. *Corruption by Design: Building Clean Government in Mainland China and Hong Kong.* Cambridge, MA: Harvard University Press.

McCarthy, Susan K. 2009. *Communist Multiculturalism: Ethnic Revival in Southwest China.* Seattle: University of Washington Press.

Mertha, Andrew C. 2005. China's 'Soft' Centralization: Shifting *Tiao/Kuai* Authority Relations. *China Quarterly* 184:791–810.

2009. 'Fragmented Authoritarianism 2.0': Political Pluralization of the Chinese Policy Process. *China Quarterly* 200:995–1012.

Mitter, Rana. 2014. *China's War with Japan, 1937–1945: The Struggle for Survival.* London: Penguin.

Moeran, Brian. 1984. Individual, Group and Seishin: Japan's Internal Cultural Debate. *Man, New Series* 19, 2:252–66.

Moser, David. 2013. An Invisible Path: 'Urban Buddhists' in Beijing and Their Search for Meaning. In *Restless China*, ed. Perry Link, Richard P. Madsen, Paul Pickowicz, pp. 167–90. Lanham, MD: Rowman and Littlefield.

Mullaney, Thomas S. 2011. *Coming to Terms with the Nation: Ethnic Classification in Modern China.* Berkeley: University of California Press.

Murphy, Rachel. 2002. *How Migrant Labor Is Changing Rural China.* Cambridge: Cambridge University Press.

Murphy, Rachel, Fong, Vanessa L., eds. 2009. *Media, Identity, and Struggle in Twenty-First-Century China.* London: Routledge.

Nathan, Andrew. 1973. A Factionalism Model for CCP Politics. *China Quarterly* 53:34–66.

2003. Authoritarian Resilience. *Journal of Democracy* 14,1:6–17.

2013. China at the Tipping Point? Foreseeing the Unforeseeable. *Journal of Democracy* 24,1:20–25.

Naughton, Barry. 2014. China's Economy: Complacency, Crisis and the Challenge of Reform. *Daedalus* 143,2:14–25.

Nee, Victor. 1989. Peasant Entrepreneurship and the Politics of Regulation in China. In *Remaking the Institutions of Socialism: China and Eastern Europe*, ed. Victor Nee, David Stark, pp. 169–207. Stanford, CA: Stanford University Press.

1989. A Theory of Market Transition: From Redistribution to Markets in State Socialism. *American Sociological Review* 54,5:663–81.

1996. The Emergence of a Market Society: Changing Mechanisms of Stratification in China. *American Journal of Sociology* 101,4:908–49.

Nee, Victor, Opper, Sonja. 2012. *Capitalism from Below: Markets and Institutional Change in China*. Cambridge, MA: Harvard University Press.

Nee, Victor, Su, Sijin. 1990. Institutional Change and Economic Growth in China: The View from the Villages. *Journal of Asian Studies* 49,1:3–25.

Nolan, Peter. 2001. *China in the Global Economy: National Champions, Industrial Policy and the Big Business Revolution*. Houndsmills, UK: Palgrave.

Nyíri, Pál. 2006. *Scenic Spots: Chinese Tourism, the State, and Cultural Authority*. Seattle: University of Washington Press.

Nyíri, Pál, Zhang, Juan, Varrall, Merriden. 2010. China's Cosmopolitan Nationalists: 'Heroes' and 'Traitors' of the 2008 Olympics. *The China Journal* 63:25–55.

Oakes, Tim. 2013. Heritage as Improvement: Cultural Display and Contested Governance in Rural China. *Modern China* 39,4:380–407.

O'Brien, Kevin J., Li, Lianjiang. 2006. *Rightful Resistance in Rural China*. Cambridge: Cambridge University Press.

Oi, Jean Chun. 1999. *Rural China Takes Off: Institutional Foundations of Economic Reform*. Berkeley: University of California Press.

Oi, Jean C., Han, Chaohua. 2011. China's Corporate Restructuring: A Multistep Process. In *Going Private in China: The Politics of Corporate Restructuring and System Reform*, ed. Jean C. Oi, pp. 18–37. Stanford, CA: Walter H. Shorenstein Asia-Pacific Research Center.

Oi, Jean C., Singer Babiarz, Kim, Zhang, Linxiu, Luo, Renfu, Rozelle, Scott. 2012. Shifting Fiscal Control to Limit Cadre Power in China's Townships and Villages. *China Quarterly* 211:649–75.

Oi, Jean C., Walder, Andrew G., eds. 1999. *Property Rights and Economic Reform in China*. Stanford, CA: Stanford University Press.

Osburg, John. 2013. *Anxious Wealth: Money and Morality among China's New Rich*. Stanford, CA: Stanford University Press.

Ownby, David. 2009. *Falun Gong and the Future of China*. Oxford: Oxford University Press.

Paik, Wooyeal, Ham, Myungsik. 2012. From Autonomous Areas to Non-autonomous Areas: The Politics of Korean Minority Migration in Contemporary China. *Modern China* 38,1:110–33.

Palmer, David A. 2007. *Qigong Fever: Body, Science and Utopia in China*. London: Hurst.

Pan, Lynn, ed. 1998. *The Encyclopedia of the Chinese Overseas*. Singapore: Archipelago Press and Landmark Books.

Park, Albert, Cai, Fang, Du, Yang. 2010. Can China Meet Her Employment Challenges? In *Growing Pains: Tensions and Opportunities in China's Transformation*, ed. Jean Oi, Scott Rozelle, Xueguang Zhou, pp. 27–55. Stanford, CA: Stanford Asia-Pacific Research Center.

Parkin, David. 1991. *Sacred Void: Spatial Images of Work and Ritual among the Giriama of Kenya*. Cambridge: Cambridge University Press.

Pearson, Margaret M. 1994. The Janus Face of Business Associations in China: Socialist Corporatism in Foreign Enterprises. *Australian Journal of Chinese Affairs* 31:25–46.

2005. The Business of Governing Business in China: Institutions and Norms of the Emerging Regulatory State. *World Politics* 57,2:296–322.

Peerenboom, Randall. 2002. *China's Long March toward Rule of Law*. Cambridge: Cambridge University Press.

Peng, Xizhe. 2011. China's Demographic History and Future Challenges. *Science* 333,6042:581–87.

Pieke, Frank N. 1995. Bureaucracy, Friends, and Money: The Growth of Capital Socialism in China. *Comparative Studies in Society and History* 37,3:494–518.

1996. *The Ordinary and the Extraordinary: An Anthropological Study of Chinese Reform and the 1989 People's Movement in Beijing*. London: Kegan Paul International.

2003. The Genealogical Mentality in Modern China. *Journal of Asian Studies* 62,1:101–28.

2009. *The Good Communist: Elite Training and State Building in Today's China*. Cambridge: Cambridge University Press.

2012. The Communist Party and Social Management in China. *China Information* 26,2:149–65.

2012. Immigrant China. *Modern China* 38,1:40–77.

2015. Communist Party Spirit Education in Contemporary China. Paper presented at the International Conference on 'The Chinese Communist Party in Action', organized by the East Asia Research Institute, National University of Singapore, 13–14 August.

Pieke, Frank N., Nyíri, Pál, Thunø, Mette, Ceccagno, Antonella. 2004. *Transnational Chinese: Fujianese Migrants in Europe*. Stanford, CA: Stanford University Press.

Pieke, Frank N., Speelman, Tabitha. 2016. Chinese Investment Strategies and Migration: Does Diaspora Matter? In *Chinese Migration and Economic Relations with Europe: The Silk Road Revisited*, ed. Marco Sanfilippo, Agnieszka Weinar, pp. 12–32. Abingdon, UK: Routledge.

Potter, Pitman. 2013. *China's Legal System*. Cambridge: Polity Press.

Ren, Xuefei. 2011. *Building Globalization: Transnational Architecture Production in Urban China*. Chicago: University of Chicago Press.

Rhoads, Edward J. M. 2000. *Manchu and Han: Ethnic Relations and Political Power in Late Qing and Early Republican China, 1861–1928*. Seattle: University of Washington Press.

Rhoads, Robert A., Wang, Xiaoyang, Shi, Xiaoguang, Chang, Yongcai. 2014. *China's Rising Research Universities: A New Era of Global Ambition*. Baltimore: Johns Hopkins University Press.

Rofel, Lisa. 2007. *Desiring China: Experiments in Neoliberalism, Sexuality, and Public Culture*. Durham, NC: Duke University Press.

Rowe, William T. 1989. *Hankow: Conflict and Community in a Chinese City, 1976–1895*. Stanford, CA: Stanford University Press.

Sahlins, Marshall. 2015. *Confucius Institutes: Academic Malware*. Chicago: Prickly Paradigm Press.

Saich, Tony. 1991. *The Origins of the First United Front in China: The Role of Sneevliet (alias Maring)*. Leiden, Netherlands: Brill.

Sassen, Saskia. 2006. *Territory, Authority, Rights: From Medieval to Global Assemblages*. Princeton, NJ: Princeton University Press.

Sautman, Barry. 2012. Paved with Good Intentions: Proposals to Curb Minority Rights and Their Consequences for China. *Modern China* 38,1:10–39.

Saxer, Martin. 2014. Re-fusing Ethnicity and Religion: An Experiment on Tibetan Grounds. *Journal of Current Chinese Affairs* 43,2:181–204.

Sceats, Sonya, Breslin, Shaun. 2012. *China and the International Human Rights System*. London: Chatham House.

Schmalzer, Sigrid. 2008. *The People's Peking Man: Popular Science and Human Identity in Twentieth-Century China*. Chicago: University of Chicago Press.

Schoenhals, Michael. 1992. *Doing Things with Words in Chinese Politics: Five Studies*. Berkeley, CA: Institute of East Asian Studies.

Schubert, Gunter, Ahlers, Anna L. 2012. *Participation and Empowerment at the Grassroots: Chinese Village Elections in Perspective*. Lanham, MD: Lexington.

Segal, Adam, Thun, Eric. 2001. Thinking Globally, Acting Locally: Local Governments, Industrial Sectors, and Development in China. *Politics and Society* 29,4:557–88.

Shambaugh, David. 2012. *China Goes Global: The Partial Power*. New York: Oxford University Press.

Sharma, Yojana. 2015. Hubs to Take Elite Universities into World-Class Club. *University World News* 286, 16 October, online at www.universityworldnews.com/article.php?story=20151015211423407, accessed 30 December 2015.

Shen, Hsiu-Hua. 2005. 'The First Taiwanese Wives' and 'the Chinese Mistresses': The International Division of Labour in Familial and Intimate Relations across the Taiwan Strait. *Global Networks* 5,4:419–37.

Shepherd, John R. 1993. *Statecraft and Political Economy on the Taiwan Frontier, 1600–1800*. Stanford, CA: Stanford University Press.

Shepherd, Robert J., Yu, Larry, eds. 2013. *Heritage Management, Tourism, and Governance in China: Managing the Past to Serve the Present*. New York: Springer.

Shi, Li, Sato, Hiroshi, Sicular, Terry, eds. 2013. *Rising Inequality in China: Challenges to a Harmonious Society*. Cambridge: Cambridge University Press.

Shirk, Susan. 1993. *The Political Logic of Economic Reform in China*. Berkeley: University of California Press.

2007. *China: Fragile Superpower*. Oxford: Oxford University Press.

Shue, Vivienne. 1988. *The Reach of the State: Sketches of the Chinese Body Politic*. Stanford, CA: Stanford University Press.

2006. The Quality of Mercy: Confucian Charity and the Mixed Metaphors of Modernity in Tianjin. *Modern China* 32,4:411–52.

Shue, Vivienne, Tao, Sun. 2010. How Many Provinces in China? Urbanization, Coordinated Regional Development, and Changing Hierarchies of Local State Administration. Paper presented at the conference 'The State of the Local State', Oxford University China Centre.

Simon, Denis Fred, Cao, Cong. 2009. *China's Emerging Technological Edge: Assessing the Role of High-End Talent*. Cambridge: Cambridge University Press.

Siu, Helen F. 2007. Grounding Displacement: Uncivil Urban Spaces in Post-reform South China. *American Ethnologist* 34,2:329–50.

Sleeboom-Faulkner, Margaret. 2007. *The Chinese Academy of Social Sciences (CASS): Shaping the Reforms, Academia and China (1977–2003)*. Leiden, Netherlands: Brill.

Smil, Vaclav. 1984. *The Bad Earth: Environmental Degradation in China*. Armonk, NY: M. E. Sharpe.

Smith Finlay, Joanne. 2013. *The Art of Symbolic Resistance: Uyghur Identities and Uyghur-Han Relations in Contemporary Xinjiang*. Leiden, Netherlands: Brill.

Smith, Graeme. 2009. Political Machinations in a Rural County. *China Journal* 62:29–59.

2010. The Hollow State: Rural Governance in China. *China Quarterly* 203:601–18.

Smith, S. A. 2000. *A Road Is Made: Communism in Shanghai 1920–1927*. Richmond, UK: Curzon.

Sneath, David. 2000. *Changing Inner Mongolia: Pastoral Mongolian Society and the Chinese State*. Oxford: Oxford University Press.

Stockmann, Daniela. 2013. *Media Commercialization and Authoritarian Rule in China*. Cambridge: Cambridge University Press.

Sun, Anna. 2013. *Confucianism as a World Religion: Contested Histories and Contemporary Realities*. Princeton, NJ: Princeton University Press.

Svensson, Marina. 2002. *Debating Human Rights in China: A Conceptual and Political History.* Lanham, MD: Rowman and Littlefield.

Takayama, Yoko. 2012. Red Tourism in China. In *India, Russia, China: Comparative Studies on Eurasian Culture and Society,* ed. Tetsuo Mochizuki, Shiho Maeda, pp. 113–30. Sapporo, Japan: Slavic Research Center, Hokkaido University.

Tan, Chee-Beng, Ding, Yuling. 2010. The Promotion of Tea in South China: Re-inventing Tradition in an Old industry. *Food and Foodways* 18,3:121–44.

Tapp, Nicholas. 2010. *The Impossibility of Self: An Essay on the Hmong Diaspora.* Berlin: LIT.

Teets, Jessica C. 2013. Let Many Civil Societies Bloom: The Rise of Consultative Authoritarianism in China. *China Quarterly* 213:19–38.

Teiwes, Frederick C. 1993. *Politics and Purges in China: Rectification and the Decline of Party Norms, 1950–1965.* Armonk, NY: M. E. Sharpe.

Thøgersen, Stig. 2002. *A County of Culture: Twentieth-Century China Seen from Village Schools of Zouping, Shandong.* Ann Arbor: University of Michigan Press.

Thornton, Patricia M. 2013. The Advance of the Party: Transformation or Takeover of Urban Grassroots Society. *China Quarterly* 213:1–18.

Thun, Eric. 2006. *Changing Lanes in China: Foreign Direct Investment, Local Governments, and Auto Sector Development.* Cambridge: Cambridge University Press.

Tilt, Bryan. 2010. *Struggling for Sustainability in Rural China: Environmental Values and Civil Society.* New York: Columbia University Press.

      2015. *Dams and Development in China: The Moral Economy of Water and Power.* New York: Columbia University Press.

Tsai, Lily L. 2007. *Accountability without Democracy: Solidary Groups and Public Goods Provision in Rural China.* Cambridge: Cambridge University Press.

Tsou, Tang. 1976. Prolegomenon to the Study of Informal Groups in CCP Politics. *China Quarterly* 65:98–114.

U, Eddy. 2007. *Disorganizing China: Counter-bureaucracy and the Decline of Socialism.* Stanford, CA: Stanford University Press.

Van de Ven, Hans. 1991. *From Friend to Comrade: The Founding of the Chinese Communist Party, 1920–1927.* Berkeley: University of California Press.

Vermeer, Eduard B. 2015. The Global Expansion of Chinese Oil Companies: Political Demands, Profitability and Risks. *China Information* 29,1:3–32.

Vukovich, Daniel F. 2012. *China and Orientalism: Western Knowledge Production and the P.R.C.* London: Routledge.

Walder, Andrew G. 1986. *Communist Neo-traditionalism: Work and Authority in Chinese Industry*. Berkeley: University of California Press.

1995. Local Governments as Industrial Firms: An Organizational Analysis of China's Transitional Economy. *American Journal of Sociology* 101,2:263–301.

2009. *Fractured Rebellion: The Beijing Red Guard Movement*. Cambridge, MA: Harvard University Press.

2015. *China under Mao: A Revolution Derailed*. Cambridge, MA: Harvard University Press.

Walder, Andrew G., Luo, Tianjue, Wang, Dan. 2013. Social Stratification in Transitional Economies: Property Rights and the Structure of Markets. *Theory and Society* 42:561–88.

Walter, Carl E., Howie, Fraser J. T. 2012. *Red Capitalism: The Fragile Financial Foundation of China's Extraordinary Rise*. Singapore: John Wiley.

Wang, Hui. 2011. The 'Tibet Issue' between East and West. *Chinese Sociology and Anthropology* 42,4:7–30.

Wang, Huiyao. 2012. *China's Competition for Global Talents: Strategy, Policy and Recommendations*. Vancouver, BC: Asia Pacific Foundation of Canada.

Wang, Shaoguang. 1995. The Politics of Private Time: Changing Leisure Patterns in Urban China. In *Urban Spaces in Contemporary China: The Potential for Autonomy and Community in Post-Mao China*, ed. Deborah Davis, Richard Kraus, Barry Naughton, Elizabeth J. Perry, pp. 149–72. Washington, DC: Woodrow Wilson Center Press and Cambridge University Press.

Wang, Xingzhou. 2008. An Investigation into Intergeneration Differences between Two Generations of Migrant Workers. *Social Sciences in China* 29,3:136–56.

Wang, Zhengxu, Sun, Long, Xu, Liuqing, Pavlićević, Dragan. 2013. Leadership in China's Urban Middle Class Protest: The Movement to Protect Homeowners' Rights in Beijing. *China Quarterly* 214:411–31.

Wank, David L. 1999. *Commodifying Communism: Business, Trust, and Politics in a Chinese City*. Cambridge: Cambridge University Press.

Watson, James L., ed. 1997. *Golden Arches East: McDonald's in East Asia*. Stanford, CA: Stanford University Press.

White, Gordon, Howell, Jude A., Shang, Xiaoyuan, eds. 1996. *In Search of Civil Society: Market Reform and Social Change in Contemporary China*. Oxford: Clarendon Press.

Whyte, Martin King. 2010. *Myth of the Social Volcano: Perceptions of Inequality and Distributive Injustice in Contemporary China*. Stanford, CA: Stanford University Press.

Wong, Bernard P. 2006. *The Chinese in Silicon Valley: Globalization, Social Networks, and Ethnic Identity*. Lanham, MD: Rowman and Littlefield.

Wong, Christine. 2009. Rebuilding Government for the 21st Century: Can China Incrementally Reform the Public Sector? *China Quarterly* 200:929–52.

2013. Reforming China's Public Finances for Long-term Growth. In *China: A New Model for Growth and Development*, ed. Ross Garnaut, Fang Cai, Ligang Song, pp. 199–219. Melbourne, Australia: ANU Press.

World Bank and State Council of the People's Republic of China. 2012. *China 2030: Building a Modern, Harmonious, and Creative High-Income Society*. Washington, DC: The World Bank.

Woronov, T. E. 2011. Learning to Serve: Urban Youth, Vocational Schools and New Class Formations in China. *China Journal* 66:77–99.

Wright, Teresa. 2004. Intellectuals and the Politics of Protest: The Case of the China Democracy Party. In *Chinese Intellectuals between State and Market*, ed. Edward Gu, Merle Goldman, pp. 158–80. London: Routledge.

Xiang, Biao. 2005. *Transcending Boundaries – Zhejiangcun: The Story of a Migrant Village in Beijing*. Leiden, Netherlands: Brill.

2012. Predatory Princes and Princely Peddlers: The State and International Labour Migration Intermediaries in China. *Pacific Affairs* 85,1:47–68.

2014. The Pacific Paradox: The Chinese State in Transpacific Interactions. In *Transpacific Studies: Framing an Emerging Field*, ed. Janet Hoskins, Viet Thanh Nguyen, pp. 85–105. Honolulu: University of Hawai'i Press.

Xu, Yi. 2013. Labor Non-governmental Organizations in China: Mobilizing Rural Migrant Workers. *Journal of Industrial Relations* 55,2:243–59.

Yan, Hairong. 2008. *New Masters, New Servants: Migration, Development, and Women Workers in China*. Durham, NC: Duke University Press.

Yan, Hairong, Sautman, Barry. 2010. Chinese Farms in Zambia: From Socialist to Agro-Imperialist Engagement? *African and Asian Studies* 9,3:307–33.

Yan, Yunxiang. 2009. The Good Samaritan's New Trouble: A Study of the Changing Moral Landscape in Contemporary China. *Social Anthropology* 17,1:9–24.

2010. The Chinese Path to Individualization. *British Journal of Sociology* 61,3:489–512.

Yang, Guobin. 2009. *The Power of the Internet in China: Citizen Activism Online*. New York: Columbia University Press.

Yang, Guobin, Calhoun, Craig. 2007. Media, Civil Society, and the Rise of a Green Public Sphere in China. *China Information* 21,2:211–36.

Yang, Mayfair Mei-hui. 1994. *Gifts, Favors and Banquets: The Art of Social Relationships in China*. Ithaca, NY: Cornell University Press.

Yang, Wen-Shan, Lu, Melody Chia-Wen. 2010. *Asian Cross-border Marriage Migration: Demographic Patterns and Social Issues*. Amsterdam: Amsterdam University Press.

Yeh, Wen-hsin. 2008. *Shanghai Splendor: A Cultural History, 1843–1949*. Berkeley: University of California Press.

Yeoh, Brenda S. A., Liu, Weiqiang. 2013. Chinese Migration to Singapore: Discourses and Discontents in a Globalizing Nation-State. *Asian and Pacific Migration Journal* 22,1:31–54.

Yeung, Arthur, Xin, Katherine, Pfoertsch, Waldemar, Liu, Shengjun. 2011. *The Globalization of Chinese Companies: Strategies for Conquering International Markets*. Singapore: John Wiley.

Zhan, Mei. 2009. *Other-Worldly: Making Chinese Medicine through Transnational Frames*. Durham, NC: Duke University Press.

Zhang, Li. 2010. *In Search of Paradise: Middle Class Living in a Chinese Metropolis*. Ithaca, NY: Cornell University Press.

Zhang, Li, Ong, Aihwa, eds. 2008. *Privatizing China: Socialism from Afar*. Ithaca, NY: Cornell University Press.

Zhang, Ning. 2012. The Wenchuan Earthquake, Social Organizations, and the Chinese State. *Urban Anthropology* 41,2–4:211–46.

Zhang, Yue. 2014. Governing Art Districts: State Control and Cultural Production in Contemporary China. *China Quarterly* 219:827–48.

Zheng, Tiantian. 2009. *Red Lights: The Lives of Sex Workers in Postsocialist China*. Minneapolis: University of Minnesota Press.

Zweig, David, Wang, Huiyao. 2013. Can China Bring Back the Best? The Communist Party Organizes China's Search for Talent. *China Quarterly* 215:590–615.

Index

216